A Complete Guide
for Location, Services,
Staffing, and Outsourcing

Designing
the Best
Call Center
for Your Business

By Brendan Read

Designing the Best Call Center for your Business
copyright © October 2000Brendan Read

Published by CMP Books
An Imprint of CMP Media Inc.
12 West 21 Street
New York, NY 10010

ISBN 1-57820-063-6

For individual orders, and for information on special discounts for quantity orders, please contact:

CMP Books
6600 Silacci Way
Gilroy, CA 95020
Tel: 800-LIBRARY or 408-848-3854
Fax: 408-848-5784
Email: telecom@rushorder.com

Distributed to the book trade in the U.S. and Canada by
Publishers Group West
1700 Fourth St., Berkeley, CA 94710

Manufactured in the United States of America

Contents

Designing Your Call Center

To my son, Alex, who, as a paramedic,
answers the *truly* mission-critical calls

▶ **Acknowledgements**

In my youth my travel was mainly "rule of thumb", that had its own
rhythm and philosophy. One of the rides of wisdom that I had picked
up was that every lift, no matter how short, slow, slightly-off-the-beat-
en path or weird, got you closer to your destination.

So it is with this book. I owe the information and lessons that I
impart to the people who have given me the lifts of knowledge and
insight in my life. Some of these individuals include:

*   John Garde, proprietor of John Garde and Company, Toronto,
    Ontario, who gave a somewhat skilled but hard working and sin-
    cere 18 year old his first start in customer service, and who taught
    him valuable lessons about serving customers;

*   Michael D. Reid, who, as then-Editor of *The Martlet*, the University
    of Victoria's student newspaper, let me stretch my fledging jour-
    nalism and analysis skills as columnist and reporter. One of my
    columns, 'Engineering for a Change' that supported administra-
    tion for an engineering school because it would attract employers,
    foreshadowed my site selection writing 20 years later;

*   Joe Krumm, Editor of *The Clackamas County Review* (now the
    Clackamas Review), Clackamas, Oregon, who gave me a start in
    business writing. One of my articles, a series on suburban
    Portland downtowns, won a first place award from the Oregon
    Newspaper Publishers Association in 1989;

*   John DeDad, Editorial Director of *EC&M* and former editor of the

short-lived *Electrical Code Watch* newsletter and Jim Lucy, Chief Editor, *Electrical Wholesaling*. Under their guidance and editing I first learned about and wrote effectively on building design and maintenance including codes and standards (including books on OSHA regulations) and about telemarketing and e-commerce. They also gave me exposure internationally, interviewing and writing about European rules and business and design practices;

- *Call Center* founder Harry Newton, Mary Lenz, the publication's Editorial Manager and Joe Fleischer its Editor. Harry inspired me for this book. He showed me that you could build up and promote an industry while not being afraid to constructively criticize it and yet have fun doing so. Mary patiently helped me refine my skills, boost my knowledge of the industry and has given incredible support for my coverage and story ideas, some of which have actually turned up worth while. Both she and Joe help me improve my day-to-day work that went into the book, and have supported and assisted it, with their ideas, suggestions and the time for me to complete it. Thanks for the foreward;

- Richard "Zippy" Grigonis, Chief Technical Editor, *Computer Telephony* and Janice Reynolds, author and consultant. Zippy let me try out (and tolerated) much of the material and angles by contracting with me to provide entries to his *Computer Telephony Encyclopedia*. The experience, of writing the articles and watching him pull his hair out in putting the encyclopedia together, proved good grounding for this book. They proved good grounding for Ms Reynolds, who calmly and very professionally edited the book, tolerating my last minute additions and revisions; the same thanks also going to Robbie Alterio in the Art Department.

I would also like to thank Christine Kern and Frank Brogan in CMP Media's books department, who after hearing me talk about it, now finally have a product in their hand and to Alison Ousey, former *Call Center* managing editor who edited the first few chapters. Finally there is not enough thanks to my lovely wife Christine, who has given me insights on the Web by doing it as a programmer and for tolerating my "terminally mad" hours writing this book.

Forward

Keeping Up in A Fast-Paced Industry

The call center industry is changing rapidly. So rapidly that some people working in call centers and IT departments have become overwhelmed with increased workloads resulting from new technology. There are more computers to support, more people to train, more ways to be reached and more on-line users with more ways of communicating, demanding quick answers to their e-mail inquiries and phone calls. Today more than ever, customers expect quick, efficient service whether they send an e-mail, request a callback or dial a customer service rep.

As their jobs expand, most call center professionals realize that systems like on-line customer service and CRM software will ultimately help them better target, retain and market to both on-line and over the phone customers.

Today it is rare to find an industry that does not require a call center. It's a bit ironic that many dot coms, anxious to set up shop, neglected to establish brick and mortar call centers to deal with customer inquiries from the start. Many thought it would be enough to offer an e-mail address to handle questions from on-line visitors. But they didn't think about how they would route and prioritize the huge volumes of e-mail inquires. They also didn't realize that not offering a toll-free number would lead to lost sales. They figured that if Web visitors were going on-line, it meant they didn't want to pick up the phone and talk to someone. But when you take away the option of live contact, you take away an important comfort level that many people want before they make a purchase. Today, many dot coms have invested in e-mail routing software and at least offer toll-free customer service numbers on their sites, even if they don't offer "click-to-call" options. And if they haven't built their own call centers, they've hired outsourcers.

The plights of the dot coms, however, has brought new media attention to call/customer contact centers; the term "call center" is practically a household name. I've never seen more analyst reports or newspaper articles threatening that on-line retailers stand to lose billions of dollars resulting from on-line visitors abandoning shopping carts unless they find a way to provide better customer service.

The industry has certainly come a long way since Rockwell built the first ACD nearly 30 years ago. The vendor choices and service options available are wide and varied. But the challenge of which products and services to buy from which vendors can become overwhelming. Issues such as tight labor and call center saturation add to the challenge of where to set up new or additional call centers. Where to find staff, how to keep them, how to ensure proper training and how to integrate new equipment with legacy data further adds to the fray.

There's also the challenge of where your responsibility actually lies or ends. The job of a call center professional today involves much more than managing an ACD and people. It often involves establishing Web initiatives; convincing upper management of the need for more labor and more software; learning how to humanize the call center and provide career paths for agents; dealing with e-mail; reducing turnover; and responding to management's realization of the call center as a key revenue source and the front-line of it's business.

This book addresses all of these concerns and much more. It provides excellent guidance and real help with all of the decisions you must make. Of course this book won't solve your every problem (you still have to show up for work each day). But it offers solid advice and provides resources for just about every situation you'll encounter in you call/customer interaction/contact center. It offers the best, most comprehensive information I've seen for what you need to know to find the best site for your center, hire the best consultants, find the right products and services, decide whether or not to outsource and find the best staff.

I've had the pleasure of working with the author for nearly four years. I actually hired Brendan to fill a writer's position when I was the Editor-In-Chief of Call Center Magazine. Brendan quickly demonstrated zealousness and passion for his work. He proved to be a strong, valuable addition to our team. His dedication and enthusiasm makes for comprehensive, objective and well-researched information — the most you can ask of any journalist. None of what you read in the following chapters has been downloaded from a Web site or taken from a press release. As a hands-on writer and editor, what'll you'll read in the following pages comes from Brendan's work in the field, his visits to countless call centers and extensive interviews with consultants, analysts and vendors. The real treat is that he takes you, the reader, along for the educational ride.

—Mary Lenz, Group Editorial Manger for Call Center,
Computer Telephony & Teleconnect Magazines &
the author of The Complete Help Desk Guide.

Why This Book Will Help You

If your employees sell products and/or services and provide customer care *without* being in the physical presence of your customers, then you operate a call center. Call centers are where these interactions take place, either over the phone or by way of other communication media.

Call centers are amazing business tools. They liberate customers from grinding their gears down a clogged traffic artery to get information, to settle complaints, or to buy products and services; all of these functions can be performed over the phone or the Internet. Say, for example, you wake up at 2 am thinking about the new video-enabled cell phone you saw on the Doggie Channel - the one that pages your Pekinese through a special chip-fitted collar. With call centers, you can instantly satisfy your desire for more info. You can call or e-mail a call center, ask about the product's features and price, and order it. If, after receiving it, the product does not work, you can bark at customer service to fix or replace it. (If you do not pay the service fee, however, the company's outbound service center may call to collect, leaving you with your tail between your legs.)

The agent who takes your order may be hundreds of miles away, perhaps even in another country or continent. A call center can connect to wherever there are high-capacity phone lines. Call centers let agents sound so close, you would swear they were right next door. And they very well could be; some call center employees and contractors work right out of their homes.

Call centers need not reside in fancy buildings, though they are becoming business showcases in their own right. The old discount department store you remember as a kid may have been boarded up for years; but today it may house a call center. Yet a call center is not a throwaway investment. The days when you can string out an armful of standard black phones over a basement card table are over. According to Dr. Jon Anton of Purdue University's Center for Customer Driven Quality (Lafayette, IN), to run a call center costs $100,000 x *** the number of full-time equivalent agents, or FTEs. This means even a small (100-FTE) center will swallow up to $10 million per year to keep going. Even if you outsource your customer service and sales to a service bureau, expect to pay more money over the long haul than if you opened a center yourself.

People are the most costly and problematic component of a call center. Agents, supervisors, managers, and ancillary HR and administrative personnel comprise over 60% of a center's operating costs, followed by technology, voice/data, utilities, and real estate (in roughly equal proportions, depending on the location and hardware/software.)

People need work space that is comfortable, safe, practical, and productive. They require washrooms, break rooms, and childcare (in cases where mothers form a large part of the workforce). These workers must also have access to quick and safe transportation to get to and from your center. And the center must be in a location that taps into enough skilled employees who are willing to work at your offered wage/benefit package for the life of the operation.

That is what this book is all about: how to find the best people and places for call centers. This way your company will always have a cheerful, helpful voice ready to serve your customers' needs — be it over the phone, on the computer, or a combination of both.

Putting people, places, and facilities together is not easy. Locations exist where labor is plentiful, but the education and skills available may not be conducive to what you need, or may be out of your price range. Language is a big issue. Many new immigrants found in high-cost cities like Los Angeles and New York prefer to speak and be spoken to in their native tongues. Yet, you may not find the requisite multi-lingual workers living in less diverse and lower-cost areas, like central Iowa or southern Alabama.

There are already proper language and skill shortages in parts of Europe; eventually this trend will extend to the Asia-Pacific region.

Although, it may be more economical to serve the entire region from one call center as opposed to several, it may not be as practical. As Philip Cohen, a teleservices consultant living in Skelleftea, Sweden, says: "It is easier to find more Spanish speakers in Barcelona, Spain than in Amsterdam, Holland."

Then you may run into issues such as: other competing call centers in, or about to enter, the same labor market as you. Some locations may meet your criteria, but may be a hassle for clients or senior management to get to. You may not be able to find suitable property within the time frame you have been given to set up the center, or there may be too much political and social instability in these areas for your comfort level. There are many things to take into consideration.

When you have found an area you want to locate to, the choices do not get any easier. Do you pick a standard office building, a converted shopping center, an overhauled warehouse, or do you have a structure built to your specifications? How much money will it cost to renovate and construct these facilities? Where are these properties in relation to your labor market? By what means will people commute to the office? What amenities, like food service or child care, are convenient, either on site or nearby?

Finding a call center involves many decisions that affect its cost, performance, and setup time frame. What should it look like? How much lighting do you need, and where? Should you have wiring under raised floors or suspended from ceilings? What workstation designs and chairs work best for your particular call center?

Put simply: if you want to run a "basic" call center, you can put a software-laden IVR system or Web server box anywhere with enough reliable power and voice/data links, where critters will not munch on the cables and locals will not "borrow" the components for home computer projects (or resell them to others). However, if you want to plan for a "successful" call center's future, you will not have the same freedom when choosing a call center location because you must carefully consider your main assets — human beings — and their own needs and requirements.

That is why I have written this book: to give you a concise, easy-to-read, enjoyable, and informative guide to call center design, site selection, real estate, staffing and training, and key legal and regulatory issues. I will also examine the equipment and technology needed for your particular call center functions and size.

Finding a location with the right amount of people and property is less of a problem for small call centers (e.g., under 50 workstations, or "seats") than for larger ones. Yet at the same time, the design, furniture, air quality, amenities, staffing, training and shutdown issues, and legal and regulatory compliance are just as important for the people working in the 10-seat inside sales office as those in the 1,000-seat inbound catalog location.

This book explores the common call center functions for both business and customers, including the major issues involved with each. For example, do you really need to conduct outbound telemarketing if your customers hang up on telemarketers? What are the risks in deploying the customer relationship management philosophy and software?

You will be asked to consider whether you actually need a physical call center for your operations. One chapter explores options and demand-shaving adjuncts to having a call center, including IVR and Web self-service, remote agents, and outsourcing. Another chapter deals with the inevitable (e.g., how you close and downsize a call center).

There is also a look at the issues involved in setting up a call center outside the US — to serve both foreign and US customers. There are unique cultural and legal factors you need to keep in mind when doing business in these markets — some of which even the largest American businesses (e.g., Coca-Cola, Disney) have tripped up on. If you work for or represent a foreign firm and have or plan to open a call center in the US, you should find this volume especially helpful. To many companies investing here, this is still the Wild West in corporate culture.

The book's focus is on call centers that provide customer service and sales, but if you have or are thinking of opening a HR call center or internal help desk, this book will also help. You can apply much of the same design, site selection, and property tips, along with the agent recruiting, training and retention techniques.

The book is organized in such a way that you can pick it up at any time and easily find the chapters you need. This means some repetition, but it is all part of the learning process; you will be surprised at how much information you retain. In the back of the book there is a handy resource guide of consultants who can help you.

With its focus on center design, location, recruiting, and call center alternatives, this book is a handy adjunct to other fine tomes that cover call center operations and technologies, such as Keith Dawson's *Call Center Handbook* and *Call Center Savvy,* and Mary Lenz's *Complete Help Desk Guide.* It complements management books like *Call Center Management on Fast Forward,* by Brad Cleveland and Julia Mayben of the Incoming Calls Management Institute.

The book serves as a reference volume to related *Call Center* articles and supplements, available at *www.callcentermagazine.com.* The call center industry changes rapidly. These readings keep you up-to-date on site selection, real estate, staffing, and outsourcing developments. You can also use both this volume and the magazine to query experts who speak on these subjects at trade shows like Call Center Demo and Conference.

Even if you have a call center and do not plan to expand, the book will prove to be valuable. It is always wise to reexamine your existing center and your customer interaction, recruiting, training strategies, and alternatives like outsourcing and remote agents, to ensure that your centers operate as effectively as possible to serve customers.

I have drawn from my reporting background in newspapers, business publications, and trade magazines in the US, Canada, and the UK. Publications range from *NorthWest Business Insider* in Manchester, England to *The Union Leader* in Manchester, NH. In the early 1990s, I wrote and edited a "series" (no pun intended) of handbooks for Intertec Publishing that explain OSHA electrical safety regulations.

How I ended up writing about call centers can be best summed up in the words sung by the Lord High Executioner from Gibert and Sullivan's operetta *The Mikado*: "a curious set of chances." I first wrote about teleservices and e-commerce in 1992, in an article for Intertec's *Electrical Wholesaling* magazine. From 1993-94 I wrote about inside sales for *Metal Center News.* My in-depth coverage of this field began in late 1995 when I joined *DM News*, then *DM News International.* When I moved to

Call Center in March 1997, I hit the ground running; I knew what a call center was.

I have also drawn from a rather unique set of life experiences, including customer service, order desk, accounts receivable, and telephone canvassing and fundraising. For fun, I have been a community activist, and director and founder of transportation users' organizations. These experiences have given me excellent insight into planning, access issues, and the hairy politics involved that can cripple and drive off businesses.

I do not claim to have run a call center. Nor am I in the consulting or site selection business. I cannot say I have the ideal call center location or building to lease, or can recommend any outsourcers (though I get quite a few requests for that information). What I do bring to the table is an objective, informed, and well-written viewpoint on the people and set-up sides of opening and expanding call centers. I will point you in the right direction so you can get the facts and the advice you need.

I hope you find this book profitable for your business. If you have any suggestions for a future edition, do not hesitate to e-mail me at bread@cmp.com. You will find a live person responding to you.

— Brendan B. Read

New York, NY

September 2000

CHAPTER ONE

What Is A Call Center? People!

When people strike up a conversation with me, they invariably ask what I do for a living. When I reply, they almost always follow up with: "What is a call center?"

I then say, "You know when you dial an 800 number to talk to someone, like in customer service or sales?" Their heads nod. "That's a call center."

Companies now realize that friendly customer service is a vital marketing tool that differentiates them from the competition. Today, many billboards and TV ads feature smiling call center agents.

The questioner smiles knowingly. Most everyone has dealt with a call center, even though they do not call it as such or know what one is.

Say you take one of those "get away from it all" trips to a place with no landline phones and terrible wireless connections. At some point, you need to check your airline or train reservation with a call center. Or, for example, you want to block out the annoying telemarketers who keep interrupting your quality family time; you need to order Caller ID through a call center. If you got a diamond-plated smart card in the mail, you probably talked to a telemarketer who called because you had a silver-plated card. And it doesn't stop there: the telemarketer was probably working off a list of names that had been matched up with data indicating an income and lifestyle to match this high-prestige (and high-interest) product.

Even at work you deal with call centers. The person who called you yesterday with a deal on copier toner dialed you up from a call center. How are you going to get back to that inside software sales rep about fitting out all your employees with video-equipped laptops that your underlings had recommended but you wanted to cut a deal on the price? By picking up the phone or sending a fax or e-mail to a rep. Where does that rep work? A call center. Many businesses or institutions with call centers refer to them by — *"customer service"*, *"sales"*, *"reservations"*, *"help desk"*, and *"collections"* — rather than as *"the call center."*

The federal government's Standard Industrial Classification (SIC) codes are considered the "Rosetta Stone" of industrial research. You can track most everything about an industry (e.g., labor productivity, statistics) by SIC code. Labor data is especially important for call centers because wages and benefits comprise over 60% of a center's operating costs. There are SIC codes and explanations for industries that provide customer service and sales and for service bureaus that use call centers, but none for call centers *per se*.

One example is electrical wholesalers, listed as: "5063 Electrical Apparatus and Equipment, Wiring Supplies, and... ." Here is how electrical wholesalers are described: "Establishments primarily engaged in the wholesale distribution of electrical power equipment for the generation, transmission, distribution, or control of electric energy; electrical construction materials for outside power transmission lines and for electrical systems; and electric light fixtures and bulbs."

Another example: steel service centers (SIC 5051). Here is how they are described: "Establishments primarily engaged in marketing semifinished metal products, except precious metals. Establishments in this industry may operate with warehouses (metals service centers) or without warehouses (metals sales offices)."

Years ago, I wrote an article for *Metal Center News* covering the operations of Wilkinson Metals in Vancouver, BC, Canada. The article described the company's use of an index that helped agents sift out the higher-profit from lower-profit customers. This index performed roughly the same function as today's customer relationship management (CRM) software. The company had a call center — only then it was called the "inside sales department."

The only SIC codes I could find that remotely relate to call centers are: a) 5961 Catalog and Mail-Order Houses, and b) 7389 Business Services, Not Elsewhere Classified — both listed under Industry Group 738: Miscellaneous Business Services. In a long list of firms are the following: "Credit card service (collection by individual firms)," "Telemarketing (telephone marketing) service on a contract or fee basis", and "Telephone solicitation service on a contract or fee basis."

There is not one word about "call centers." There is also no mention of customer service or technical help desk, which are quite different in cost, responsibility, and productivity from agents making outbound calls or taking inbound sales. An agent who is on the phone for 10 minutes trying to fix a problem with the caller's video-enabled palmtop PC is not measured in the same way as an agent who is trying to sell Hello Kitty hood ornaments to a list of Cadillac owners.

▶ Defining Call Centers & Call Center Employees

Call centers are *where* activities such as customer service, sales, help desk, and collections take place — without physical contact with the people who are initiating or receiving the transactions. *In Newton's Telecom Dictionary, Call Center* founder Harry Newton defines a call center as "a place where calls are answered and made."

This book goes farther, defining a call center as also a place that answers and initiates e-mail, and handles other online communications such as Web chat and escorted browsing. Today, some call center employees even assist customers by way of "snail mail" and video contacts. *Call Center* contains articles on online and video customer service and sales, on the services and technologies that support them, and how to screen and train agents to use them.

"Call center" is a foundation phrase — one that describes an object when it is created, becomes established, and is in widespread use. One of my favorite examples of a foundation phrase is "carfare." Carfare refers to the money people pay for transportation — usually mass transit. But its origin dates from the streetcar era, which still lives on in many cities. Do you pay "carfare" when you board a bus or subway, or on the revived and upgraded streetcars known as "light rail transit" (LRT)? I paid "carfare" when I rode the King streetcar line to Spadina Avenue when I worked in Toronto years ago. Was it still considered "carfare" when I changed to the Spadina bus to go to my stop? Is it "carfare" now that the Toronto Transit Commission replaced the bus with a restored streetcar (a.k.a. LRT)?

Moving forward, think of the term "dial-up" (as in "dial-up modems"). Do you actually use touch-tone signals to connect to other computers rather than rotary pulse dialing? Today, do you *really* put your finger inside a hole over a number, yank down, and let it click back when you "dial" someone on your cell phone? Growing numbers of cell phones accept e-mail through unified messaging and have Internet access. Are they still "phones" if you do not engage in telephony on them? Or should we even call it a "phone," as these radiotelephony devices become as popular as wired telephones?

I stay away from other attempt-to-be-evolutionary phrases for call centers, such as "contact centers" and "customer interaction centers." So does *Call Center*. Contact centers sound a little too personal, like someone poking me in the arm. "Customer interaction center" is too nebulous, too touchy-feely, like New Age group therapy sessions.

I talk, e-mail and text-chat with someone, and that's how I refer to these functions — not "contact" or "interact." I simply want to talk to someone about a problem I may have with my dial-up Internet connection, or simply send an e-mail to find out when those luminescent garden gnomes will arrive to complement the pink flamingoes outside my home office.

There is also no agreement on what companies should title their employees that work in the call center. Some of the more common terms used include "account representative", "agent", "customer care specialist," "customer service representative," "help desk rep," and "telephone sales representative," often known by their abbreviations: "AR" and "CSR" and "TSR."

For simplicity's sake, in this book I use the term "agent" — in a general sense — just as I use "call center." An "agent" can be a "representative" just as a service bureau's agent represents its employer's clients to the clients' customers. Given that, "help desk reps" also perform essential customer service, I call them "agents" too.

▶ How Many Call Centers Are There?

I get many inquiries from public relations firms, researchers, and suppliers who ask, "How many call centers are there?" I reply that describing the call center "business" is like the blind men describing an elephant. There is no agreed-on minimum size for a call center. For example, when I was 18, I was a one-person "call center" for John Garde and Company, a small family-owned firm that assembled and serviced factory sewing machines in Toronto. I answered the phone, took orders, arranged for repair calls, and called delinquent customers — the same *functions* that many call centers provide. Only I was known as an accounts receivable clerk, not an agent.

Technology has brought us a long way. Today's telecommuting agents make and take calls and perform other related functions, working right out of their homes. Do you count their houses or apartments as call centers? Willow CSN, a unique and innovative Miami, FL-based firm, sets up independent contractors who take calls part-time from their homes. In this scenario, where is the call center — at the client's house or at Willow's offices?

Or what if employees work at their desks for only part of the day? *Call Center's* ad sales office is a call center. Sales reps make and take customer "contacts", yet they are also in the field, visiting suppliers at their offices and at trade shows. When at John Garde and Company, I did not answer calls all day. I served customers at the counter, lugged parcels to the post office, delivered machinery, and collected on accounts in person.

You cannot fairly compare call centers to service bureaus providing call center services. For example, a 10-agent business-to-business call center that sells networking products can make more money in a year than a

1,000-agent call center that takes orders for garden gnomes. Yet the center serving the lawn ornament industry may be the market leader.

Just as you cannot lump customer service and outbound

Service bureau Convergys (Cincinnati, OH) has domestic and international call centers; the firm also handles online communications. Agents at its modern, over 800-seat Heathrow, FL call center, handle customer service. Call centers come in different sizes, shapes and locations. Beautyrock, based in Cornwall, ON, Canada, is an outbound-only service bureau with two small (36-seat) call centers. Agents make calls from desks in an older building in the small Canadian city's downtown.

sales into labor productivity data, it is unwise to place a direct comparative monetary value with different customer service and information call centers. You cannot equate a 10-minute call to fix a computer bug with a 10-minute hassle over an airline travel reservation.

Each call is equally important to the business and, most importantly, to the customer.

For these reasons, the magazine and I do not attempt to "rank" call centers or even service bureaus. Pseudo-measurements (e.g., billable hours from carriers) that others may use say nothing about what went on during those calls — especially today when companies train agents to take a customer service or help desk call and turn it into a sales call.

You can, however, benchmark or compare your call center's existing or expected performance against others in your class. Purdue University's Center for Customer Driven Quality (Lafayette, IN) and consulting firms, such as Response Design Corporation (Ocean City, NJ), have benchmarking programs on a shared-information basis.

The only objective criteria for call center measurement that I prefer to use is "seat", or its longer synonym "workstation." Seats are considered a call center's "machinery." The number of seats in a call center determines its maximum output, just like the number and capacity of furnaces in a steel mill, or sewing machines in a clothing firm. In call centers, the production rate varies on the type and volume of calls and contacts received and the number and efficiency of employees at the workstations to process them.

There are variations, of course, depending on a center's functions and the equipment at the workstation — just as there are in steel mills and garment makers. A rolling mill that reduces shiny stainless steel castings into thin, coiled sheets will often produce less, but almost always offers a higher-value output than one that presses and coils dull carbon steel plate. A heavy-duty machine that sews a $500 leather coat is slower to operate than a high-speed machine than zips through $19.95 shirts.

Machines and their operators, like call center phones and terminals, also need downtime. If you manage a call center, make sure you have backup. At the very least, you need to let your customers know when there are delays or if your office is closed.

And as the economy expands and develops worldwide, so too will the number of workstations and call centers to house them. This increase will occur even as self-service media such as automated e-mail transmission and response, IVR systems, and Web sites become more sophisticated and user-friendly.

Dr. Jon Anton of the Center for Customer Driven Quality predicts there will be 3.45 million workstations in North America and 1.625 million workstations outside of North America in 2003, compared with 2.75 million and 1.224 million, respectively, in 1999. This assumes the current economic boom holds, migration of calls to Web and e-mail contacts continue at the same current pace, and the trend towards "off shore" call handling does not accelerate.

▶ People Are What Make A Call Center

Even as the Web takes center stage and IVR systems become commonplace, call center workstations will continue to grow. This is because people prefer to communicate with other people. They are what make a call center, and a call center cannot run without them.

How an agent treats you — be it over the phone or through e-mail — usually determines whether or not you do business with that company again. Try to think of it in terms of the way a salesclerk or waitperson can make a difference in the amount of time you visit a store or eat in a restaurant (unless you're a true New Yorker and are used to getting lost in the shuffle).

Never mind the sophisticated and heavily promoted e-mail and Web-based self-service, nor the speech-recognition-enabled IVR units that promise to do everything except take Rover for his morning walk. These systems are not call centers, and they will never totally displace the agent on the keyboard or the phone.

Who but a friendly call center agent, with his or her unique personality coming out through their words, will understand the customer's tone of voice and can say, "Yes, the 18k gold necklace in the catalog will go with that black pique cotton dress on page 53"? Who else draws from their experience and knowledge to come up with a bug fix that was not curable from the solutions written into the online problem-management system? Or recommend a competing dealer in the same caller's neighborhood who has in stock the Michelin tires they wanted, knowing that this positive customer service experience will bring that caller back? (Progressive Insurance made this point in recent TV ads, where its agents told callers that their competitors had lower rates.)

Admit it. How many times have *you* zeroed-out of an IVR system, or said "to the devil with it" and clicked the "call me" button or dialed the toll-free number on a Web site? Machines, no matter how clever, cannot show empathy or understanding. They cannot discuss last night's Yankees-Texas game, inquire about grandkids, or put a smile on a customer's face as they wait for an order to be traced.

Much of this IVR technology has its limits. Take natural-language-fitted IVR systems, for example. Talking to a machine is easier, faster, and, well, more *natural* than keying in letters or numbers on a handset. The vocabularies developed by firms such as Nuance and SpeechWorks are expanding by leaps and bounds. Yet there are many expressions and words they cannot understand, for many reasons. One main problem: they cannot think out of the people-programmed box.

When my wife, a self-taught programmer, gets angry with her PC, she calls it every name in the book, and then some. But she uses her own phrases she made up when she was raising our son, to express anger and frustration without resorting to obscenities. She also uses them in neutral tones. No computer in the world can understand *those* words.

I am also guilty of getting angry. My favorite word is "bloody." Yet "bloody" is interpreted differently in the US, Canada, and England (I have lived in all three countries). An American, like my paramedic son, takes it literally (as in the "bloody" patients he picked up and performed triage on). A Canadian uses the word casually, like I did when I worked as a small-town reporter in the Rockies. During a week of 20 below weather I'd say to someone in the town's Husky truck stop, (where you literally ate there and got gas): "bloody weather, eh?" Yet a Briton, like my mother, uses it when she's furious, as in "you bloody fool!" Even as my wife has difficulty understanding which way I use the term sometimes, there is still not a program that can differentiate the meaning.

Consumer banking is one example of an industry with technology limitation issues. Banks can be called the "Titans of Technology Adoption" to cut costs, and the "Counts of Call Center Applications". But these "Wizards of Negotiable Wads" know that most people do not have to be in a bank branch — which costs a lot of money to build, operate, keep secure and maintain — to conduct business. Most of what is involved is making deposits, withdrawing cash, and finding out which checks cleared.

That is why banks introduced telephones, then PCs, and now Web banking and automatic teller machines. In exchange for the live, face-to-face interaction banks provide, you can now get 7x24 service, liberating yourself from the dreaded "bankers hours." Telephone banking systems now have vast IVR menus; some banks fit their IVR system with speech recognition, minimizing the personal contact even further.

Yet even with all this very convenient technology, banks still rely on people. I bank with Citigroup. If I am on the phone and I have a problem that needs to be answered I can still talk to a live agent. If I am at an ATM there is a handy phone for me to pick up and speak to a live agent. I can do that if I am at another bank's ATM, by "dialing" the toll-free number on my cellphone. I can still go in and conduct my transaction with a teller.

This is not to say that technology does not have its place. IVR and Web self-service systems are essential, efficient, and cost-saving channels and adjuncts to live agent call centers. They are also speedy. It is rare today to be put on hold for seconds that seem like hours, listening to elevator music. These systems take and deliver many things, such as account and general information, dealer locator services, order and reservations taking, ticketing and tracking, and problem management and resolution.

The Web has become a virtual store where you go in and do nearly everything except kick the tires. You can see a product or hotel room from every dimension, and hear and see video clips, downloading the ones you want.

There are some products that people do not want to talk to an agent about, like buying underwear for your lover. On the other hand, there is nothing like an understanding agent to help find the right size and perfect gift based on the individual's preferences. Only if and when videophones become popular, red faces won't be seen.

▶ Lessons For Internet Companies

E-commerce firms (a.k.a. dot-coms) are sometimes started up and managed by people with no customer service experience whatsoever. They learn the hard way that they need call centers, or at the very least, to outsource their call and contact handling to a service bureau with experienced agents. Studies and consumer complaint columns regularly blast dot-coms for terrible customer service and sales. Little wonder many of them are going under or are being bought up by the competition: a few smart online firms, brick-and-mortar businesses, and catalog companies who know how to deliver people-based service. The lead paragraph in the *New York Daily News'* May 16, 2000 "Ask Asa" feature says it all: "Emily Smith of Manhattan has a word of advice to retailers: 'A product is only as good as the customer service offered with it.'"

The International Customer Service Association (Chicago, IL) and E-Satisfy, a unit of service bureau Telespectrum Worldwide (King of Prussia, PA), revealed in a recent report that only 36% of Web-using customers were completely satisfied with their electronic contact experience. Only 40% of electronic contacts were resolved online; almost half required a telephone call from the customer to resolve.

The reports says this poor handling of online contacts creates at least 30% lower customer loyalty among the two-thirds of online users who are not satisfied. This leads to a high level of negative "word-of-mouse," with dissatisfied customers telling twice as many people about their experience (both online and off-line) than satisfied online customers. Reflecting the truism that bad news travels faster than good news, the ICSA/E-Satisfy paper reports dissatisfied online customers are almost four times more likely to discuss their experience in an online chat room than satisfied ones.

Chris Gongol, Telespectrum's executive VP of business development, knows both sides: self-service technology and live agent interaction. He was a partner in Voice F/X, a clever IVR service bureau later acquired by the outsourcer. It developed neat projects such as installing and maintaining telephone lines in colleges for students to call in about their grades or register on IVR systems, in exchange for up to a minute of ads with touch-tone acceptance as the records are being obtained.

"The problem many dot-coms have is that their customer service model was self-service — with no live agents," says Gongol. "They kept saying to us that live agent service is not scalable. Now they are learning that they need a human component to keep their customers, and surprise — live agent service is scalable."

Another outsourcer, LiveBridge (Portland, OR) says it all: "Ninety percent of online buyers prefer the option of human contact. With LiveBridge, you can give it to them. BridgeReps [agents] will take their calls to both answer their questions and take their orders."

CHAPTER TWO

Why You Need a Call Center

Call centers are the most versatile business apparatus around. You can use them for nearly every type of person-to-person transaction that does not require physical interaction, including sales, service, and collections, and business-to-business or business-to-customer. Call center interactions may range from something as simple as discussing recipes to something as complex as servicing industrial machinery.

Call centers are far more flexible than retail outlets or showrooms; customers do not have to wait until they open to shop. You can also

Call centers' presence is everywhere – even on the rolls of Scott's toilet tissue. If you should ever have a question or comment about the product, the toll-free number is right there on the packaging.

save money with technologies such as Web and IVR self-service, according to The Center for Customer Driven Quality at Purdue University (Lafayette, IN). These time-savers cost 5 cents and 50 cents per transaction, respectively, compared with $5 per phone call. And if you want that human touch, live agent handling through a call center is a bargain compared with $50 per transaction for retail.

A call center's low operating costs let you turn the lights on earlier and switch them off much later. This provides customers greater convenience; many call centers never close. But that doesn't mean they are open all of the time, staffed at full volume. Many companies run call centers located in different time zones, including other countries, and shift calls to these places in a practice known as "follow the sun." Customers do not even realize they are being routed elsewhere.

This is how it works. Say you have a travel service, such as an airline or bus charter. If inbound call volume trails off after 9 pm in your Scranton, PA call center, you can shut the center down and shift calls to your Enid, OK center at 8 pm CT. When Enid shuts down at 9 pm CT, you can route calls to your Fresno, CA center, which is two hours ahead and stays open until midnight. If you reopen your Scranton center at 6 am ET, you only need to cover the three-hour period when all three centers are closed; just use an auto-attendant with an opt-out to an on-call emergency supervisor. This three-hour period varies per time zone (e.g., 3 am to 6 am ET, 2 am to 5 am CT, 1 am to 4 am MT and 12 am to 3 am PT). Your customers are always taken care of, no matter where they are routed to or what time it is.

Call centers help your business in other ways. For example, if a retail shop has long lines or is not fully stocked, customers are stuck. The next branch may be miles away and there's no guarantee that items will be in stock when customers come back (if they have not gone to your competition already). A call center has access to your central inventory, so it can pick and ship goods; agents can take pre-pay orders and ship goods as soon as they are in stock. If you have more than one call center, you can set up routing to send incoming calls to the first available qualified agent — wherever he or she is located.

If your customers are experiencing long hold times and it is too costly or not feasible to hire more agents, you can always outsource the overflow to a service bureau that will handle calls and contacts on contract. Or you can install an opt-out to an IVR self-service menu, invite callers to leave a call-back message, send e-mail to an automated response database, or invite callers to visit your Web site. All this beats customers having to stand in line, twiddle their thumbs, and walk out the door, never to return.

The savings are even greater with business-to-business sales. If an agent or inside salesperson makes a sale, it costs a fraction of what a transaction made by a field sales rep would be ($500, estimates The Center for Customer Driven Quality.) Also, if you sell b-to-b through a call center, you know where your agents are. This cannot be said for field salespeople, unless you have tracing devices implanted into their bodies.

If you make purchasing decisions for your business, you may prefer to be in contact with people through a call center rather than in person; you can put a sales call on hold, tell your secretary to call people back, even temporarily ignore your e-mail. By going through a call center, you and your staff can avoid dealing with that well-dressed, briefcase-burdened character who is checking her voice mail and e-mail simultaneously, or playing Internet poker on a laptop. Your company can also "save face" with a call center — you will never have to tell a visitor waiting in the reception area that "something just came up" and they cannot be seen.

Thanks to their versatility, call centers have come a long way from outbound cold-call telemarketing, collections, and airline and hotel reservations — which is what they were originally used for. Now they are virtual storefronts, with sales and service shops located in buildings that may be thousands of miles away from customers. As mentioned, e-commerce firms now realize they need these human "virtual sales associates" to assist customers with online shopping.

Call centers may also make or break a sale. By tapping into the same software, dealers and outside salespeople can pick up leads and new customer info from agents, be it in real-time off their cell modem-fitted palmtop or from a just-off-the-Interstate payphone. The call center's unsung workers — agents — can also save their tails.

Darren Nelson, founder of GWI Software (Vancouver, WA), knows the consequences of not collecting up-to-date customer information. He once worked as a salesperson for several large, high-tech firms. When he made a sale, he would turn over the contracts and details to his company's implementation department. Several times he returned to clients only to discover problems that could torch future sales and commissions. "I looked stupid going in there," recounts Nelson. "I'm selling the clients better connectivity, and I didn't even understand the problems they were having with the products they were already using."

Call centers are advertising, sales, and market research channels in their own right. Companies use the information agents collect to improve products and services, uncover problems, and, more accurately, target customers, to deliver what people will buy.

Call centers and their agents are also the first lines of defense when a firm fouls up. Certain situations prompt people to call or send e-mail more quickly than others, such as a software bug, a toxic waste spill, or a defect that a safety expert alleges could injure a child. How you instruct your agents to respond determines whether or not the public and its government agents will tear off your hide.

Call center agents are corporate windows to the customers. The customer service they supply is now a vital marketplace differentiator. It is no coincidence that many TV ads and billboards show a smiling, headset-wearing agent engaged in conversation. Call centers have become customer and senior management showrooms for service bureaus and in-house firms alike, with corporate-style furnishings.

More companies are finding new ways to use call centers. Take the automotive industry, for example. The traditional way to buy a car is to drive down to your friendly dealer, see what's in stock, kick the tires, and rip through the lot to see if the beast works. If there is one you like, you haggle on price and extras with a salesman, sign the deal, and drive out with the fume-spluttering machination. Hopefully you won't have to drive back to have the darn thing repaired.

When you buy a car about the only time you generally come in contact with a call center is the finance company (unless you pay cash), when it calls to verify info or hassles you about late insurance carrier payments, with your insurer or with an automotive service like the American Automobile Association's

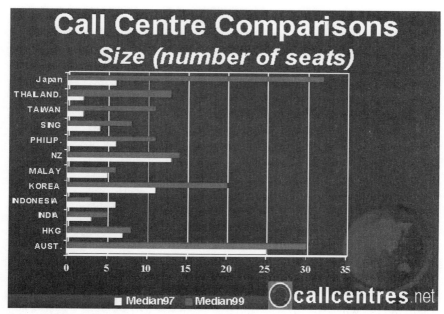

Call Centre Comparisons
Size (number of seats)

Because call centers save money over retail and field sales channels, you should not put off opening a call center or adding seats – even if there is a downturn. Martin Conboy, director of ACA Research (North Sydney, Australia), saw the number of workstations and call centers grow during the Asia-Pacific downturn in the late 1990s.

Emergency Roadside Assistance or the OnStar system. Should a tree ever get in your way, you hope that a helpful agent gets to your call immediately and does not leave you sitting on hold for half an hour.

Things are changing. Automakers now want to reduce the time it takes to get a car to the customer. They want to enhance customer loyalty. Instead of relying only on fancy ads and hoping the dealers will hustle for customers, they are reaching directly to buyers. They are also looking at online ordering and customization, just as computer makers such as Dell have successfully done with PCs. The key? Call centers.

▶ What Do You Need a Call Center For?

Call centers are not a low-cost investment. Web and IVR self-service cost cents per transaction compared with the dollars per interaction involved with a live call center agent — either on the phone or online. As noted, the

Center for Customer Driven Quality calculates that a center with 100 full-time-equivalent (FTE) employees (a FTE can be one full-time or two-part time agents) costs about $10 million to operate. To set one up costs about $40,000 per seat for a small (under 50-seat) center, used for business-to-business sales and external help desk, and $25,000 per seat for a typical medium size (200-seat), general purpose customer service/sales center.

The cost and time involved does not include the substantial IT, HR, legal, and other corporate resources needed to commit to making a center work. The following chapter discusses technology, outsourcing, and remote agent alternatives to owning a call center.

Also, call centers have their limitations. The main one is that they can't fix inherent problems with your product or service. They can't turn a sow's ear into a silk purse. By themselves they can't make software easier to use, remedy production flaws (like introducing better grade materials), make the planes run on time or lower prices. Many telcos have excellent call centers but the fine agents can't replace the bad wiring from the CO to your house; they can only relay the problems to the repair department.

After awhile customer complaints will get to the agents; that is human nature, and customer service will deteriorate. The solution: make sure the product or service that you make, sell and are responsible for is the best quality it can be at the pricepoint your customers will accept, and that your agents will be proud of.

To find out what type of call center is right for you, examine your existing and future needs closely. You do not necessarily need a center to sell, survey, or service customers. Customers can come to your store, office, movie theatre, or other physical place of business, and buy from (or yell at) you and your staff in person. You can obtain customer response information through focus groups, market through brand advertising, and sell through dealers and retailers.

For example, few people today place orders for their cereal, coffee, or Thanksgiving turkey through a call center (except for gourmet foods like Balducci's Kobe beef and the pre-packaged clambakes found in airlines' SkyMall catalogs.) Most shop for food at supermarkets but, increasingly, shoppers are going through online delivery services, such as Peapod — that need call centers.

You can program Web, e-mail, and IVR self-help systems to handle many inquiries, even take sales. Some sophisticated set-ups like TrustedAnswer.com have supervisors who solve out-of-the-box questions and update databases.

Yet at some point you need to communicate directly with your customers. Through small in-house or outsourced call centers, food manufacturers provide info (e.g., recipes) about their products. Butterball's popular bilingual Turkey Talk Line, staffed by a team of home economists, handles calls from Thanksgiving to Christmas on topics ranging from the best way to thaw a turkey to knowing when one is done.

Some of these calls can get weird. A trucker, for example, wanted to know if his turkey would cook more quickly if he drove faster — he planned to roast the bird on his 18-wheeler's engine block. A California restaurant owner wanted to know how to roast a turkey — for a vegetarian meal. When one woman called to find out how long it would take to cook her gobbler, the Talk Line economist asked her how much it weighed. The woman replied: "I don't know. It's still running around outside."

If you sell through a dealer channel, chances are you will need a small call center for service, as a supplement to an outside sales team. But as Jon Kaplan, president of consultancy TeleDevelopment Services (Richfield, OH) discovered when he was hired by B.F. Goodrich over 20 years ago, your customers may *prefer* doing business with call center agents rather than sitting down with a field sales representative.

B.F. Goodrich had Kaplan develop an inside sales call center to obtain dealerships where the tire giant did not have them. The firm franchised 16 dealers through the inside sales call center within the first 10 months. The inside salespeople (e.g., agents) would say, "We don't have distribution in your area, but you're a big player in the market, we know you carry x, y, z and brands, and we'd like you to carry the B.F.Goodrich brand for these reasons ..."

"The company had a philosophy where, if a franchisee reached a certain size, it would turn them back to the field sales rep," recalls Kaplan. "At this point they deserved a field sales rep's time and attention. Yet guess what? We gave dealer customers the option of having a field sales rep or continuing the inside sales relationship they had. Nine times out of 10 they wanted to continue the relationship they had. Why? If the company turned them back to the rep, the rep would visit them maybe once a quarter. In the grand scale, they were still small fish in a big pond. But for me they were a large account. And they could call me on a toll-free number at the B.F. Goodrich building world headquarters, where I had access to product managers, R&D, and price people, and get answers right away."

▶ Major Call Center Functions

To help determine what a call center can do for your business, let's look closely at the major functions one provides:

Telesales: Outbound & Inbound

Any time you buy a product or service over the phone or online, you are engaged in a telesales transaction. Commonly known as "telemarketing," telesales comprises *outbound* calls and e-mails from centers to targeted prospects and existing customers, such as for Internet services, steak knives, and Hello Kitty hood ornaments.

Telesales, like "call center" is another foundation phrase. According to my trusty Concise Oxford Dictionary (New Edition), the prefix "tele" is from a Greek phrase meaning "far off." Therefore, telesales can include, by definition, a way to sell by way of online, video, fax, telegraph, Telex, flashing lights and semaphores — in addition to by telephone.

Yet telesales also includes taking *inbound* calls from customers, such as when they place orders by phone, e-mail, from a Web site for an Internet service provider, or from a tasteless kitsch catalog. Customers may be responding to a print, radio, TV, Internet banner ad, a direct mail piece, an outbound e-mail, or from a print or online catalog.

The key to driving outbound and, to a large extent, inbound, are *lists* of consumers and businesses. These lists include both existing customers and those likely to buy products and services similar to yours; they have also been put through sophisticated analysis. By examining past buying patterns, you can not only determine what they might acquire and at what price point, but when. Outbound telemarketers call and e-mail from lists; inbound telemarketers send direct mail, which includes both snail mail, like catalogs, and e-mail. Telemarketers may also pop offers if you visit their Web sites, asking you to visit a certain page, e-mail, chat, or call them.

There are two types of lists: *compiled* and *response*. The American List Council, a big Princeton, NJ-based list marketer, explains the differences between the lists and their pros and cons. Compiled lists are general lists, pulled from sources like directories, phone books, public records, retail sales slips and trade show registrations. Firms can use them to reach entire markets. That's why if you came to Internet Telecom, chances are you'll get a mailing to come to CT Expo Spring.

With compiled lists, marketers usually know your name, family, lifestyle, and neighborhood characteristics, and they match them against demographic and geographic profiles. When you call up a marketer, they are one example of a source that has information such as your name and telephone number.

Response lists are those which contain consumers that buy regularly through a certain channel, like by phone. The telemarketer may have rented this list from a magazine, or even from that online garden center where you bought the pink flamingoes for your front lawn, after being drawn in by the free John Waters movie offer.

Compiled lists give comprehensive, specific market coverage, like if a firm is opening a new store and wants to drive business into its catchment area — the area where it expects the bulk of its customers to come from. Response lists generate higher response per name. Compiled lists' selections are more demographic while response lists are more psychographic, including attitudes and buying patterns. Compiled lists are also less expensive than response lists.

Marketers append information to their lists. They will add phone numbers if they only have your address, and vice versa. They also append buying data and demographic and geographic changes to your file. If your wife just had a baby, you'll get showered with offers for goodies like infant-safe toys and teddy bears. Marketers know when you move; they obtain public-knowledge US Postal Service National Change of Address lists.

The marketers' reason for gaining such information is to find out what, when, and how much you want to buy because you will buy something, sometime. They want to target only the offers that you are mostly likely to accept. Smart marketers don't want to waste time and resources buying lists and paying agents, along with ancillary facilities and technology costs, trying to sell you something you don't want or need (e.g., sending you baby clothes promotions if you don't have kids. Unless wearing them is your thing and your name is on a targeted list that we don't want to know about.)

Yet telesales also encompasses cross-selling and upselling. This is when you dial into a center to get information or obtain a service (e.g., activating a credit card) and an agent suggests or offers a product or service like an awards plan.

The other day, for example, I called American Express to inquire about payment arrangements. The agent, after looking at my transaction record, suggested that because I was such a good customer, I should sign up for its "Membership Awards" program, in exchange for a service fee. I asked myself why not? I get benefits. Meanwhile, American Express made a sale, lined up new customers from their points sponsors, and locked me in tighter as a card consumer.

This also occurs online. You can be browsing or shopping on a Web site, then suddenly see an "intelligent agent" icon (similar to the animated paper clip on Microsoft Word) that asks if you need assistance, tells you of sales or makes you an offer. Say you're on "vroompersonalizations.com". An intelligent agent shaped like a car pop ups and blurbs: "I noticed you're looking for hood ornaments. We have a limited edition Darth Vader that fits all SUV models for $59.99."

When you call to make airline, Amtrak, hotel, or rental car reservations, or if any of these companies contact you with an offer and you accept, you're also in telesales. You made a commitment to purchase services, and the tightness of that agreement depends on the contract terms. When you reserve a flight on Golden Parachute Airways from Newark to San Jose at a one-way $99 nonrefundable fare, that amount gets taken off your credit or debit card automatically. Even if you cannot shrink your frame into the eight-across seating on the 737 and do buy that bag of snacks for $3.

There are growing numbers of domestic and foreign laws and regulations that affect telesales. Many of them govern when and how you should call, with what means and to whom. They also tell you what data you are allowed to keep and how you should use it. (Read more about these laws in Chapter 4.) For example, the federal Telephone Consumer Protection Act (TCPA) and the Telemarketing Sales Rule (TSR) require you to maintain do not call

(DNC) lists. When a consumer or consumer representative tells an agent they or the person whom they are representing do not wish to be contacted, the agent must put those names on that list. Many states have DNC lists that consumers can place themselves on; all marketers that do business with those residents must scrub their database against those lists.

Also, the Direct Marketing Association has three databases of consumers that do not wish to be contacted for marketers to use: the Mail Preference Service (MPS), for direct mail that also impacts on inbound calling and contacts; the Telephone Preference Service (TPS); and e-mail Preference Service (eMPS). DMA business-to-consumer selling members must comply with its Privacy Promise, a set of consumer protection guidelines that says they must remove the names of consumers who are on federal, state, and the DMA's DNC databases. The Canadian Marketing Association requires its members to comply with Canadian laws and its practices.

Customer service

This includes inbound from businesses and consumers who have concerns, questions, or a problem with products or services. It can also be outbound, which is by far the most common usage. These are known as *outbound customer care* contacts. My wife and I live in Staten Island, the most suburban of New York City's five boroughs. When we had fuzzy signals from Staten Island Cable, I called in to point that out. About an hour after they fixed the problem, the center called back to see if everything was fine.

For companies providing complex products and services like appliances, computers, cable, and Internet services, a common and essential customer service function is *external help desk*. In an external help desk, highly-trained agents help fix customers' problems either by offering suggestions, working remotely from their desks to diagnose machine bugs — or performing a combination of the two. Using sophisticated software, they can get inside your computer, figure out what is going wrong, and zap bug fixes. An external help desk resolved the aforementioned Staten Island Cable problem.

Smart companies offer their customers who have difficulties with their products or services discounted or free items, like a month of free Internet access, 40% off of their next software purchase, or an upgrade to business class. This way they can retain customers by giving them a little in return for the time-sapping inconvenience. This practice is based on the customer relationship management (CRM) philosophy; at the core of this is the belief that retaining a customer is much more profitable than finding a new one. This means that current customers are worth the investment. (More about CRM later.)

Lead generation/qualification

This is a prime rationale for running a b-to-b call center, and is also used for large-ticket consumer sales. Lead generation/qualification is inbound and outbound. Here is how it works: you generate interest in your product or service by advertising, sending a direct mail piece, or outbound e-mail, and enclosing your phone number, e-mail, Web site and/or mailing address. Or, your agents call or e-mail from targeted lists.

When customers and prospects reach out to your firm or when agents make outbound calls and contacts, agents ask questions on job title, if they buy or specify products, and to what dollar value to qualify them. If the customers/prospects ask your agents to send them literature, the agents make an offer and close the sale, or pass the lead to your inside or outside account representatives, depending your program. If the prospects have any technical questions, you can conference in your experts. The call center should then follow up to see if the inside or outside salespeople and dealers contacted the lead, and find out if the contact had been satisfactory.

Customer and market surveys

These outbound and inbound calls and contacts are important business development tools. Businesses use them to find out what customers and prospects are looking for, what their attitudes would be to the firms' products and services, and what their experiences have been with them. Call centers try to implement surveys when a customer calls in for service or sales; they usually take place at the end of the call.

Collections

This is the essential call center function that recipients always dread. These types of calls traditionally have required agents to be sharp, tough, and to the point — to impart fear without breaking the law. The called party owes the company money, and agents need this money to get paid (sometimes so they can pay the collectors that have been calling *them*.)

The stereotypical collection guy with a baseball bat no longer proves effective in collections. Instead, for some, it is hearing that if they don't arrange payments on that washing machine, anonymous faces in the credit bureaus may make it impossible for them to buy that monster house with the security system. Collection agents are becoming credit advisors, helping people stay on the right side of the bureaus and ensuring the money keeps coming in.

Business-to-business marketers also rely on call centers to sell and service customers. Some make outbound cold calls. Many, like *Call Center*, rely on printed and online business reply cards to generate leads. Agents in call centers verify and, in some cases, make outbound lead qualification calls. Other businesses, like Stratasoft, which makes predictive dialers, encourage prospects to call and contact them directly.

▶ Going From Small To Large Call Centers

Nearly every business has a call center. But there is a difference between call centers where there are a dozen people that make and take contacts and supply sales and customer service, and call centers where there are over 50 agents in a room or two, technically chained to their workstations. Some consultants and publications use figures like 25 or 50 agents or seats as the benchmark between formal (50-plus seats) and informal (under 50 seats). Site selection experts say that it is easy to find people and places for informal call centers, but the task becomes more challenging for formal ones.

Andrew Hewitt, principal with consulting firm Pittiglio Rabin Todd and McGrath (Mountain View, CA and Waltham, MA), recommends that you ask yourself several fundamental questions before choosing to open a formal call center:

- Does your product or service require any level of pre- or post-sales support?

- Have you sold, or are you going to sell, a sufficient unit volume to require dedicated resources to address customer issues?

- How important is it that your customers have an avenue to get their questions answered or get their issues resolved in a consistent and efficient manner?

"In today's hyper-competitive marketplace, attracting and retaining customers is a constant challenge," says Hewitt. "For many businesses, the call center is your face to the customer. It's responsible for maintaining an ongoing relationship. Call centers should be in the business of enhancing the overall customer experience and value of the product. A call center can also provide a wealth of data about your products and services."

▶ Justifying A Call Center

As noted earlier, building, outfitting, and operating a call center is not cheap — justifying adequate financing for call centers can be challenging. While most firms now recognize that effective customer service from a live agent phone and online center is essential (if only to have people there to apologize for the company when it screws up), obtaining the funds to build, expand, and improve is another matter.

The problem is that it is difficult to quantify the results from investing in a call center, or buying call center services from an outsourcer. On the other hand, some activities are easy to justify, such as outbound sales, inbound order taking, and collections, and in cases where an agent cross-sells and upsells on customer care or service calls.

Attributing a sale is more difficult where there are many channels, such as business-to-business, where the call center generates and qualifies the leads, then forwards them on to a field sales rep or a dealer, and in business-to-consumer, where the call center literally drives callers to the sales floor. Which person in the transaction process convinced the customer to buy the product — the agent or the dealer? Or did the customer already decide before contacting the company?

Justifying a center becomes more challenging, especially if it is for customer service and help desk, where no money is involved in the transaction. Such call centers become an expense, or a "cost center," even when they are outsourced. In today's hyper, bottom-line sensitive environment, anything listed as an expense is usually marked for a slow or a quick death. If this rings a bell, you need to show how customer service contributes to overall profitability.

According to Response Design Corporation's (Ocean City, NJ) LeapFrog! call center metrics database, 61% of companies currently consider their call center a cost center and 2% as a cost reduction center, compared with 27% who regard it as a profit center and 9% who treat it as a value-add center. In a recent benchmarking study with the American Productivity and Quality Center, RDC found that more companies want their center to be value-add centers, and calculate their value based on how they improve customer retention.

"If a call center is not a direct revenue generating department, then management should move toward calculating their value based on customer retention," says RDC associate Kathryn Jackson.

At a recent conference, Rudy Oetting, president of marketing consultancy Oetting and Company (New York, NY), said that the "cost center" approach — meaning shorter calls, lower pay, high supervisor ratios, and high agent turnover — leads to higher customer acquisition costs, fewer dollars per sale, and lower retention rates caused by bad customer service.

Chad Burbage, president of consulting firm BC-Group International (Dallas, TX), believes that treating call centers as cost centers blinds management to new opportunities. Unfortunately, most call centers are viewed as a necessary evil. "Many firms place call centers at the bottom of the organization, not because of corporate strategies, but because it maintains the status quo," says Burbage. "Those firms will not achieve the excellence of firms who view the call center as an opportunity for increased profit."

Susan Jacobsen, as Monsanto's consumer affairs manager, contracted with Affina-The Customer Relationship Company (Peoria, IL) to handle first-level customer inquiries about its Equal artificial sweetener. She reports that it was the few times the call center sold the product directly to customers that helped the company appreciate her department. Monsanto later sold the sweetener line to Tabletop Acquisitions. "While the sales are small compared to what we do as a company, that money goes directly to consumer affairs," says Jacobsen. "It lets us run more programs and underscores our value as a department."

Smart companies realize that customer service and support deserve the same attention as sales. According to PRTM principal Andrew Hewitt, customers will spend over $50 billion in 2000 for maintenance, support, and other services related to the purchase and ownership of technology-related products alone. He says large, well-established firms such as Cisco, Hewlett-Packard, and IBM rely on the revenue stream from customer service and support for a major source of growth and profit.

Nothing catches senior management's eye faster, he says, than a consistent high margin revenue stream. It is not unusual for organizations that run their customer service and support operations *as a business* to enjoy margins that are over 30% higher than the products they sell. "The bottom line is the bottom line, where customer service and support are concerned," says Hewitt. "Good customer care makes customers successful, wins business, and pays for itself. This only occurs when executive management treats customer service and support strategically, and gives it the attention it deserves."

There are pitfalls to moving too far in the profit center/sales center direction. Steve Murtagh, principal with consulting firm North Highland (Atlanta, GA), says that treating a center strictly as a profit center ignores vital activities such as customer service or support that benefits other direct revenue-generating functions like manufacturing, product development, and sales. "A call center that is only a selling channel is not living up to its potential," says Murtagh. "I often find it best to treat the call center as a cost center, but with specific revenues objectives and responsibilities."

Mark Schmidt, VP of TeleDevelopment Services adds that you should not neglect cost center functions like external help desk. "Even though these functions are cost centers, the service they provide is important to customer retention over the long haul," Schmidt says.

If you want to help your center — even one engaged in sales — get credit where it is due by establishing sound cost and revenue allocation methods. Jon Kaplan, president of TeleDevelopment Services, advises creating predefined standard operating procedures and key performance measurements to allocate revenue targets and operating expenses.

To work in that framework, you must set up back-end measurements (e.g., closed-loop lead tracking processes, cross-selling activities) to track results to recognize what is driving the business, and break down all process components to clearly allocate credit. Once done, you can determine how each sales and service step contributes to revenue, then allocate a percent of revenue to the appropriate department. "It is much easier to get time, attention, and resources from top management when you can demonstrate a corporate contribution," says Kaplan.

CHAPTER THREE

Call Center Alternatives and Adjuncts

Before you start planning or expanding your call center, with visions of happy agents saying, "Thank you for calling America's Classic Septic Service, how can I help you today?" take a hard look at whether you need to service your customers with such an in-house investment. You are looking at anywhere from $40,000 to $80,000 per seat to set up a call center: the smaller (-50 seats) the center the higher the cost per seat because of economies in scale in facilities and technology expenses. You're also facing from thousands to millions of dollars in annual operating costs, mostly wages and benefits, to operate a call center depending on how many agents you have.

Labor alone accounts for 60%+ of your operating costs. And finding enough qualified people who will work in your center, when you want them, at the compensation package your firm has budgeted, over the period you expect to keep it operating, is the biggest challenge you face.

▶ Your Choices

There are several alternatives and adjuncts to expanding and opening call centers that you should examine before going forward. They will help you spend your resources wisely while ensuring that there is the flexibility necessary to handle fluctuating customer contacts and demand. The key ones are *self-service, teleworking* and *outsourcing* Make sure you thoroughly examine them before signaling the work crews to begin ripping out walls or erecting new ones for your new call center.

Customer self-service includes automated inbound voice, known as interactive voice response (IVR), Web self-service, automated outbound voice messaging (OVM), fax and automated inbound and outbound e-mail response and straight outbound e-mail. The powerful software that drives most of these applications enable customers to perform much of the same tasks as with live agents, such as placing, changing and canceling orders, managing accounts and transactions, requesting and obtaining information, solving problems, locating dealers, entering contests and filling out surveys.

This book and this chapter are not about the details of the technologies that enable the self-service functions used to support customer service and sales. There are other books like the *Call Center Handbook, The Complete E-Commerce Book* and *Computer Telephony Encyclopedia* also offered by CMP, plus numerous articles in CMP magazines like *Call Center, Computer Telephony* and *Teleconnect* that can give you that information. I will instead briefly describe them, their applications and their advantages and weaknesses.

IVR is a very sophisticated software application that captures and recognizes input from telephone keypads. Customers hit the keypads to make menu selections, answer yes or no questions and spell out names or words. Speaking is more "human" than punching in letters or numbers on a telephone touchpad to make your way through long, complicated menus that can get you lost quicker than shopping at Macy's at Christmas. Therefore, increasingly, IVR systems are coupled with speech recognition software that recognizes parts of human speech, and looks for key spoken numbers and words, then responds in kind.

Web self-service is where customers access your company via the Internet or internally through your corporate network or 'Intranet' to obtain assistance, including help desk and buying products and services. Users point-and-click, and/or key in information.

OVM systems dial up numbers from databases and deliver pre-recorded messages. Some OVM systems connect called parties to an IVR menu or to a live agent.

Fax systems let you send broadcast faxes or let callers request faxes from a keypad menu or leave a message to have the fax sent at another time or to a specific location, such as a hotel room or business, like a Mail Boxes Etc.

Automated inbound and outbound e-mail response receives and sends text and graphics. The software searches for words, numbers and phrases and generates a response on set templates. Straight outbound e-mail consists of text and possibly graphics transmitted from one computer to another computer, which can be a cellphone as well as the more conventional desktop, laptop, notebook and PDA. Customers can respond by sending an e-mail back, or by calling, faxing, or in person. All outbound e-mail can have links to your Web site, thereby driving traffic to it.

Outbound e-mail that is sent without being asked for is known as unsolicited commercial e-mail (UCE). Unwanted UCE is known as "spam," after an infamous Monty Python restaurant sketch where a hapless diner has been told that everything on the menu has Spam® in it.

A faxback self-service program by IVR or Web is another handy service. It lets your customers obtain documents, without the necessity of having someone write down the order and/or send it out.

Self-service systems that conduct transactions, be it for information, selling, or service must rely on databases. The information or responses that are entered are automatically "read" by machines that extract what the person is looking for, i.e., flight times, product availability, or answers to questions, such as "my PC won't boot up." If what is being sought is not there, most self-service systems can hook the person up to a live agent, and transmit the corresponding file or what is on the computer screen to an agent for further assistance.

There are some differences in how various self-service technologies operate. If a new customer and the company they're contacting don't have a file on them, they must fill out a form, which can be via an IVR or a Web form. In some cases with an IVR (such as dealer locator), their phone number is picked off by automatic number identification (ANI), giving all the information a system needs. By matching the number, such as the exchange (the first three digits) with the area the exchange covers, the system can locate the nearest store and "tell" its location, hours open and contact information. This doesn't work, of course, with cellphone numbers and cell and pager exchanges that are also used by landlines.

If the person has called before, the company will have a record on them, then an IVR system will "recognize" the caller based on their phone number and can (if so programmed) present customized menus, offers and/or pop their information to an agent. If a person has previously visited a Web site, software known as a "cookie" will have been placed at that time on their computer, allowing the Web site to "know" them the next time they visit the site.

Teleworking is having your own employees answer and make calls and contacts from their home, on computers and phones that are monitored by a principal call center or office. Attributable operating costs, such as voice/data charges are expensed.

In this book, *outsourcing* means having another company, known as a *service bureau* handling all calls and contacts with their employees off your premises at centers they own and operate at locations they select — though bureaus will open a call center where you want if you're willing to pay for it. Service bureaus will also manage, including hiring/firing, on your premises in an arrangement known as *insourcing*.

A few technically adept bureaus will host complex technology like customer relationship management packages, IVR, e-mail and Web self-service technologies along with online handling and as such become an application service provider (ASP). They can provide any of their proffered services at your in-house or insourced center as well as at theirs. IVR ASPs are known as *IVR service bureaus*.

A cross between teleworking and outsourcing is *remote agent contracting*, where you contract with independent freelance workers to provide call center services from their home on a network maintained and organized by a third party. Because this is a contractual relationship with someone who is not an employee I treat this under outsourcing.

▶ Why the Alternatives Should be Part of Your Call Center

As the global economy expands there is more focus on services. This means that there are strong financial, operational and customer-satisfying reasons why you should carefully examine and incorporate some, if not all of these methods into your call center planning.

No longer do agents, who work for little more than minimum wage, just take down orders; provide simple replies to questions like "what time does the next train leave?"; or even supply basic information to queries such as "where is the nearest dealer?"; or pitch a product or service off an acquired list. Instead more agents are using their innate, unduplicated human intelligence to solve complex problems, asking the rights questions to find out what customers and prospects need, so that they or an outside sales rep can make a sale. The challenge is finding and keeping enough of this type of employee.

You can use all three: self-service, telemarketing and outsourcing and their variations in various combinations to replace part or most of a physical call center, leaving the remaining live agents to handle the most demanding contacts, it all depends on what you need your center to accomplish. If you make the right decision concerning the most suitable options or combination of options you will save, in most cases, on labor costs, facility and real estate expenses and numerous hassles.

If you are not comfortable in having self-service handle your first level customer contact, lead generation and response, or making outbound sales and service contacts, you may find live agent outsourcing more economical, flexible, yet equally as effective as hiring agents for these functions in-house. If your call center is at its physical limit but demand for your top level live agent service is growing you may discover that offering teleworking will not only excite your agents but the possibility of it may attract new recruits to your company. You could have calls and contacts routed through the IVR/Web, to a first level provided by a bureau and then possibly escalated, if need be, to an expert or account rep working out of their home. If that customer wants another service, say customer service or order desk, the expert or the bureau can route them to that department's agent at your call center.

All of these methods are scalable to meet your needs. They can help you not only manage expected but sudden call and contact volume peaks, like for seasonal and limited-time-offer products and services, saving you from investing in workstations, building capacity and operations over and above your normal demand flow. And also from lawsuits and

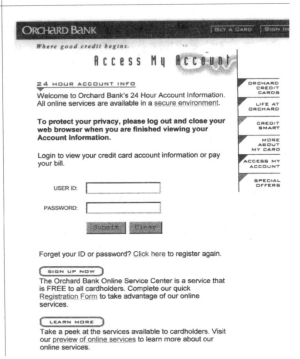

Self-service is convenient, when implemented correctly. Orchard Bank gives credit card holders who access their accounts online information that they could not get on their statements. In exchange such companies, recognizing that DIY costs pennies compared to dollars per transaction for live agents and tellers, are eliminating toll-free numbers as well as closing branches to encourage self-service.

bad publicity if and when you have to cut back your call center.

▶ Self Service Advantages

Cost savings

The most important of the three options is self-service. The principal reason is cost savings. IVR, Web self-service technologies and e-mail can provide most of the basic functions at a fraction of the cost of a live agent. Again, according to Purdue University's Center for Customer Driven Quality (Lafayette, IN), to engage in a self-service transaction costs 5 cents for Web self-service, 50 cents for IVR, $5 for a live agent, $50 for a retail clerk and $500 for a field sales visit. Moreover, CRM contact management software coupled to computer telephony links, can cull lower-valued contacts and stream them through less costly self-service media before resorting to live agents, allowing you to obtain greater profit and lower your cost per customer transaction.

Self-service, such as outbound e-mail costs virtually nothing to send, compared with white or "3-D" mail. Acceptance and rejection is immediate, instead of waiting several days for an e-mail, fax, phone or white mail response.

You can easily customize outbound e-mail. To do the same with "white" or "snail" direct mail is expensive and sometimes impossible since it is dependent on large mass volumes of the same pieces to keep printing costs down. Changing and dropping in text and zapping them out electronically is far faster than redesigning and laying out new copy, plates, and cranking out separate press runs. Outbound e-mail is especially important if you're targeting niche markets with small numbers of potential customers, using direct mail may eat up your entire profit margin.

The savings also apply when you outsource IVR compared with doing the same via live agents. When Office Depot outsourced its IVR system to Registry Magic's (Boca Raton, FL) Virtual Employee Teleservices division, it saved 50% over having a live agent service bureau take the calls. Virtual Employee Teleservices can answer 2,000 ports at once; of course, this method can offer live agent opt-out.

One highly useful, cost-saving option is hybrid outbound live/automated messaging and response for high volume of simple-message outbound calls, such as for temporary campaigns or when you need outbound overflow capacity. Agents ask the called parties whether they want to hear the message.

IVR service bureau Intelogistic's (Fort Lauderdale, FL) *Rapid* program lets you connect your phone banks or remote agents' phones to its dialer. The dialer rings the number and your agents ask the called parties whether they want to hear a message, which is then played. While this is happening, the dialer rings the next number. The IVR offers callers the option of returning to a live agent at the end of the message.

The savings over live agent-only calls are significant. You can send out 60 calls per hour with the blended program compared with 15 calls per hour with live-agent only. The savings total around 60% per completed call, with costs as low as $1 per call.

And cost saving advantages are why companies want customers to visit their Web sites rather than phoning them or going to their stores. Many companies no longer offer toll-free numbers — for example, the computer hardware and software makers have dropped toll-free support for pay-as-you-talk 900 numbers.

Consultants like Jon Kaplan, president of TeleDevelopment Services (Richfield, OH), believes non-high tech firms will soon start charging calling fees, just as banks and travel agencies have introduced service fees. While buyers have been known to balk and complain to government offi-cials — like when the airlines raise their fares — banks add fees and tel-cos do play with phone rates, so customers may acquiesce to the new real-ity of calling fees.

"Reaching a live agent is a value-add service," Kaplan points out. "Therefore it is not unreasonable for them to pay."

Better live agent utilization

There is a second key advantage of self-service: better live agent utilization. Given that people are expensive, you want to use them as efficiently as pos-sible. The people who work for you feel the same way. Basic tasks like order taking and dealer locator does not tap into the creativity, intelligence and customer service skills of your agents. They get bored quickly, and that usually means lowered performance followed by a door slamming "bye!"

Improved customer service

Assigning these tasks to lower-cost self-service saves money; and your agents can be used for complicated value-added and mutually rewarding sales and service tasks. A win-win for you, your employees and your cus-tomers, since a third important reason for adopting self-service is improved customer service. When faced with growing call and contact volumes and static agent supply because you can't find enough people when you need them, self-service can fill the gap. Whether you have all calls hit an IVR/auto-attendant or have online contacts go through your Web site before inviting them to contact a live agent either by voice (phone and voice over IP), e-mail or chat, you can to vent a certain per-centage of them through self-service venues.

If a caller is on hold you can invite them to go through the IVR, some-times without losing their place in queue should they wish to return to it and speak to a live agent. This is similar to the practice where airline staff ask passengers in long airport lineups if they are walk-on or have an e-ticket, so they can get them out of the queue.

OVMs, automated e-mail and faxing also deliver acknowledgement, marketing, reminder messages and customer care confirmations. IVR systems that are hooked up to OVMs can deliver interactive outbound messages to your customers, such as notifying them of software bugs and reminding them to activate their credit cards. You can also use self-service media to drive callers and contacts to your live agent call center.

Disaster recovery

Self-service systems are vital for a fourth function, disaster recovery. There is no faster, more economical way to warn of a computer virus and or service disruption, like when a hurricane or tornado hits, than by sending out OVMs, e-mails and faxes. A set of wired-in IVR boxes in a remote location in a safe and secure closet or additional e-mail and Web servers, or contracting for them, is less costly, faster and involves less hassle to set up than emergency phone banks and the people to staff them.

Product delivery

Web self-service has a fifth advantage: product delivery. Chances are that the last time you bought a new piece of software or upgrade you downloaded it into your PC instead of trudging off to the megashop or waiting for the UPS guy.

Customer acceptance

The sixth rationale is customer acceptance. As these technologies improve, they are becoming more acceptable by customers, hence increasing their opportunities for use. E-mail is now in widespread use; the nice aspect about it is that everyone involved can have a record of what was communicated. The Web's popularity as a channel need not be expounded on here. People like surfing and doing business on the Web, provided they can reach a live agent when they seek one.

IVR, seen as the least customer friendly because of the hassle of pushing buttons and navigating complicated menus, is getting a face lift with speech recognition technology that permits customers to have a near natural conversation with these machines. This leads to fewer live agent opt-outs and greater savings. IVR with speech recognition also taps into the consumers and businesses that still use rotary phones.

Customer preference

This leads to a seventh reason for self service: customer preference. Customers may prefer self service because it is quicker and easier. Why be on hold for ten minutes when they can find out what they need with an IVR or on the Web in two minutes? With the Web they can also see the product and find out more information about it. With the aid of video, the Web can give the consumer an experience that is the next best thing to being there.

Through the use of a simple speech recognition application developed in-house by Call Interactive, an IVR service bureau (Omaha, NE), Kraft Foods discovered in a promotional campaign for *Jell-O Jigglers* gelatin molds that a surprising 73% of the callers chose the IVR system over going to a live agent. The IVR system completed over 99% of the 73% of calls it handled.

The automated script thanked callers, then invited them to place orders, request more information or reach a live agent. The script then asked callers to state their mailing information. If the caller chose to buy the molds, the system asked them to key in their credit card number. It then read the number back to verify. The system handled most calls in two to three minutes.

Self-service is especially important if you are marketing personally sensitive items, such as clothing and personal hygiene supplies like incontinence pads. Online shopping at sites such as Fredericks of Hollywood and Victoria's Secret, where the customer can just basically point and click, is the best thing for guys who'd choke if they tried to order the same allegedly sexy flimsy or excruciatingly tight and sweaty garments over the phone, let alone walking into a store.

And, many women like to buy clothes online or use an IVR, for the same reasons. According to my wife, no woman (notwithstanding the fact that many are objectively in good shape) likes to reveal their size to another person, even if it is over the phone.

Transaction traceability

Lastly, with e-mail and Web-based self-service you have transaction traceability. You can keep a permanent instantly accessible record of what was said, promised, ordered and delivered and the price, compared with the slower, clumsier method of listening and reviewing tapes with call monitoring, which also may be legally restricted to protect privacy. You will find fewer 'he said/she said' disputes. The records enable easier escalation of leads, issues and problems to higher-level agents and management.

▶ Self Service Downsides

Self-service technologies like IVR and a fully interactive Web site, with ordering and problem resolution are not cheap and take months to go live reliably. Then you must have the funds and the financing in place when you acquire the system along with bearing the costs of the inevitable installation headaches.

To buy speech rec-enabled IVR costs 10 cents per minute, including capital and installation costs (around $500,000+) — spread out over four years. The Internet/e-commerce software and servers cost tens to hundreds of thousands of dollars and take months to install and debug. According to teleservices consultancy Kowal Associates (Boston, MA) at the lowest end a company could spend $100,000 for an e-mail-enabled Web site over the first year, and more than twice that for an e-commerce site. The more features you add, the higher the price. Experienced Web programmers don't come cheap, especially those who are experienced at back-end integration of databases and fulfillment.

And it isn't a one-shot deal; Web technology becomes obsolete very quickly. To keep your Web site fresh and attractive, you have to redo your site and your offers often.

IVR (and to a lesser extent the Web) has suffered from poor implementation. Few aspects annoy customers more and prompts them to zero-out more often than long and complicated IVR menus — people cannot remember more than a few options at a time. Web sites that have broken links and Javascript errors will also make surfers reach for the phone.

Web self-service is also a lot more complicated than it looks, especially if the customers are conducting transactions online. The data can sit on many different computers, from servers to mainframes, using different operating systems and database software, strung out over thousands of miles connected by complex networks. Often the computers belong to other companies, like a bank or finance firm. Somehow they must all communicate to each other. If they don't then there are problems and customers will get annoyed because they don't care about how complex your systems are; it isn't *their* problem.

My wife is a programmer with a large healthcare company. When she shows me the complex coding behind one seemingly simple Web page, such as a member enrollment form, I understand why she gets paid as well as she does. This isn't kid's stuff. Programming is painstaking rigidly logical math. Make one error in the equation and the answer will be wrong. Even the simplest error will cause a program to fail or a Web site to crash. As I was writing this section my computer died, a "fatal error" in Windows.

The worst mistake you can make with self-service is not allowing callers and surfers access to a live agent; it will probably ensure that they'll never call or shop on your site again. Yet, I've come across IVR menus with no zero-out; there are also too many so-called interactive Web sites that lack phone numbers, e-mail addresses or even white mail addresses.

Web self-service may lull you into thinking that's all you need. Wrong — you're going to need live agents.

That's the trap the dot-coms fell into, and they are now scrambling to get live agent services. Studies poured out of the research firms in 1999 and 2000 about customers abandoning online shopping carts because they could not get customer service. Paul Kowal cites studies that show that 65% of e-commerce site visitors who initiate live agent contact complete the sale. You'll also need Web-enabled agents who can read and push Web pages and undertake text chat. An e-commerce site offering only automated self-service will annoy consumers; you can't program an automated e-mail response or FAQ as well as you can train a truly interactive agent.

There are many excellent companies that offer the best of both worlds — self-service and live agents. Two that I can recommend, from personal experience, are QVC and Archie McPhee. QVC is known for marketing to

Middle America — through its TV channel — consumer goods, such as, jewelry, gift items and increasingly clothes and household products. But the actual sale is accomplished through a mixture of live agents, IVR and its Web site. My wife does much of her shopping on QVC. I occasionally shop for her through it. The customer service, through *every* channel is excellent.

At the other extreme, Archie McPhee sells strange 60s-styled novelty items like boxing nun and rabbi puppets, lava lamps, lunch boxes (with or without plastic roaches) and pink flamingoes — both online and over the phone as well as through a store in Seattle. I've just given away where I do my Christmas shopping... In a *Call Center Magazine* article on catalog companies that ran in the May 2000 issue, David Wahl, the company's Web and catalog manager said that self-service and e-mail messages have been supplanting phone calls for orders.

Yet Wahl doesn't believe that Archie McPhee's Web site will completely eliminate its need for a call center. For example, the agents can direct callers to other firms if they can't find what they want, such as plastic false teeth. "It really makes people more confident in a Web-based business if they can actually contact the company," he says.

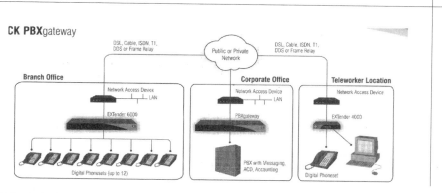

Switching technology such as MCK Communication's EXTender 3200 make teleworking agents appear to your customers like they're in the typical noisy high-stress call center bullpen, instead of in the more relaxed, less frazzled confines of their home, free of the fender-bending, nose-in-the-other's armpit commute. Yet you can monitor their performance just as if they were in your center, with call monitoring, ACD Reports, Assigned Queue Performance, number of calls-handled and time spent on after-call, i.e., wrap-up activities.

▶ **Teleworking Advantages**

Teleworking is having your agents take or make calls on your premises, or from sites that are closer to their homes than your primary call center operation. High-speed services, such as ISDN, digital subscriber line (DSL) and cable modems make teleworking feasible. There are many products available for switching calls to agents who work from remote locations and for monitoring these calls.

Frees up seats and facilities

The principal advantage of teleworking is that it frees up seats and facilities. According to John Heacock, vice president of TManage (Austin, TX), a teleworking consultancy, and a former official with the International Telework Association and Council, a trade organization, there is a *cost avoidance of about $25,000 per teleworking agent*, when measured against $35,000 for the traditional in-center agent. This is achieved by avoiding the one-time and on-going costs necessary to build and maintain in-center workstations, lunchroom, parking spaces, and other amenities often designed-in to attract and retain agents.

Heacock recounts that there once was a large gas and electric utility company which owned two call center facilities and leased a third. When the 'landlord' of the leased facility found it necessary to raise the rent three-fold, the utility thought its only choice was to either pay the higher lease cost or bear the cost and disruption of moving it to a new location, with the hope that they could keep their existing agents.

"I recommended a 'New Alternative': reconfigure the two 'owned facilities' to focus more on new agent selection and training, and to service as fully-redundant technology 'bases' for their new Remote Agent [teleworking] Program," says Heacock. "This completely eliminated the leased facility and associated expenses, thereby avoiding the facilities cost of the third center, and improved customer satisfaction, agent productivity and reduced 'churn' all in one bold vision!"

Teleworking also permits you to tap into low-density remote locations where the workforce is too spread out to effectively commute to one site. However, to make this work, there must be excellent, reliable high-capacity lines to each home, although there are experiments with wireless data transmission to avoid that problem.

"Given an established 'traditional' call center facility, agent capacity can be expanded by at least one-third (without any 'brick and mortar' investment) through an effective remote agent program," says Heacock. "Depending upon the efficiencies of the computer telephony system and the sophistication of the mainframe applications, remote teleworking agent populations beyond 40 percent are possible."

Labor attraction and retention

A second key advantage of teleworking is labor attraction and retention. Literally driving teleworking is the hassle of commuting, with growing traffic congestion even in the smaller cities, creating up to 60 to 90 minutes of pollution-creating nerve-destroying "drive time," and delays that make workers late. This costs them wages, inconveniences their reliefs and costs you productivity.

Where it is available, travelling by mass transit isn't a barrel of laughs either. The bus or rail routes may not go conveniently close to where employees live and where employers are located, especially in the suburbs. Service may be slow, infrequent or not run at all in the evenings and weekends; connections and transfers may be poor or nonexistent. Stations and stops may be unsafe, especially at night. Also, employees cannot easily handle important chores, such as picking up the offspring at the child care, if they take transit.

John Heacock points out that teleworking agents are 7% - 25% more productive than their "In-Center" counterparts. With teleworking there is greater job satisfaction, reduced absenteeism and fewer illnesses. Offering teleworking is equivalent to a $4,000 indirect pay raise per full-time teleworker, through lower car insurance, less gasoline, reduced clothing expenses and more economical lunches.

If you have a high-level sales or external help desk with professional people, you will find offering teleworking extremely critical to fulfilling your staffing requirements in today's hot labor market. Teleworking is growing at an annual rate of more than 20%, says Cherry Anderson, an analyst with the Gartner Group, driven to a large extent by the IT industry. IT workers have been a key driver because there are only seven available workers for every 10 job openings in that industry, says Anderson.

"So when most companies initially considered telecommuting, they tapped the IT workers," says Anderson.

Yet teleworking isn't just for the IT professionals. To maintain good service levels you may need it to draw in potentially fine workers who cannot, for mobility reasons, or who have childcare and senior care responsibilities, access your call center.

You may also have evening and night shifts that are difficult to staff. Who wants to be out at night, especially in larger metropolitan areas, where it is impossible to know who or what is lurking in the parking lot or at the bus stop? Teleworking is an option for those agents whose home environment is such that they can make and receive calls even at 2am.

Disaster survival

The third edge with teleworking is disaster survival. Your call center can be hit by bad weather that not only knocks out the power and voice/data but can make it impossible for the agents to get to it. Agents who telework can't use bad weather as an excuse for not showing up for work. Then, because not everyone lives in the same area, if a few of the teleworking agents' lines are down, there are others that will be connected.

"During the Blizzard of `96 Pennsylvania's governor closed the highways for three day, with one 400+ seat call center that had 32 'snowed-in' agents," Heacock points out.

▶ **Teleworking Downsides**

Teleworking is not for everyone: maybe about 35% to 40% of your workforce. You have to know your staff well enough to determine which agents function best away from your direct supervision.

Among the agents who indicate that they want to telework you need to select only those who have sufficient training and experience, who demonstrate that they can manage their own time and who know how to resolve problems with customers on their own. After you make your decision, you have to adapt your managerial approach so that you can supervise and train agents whether they work inside or outside your center.

Teleworking also introduces technological issues and expenses. For example, you have to provide special equipment and software so that they can handle calls and collect information about customers as though they were in your main center.

"Teleworking can work where agents are highly motivated and need little supervision," Ron Cariola, vice president with Equis (Chicago, IL), points out. "These include help desk reps and high-level customer service reps. However, if from experience, your call center requires high supervision, such as outbound sales, credit and collections and lower-level customer service and order taking, then the agents shouldn't telework."

Perhaps the most serious limitation to teleworking is the availability of the proper teleco service to the home. Neither ISDN nor DSL is available everywhere; DSL services require subscribers to be within about a mile, as the cable is hung, from the central office. About 1/3 of US homes are in that range. The wires could be great or rotten, as is the installation and repairs by the incumbent local exchange carrier (ILEC). Competing DSL offerings do little good; they must use the ILEC equipment to reach the premises.

The sad fact is that too often ILEC service stinks. *Call Center* founder Harry Newton has raged against telco, pre- and post-deregulation stupidity. They dropped the ball on ISDN: I heard near-endless complaints about ISDN setups and costs from co-workers. In a story appropriately titled "DS-Hell" the August 1, 2000 *America's Network* reported of DSL delays, plus bad service, untrained technicians and poor performance, growing complaints about ILEC residential service causing, not surprisingly, a decline in satisfaction rates.

It doesn't have to be this way. For example, I have heard excellent reports of carrier cooperation with call centers and small businesses and of excellent networks, even into remote areas in Canada. NB Tel in New Brunswick has been working on teleworking agent programs in that province. There are also reports of carrier interest in teleworking in Australia and in the UK.

Before embarking on a teleworking program that involves sending voice and data, you should check out the technology feasibility and talk to the local users about their experiences. Local Internet service providers and Internet user groups are a great source of information. They will know firsthand how good the local lines and the carriers are. Because bad phone service makes news, check out local news coverage. If there are competing cable modem services available, such as Time Warner/AOL's RoadRunner, and new wireless alternatives, look into them.

▶ Outsourcing Advantages

Cost and hassle savings

The principal reason why you should consider outsourcing to a service bureau is cost and hassle savings. Outsourcing saves money. The global consultancy PriceWaterhouseCoopers (PwC) (New York, NY) estimates outsourcing can slice your call handling costs by up to 30%. You also save the cost-riddled hassle and drain on your staff, facilities and IT resources, especially if your alternative is building another call center.

Service bureaus can help you cut down on the size of a call center or eliminate existing and future call centers, depending on how much of these functions you want and how much you can outsource. You may want to have a few top-level agents in-house to handle tough-to-answer questions, or to patch in engineers and developers, or to have senior account managers give personalized service to top customers who appreciate dealing directly with your company.

Outsourcer agents work for you. When outsourcing, make sure that your partner educates and instills in their agents that they are working as *your* representatives. Mostly do by methods such as hanging banners with the client's name, such as what Convergys had done for Hallmark. This also goes for shared agents. When a call or contact comes in about your company at that moment they're *your* agents.

If you are with a growing new or capital-husbanding company, like a dot-com, your best bet is to outsource your customer service and sales. You buy the agents and services as you need them, without investing any resources in the hardware, software, facilities and people.

This also goes for growing "mainstream" companies. For example, agents employed by Convergys (Cincinnati, OH) at its Omaha, NE call center have been the voices most consumers have heard when they dialed 800-HALLMARK since 1995 and when they called up Hallmark's store locator service since 1991.

"We soon realized the call volume was too great to handle on our own," says Sonie Wines, Hallmark's consumer affairs manager. "We evaluated our budget and made the decision to outsource."

Service bureaus achieve those savings because they have the expertise, flexibility and contacts to staff and set up quicker with less cost, even though they face the same labor/facilities/technology pressures of in-house centers. Yet they deliver equal or better service, and equal or more sales, usually at a lower cost per sale than agents can in your own center.

Bureaus can pick and choose the best, most economical locations, not limited by your internal factors such as union considerations or by the condition of the fairway at the 19th hole. Also, if you have a large contract that demands a center dedicated to you, a service bureau will work with you to open it in a mutually-agreeable location.

Their nose for locations is why you find service bureaus in less costly, higher unemployment, areas of the US. For example, Maine, the Appalachians (eastern Pennsylvania, western Virginia, West Virginia, eastern Kentucky), Arkansas, east Texas and Louisiana, California (both northern and the San Joaquin Valley), eastern Oregon and Washington State. You will also find service bureaus where there are workers with specific skill sets, such as computer knowledge, sales culture and multiple language abilities.

As the US becomes more polyethnic, with increasingly affluent immigrants preferring to communicate in their native tongues, outsourcing programs and services to reach them may be less expensive than handling these customers in-house. The Hispanic market alone is about 20% of the US population, yet you may not have enough of these buyers and prospects to warrant hiring and investing in in-house Hispanic-speaking agents and centers. So you contract with service bureaus like Precision Response, ICT Group or Convergys.

Miami, FL is home to Precision Response, giving it the means to serve the Hispanic market. ICT Group's (Langhorne, PA) Spantel division is also based in Miami. For that same reason companies like Convergys have opened bureaus in small south Texas cities such as Brownsville. But Convergys also recently opened a new call center in Fremont, CA, close enough to tap into Silicon Valley's computer-soaked workforce and to the San Francisco Bay area's Asian-speaking workers.

Service bureaus are also set up to handle US calls from foreign countries where labor is less expensive and more plentiful, and where there are educated workers who can speak other languages, such as Canada, India and The Philippines. For example, if you drive on Highway 17, the principal road and for most of the way the route of the Trans Canada Highway, across northern Ontario west of Ottawa, you will travel through several small cities that have become home to US-owned call centers. These include, at present North Bay, (TeleSpectrum Worldwide, King of Prussia, PA), Sudbury, (TeleTech, Denver, CO) and Sault Ste. Marie (RMH Teleservices, Bryn Mawr, PA).

There are also foreign service bureaus that market themselves to US businesses as having the same advantages as their US counterparts. For example, vCustomer (Bellevue, WA) handles calls and contacts from a call center in New Delhi, India while Transworx (Sunnyvale, CA) has theirs in Mumbai. Large and small Canadian outsourcers such as Beautyrock and ClienTelPlus (both of Cornwall, ON), Capreol Connex (Capreol, ON), Conduit (Thunder Bay, ON), CorporaTel (Halifax, NS), Minacs Worldwide (Pickering, ON), Optima (Toronto, ON) and Watts (Toronto, ON) compete with US firms for American business.

Says Geri Gantman, who once ran a service bureau and is now senior partner with marketing consultancy Oetting and Company (New York, NY), "outsourcers are not as tied down to locations as your company may be."

But what really gives bureaus their financial edge is that they have seats to fill and people to fill them. Unlike if you opened your own call center, these contractors can keep their agents busy, phones flashing and screens live at all times, maximizing productivity.

One common way bureaus can cut cost is by sharing your program between different companies so you are not paying for idle time. Known as "shared agent" this feature enables companies to benefit from high quality call center services that they might not have been able to afford.

Shared agents cost less than agents assigned to one account (a "dedicated agent"). They represent excellent value for standard services that do not require highly specialized client-specific training such as inbound dealer locator, basic customer service and appointments and outbound customer care and telemarketing. The bureau can connect them in to your program for short periods of time to handle call peaks, including supplementing dedicated agents. You pay for what you need.

For example, Affina-The Customer Relationship Company (Peoria, IL's) *Affina Select* program offers shared-agent CRM services during weekdays from 7am to 7pm to small/medium-sized companies that do not have the budget for dedicated agents let alone for a megamillion dollar in-house CRM software and call center installation. Yet Affina Select allows the clients to monitor agents making/taking calls on their behalf just as the larger ones do with dedicated agents.

On the other hand dedicated agents give greater customer service depth and build true long-term customer relationships. Agents stay longer, and develop their expertise in your products and services. For example, one of Affina's accounts is customer service for Equal artificial sweetener. Two of the seven agents dedicated to that account have been with it since its start in 1996.

To reinforce this connection outsourcers will dedicate areas, rooms, or even buildings to these agents. In these spaces they will often have product samples, signage and, in the case of GM's Tampa, FL call center run by Sitel (Omaha, NE), elaborate mural panels. Outsourcers will also supply t-shirts and other apparel with the clients' logos to those agents. Centralized Marketing Company (CMC, Cordova, TN) sent its agent to a client's Memphis branch to see how it operated and to gain a better understanding of how the client would benefit from CMC's services.

How can service bureaus achieve all of these results? Because as contractors they have to be efficient and effective. That is their culture. Setting up and managing call centers and running programs is *their* core competency.

"The outsourcer call center culture is more productive than many in-house call center cultures," Paul Kowal points out. "With an in-house call center when agents come to work they expect to get paid from the time they show up. There may be a time lag between the time they punch in and when they get on the phones. With an outsourcer because the client is paying by the minutes its agents get on the phones right away."

Flexibility

The second key reason for outsourcing to a service bureau is flexibility. Service bureaus are there *when you need them.* You can contract with them just to handle disaster recovery, overflow or after hours calls or you can turn over your entire multimedia customer service management to them. While outsourcers handle medium to large contracts they also take on small ones, especially from the dot-coms.

If you make ski equipment why have a big call center if it will be mostly idle in spring and summer, unless you have customers in Australia or South America? If you run promotions sporadically, like direct response ads for plastic pink flamingoes and other similar tasteless ornaments during a John Waters film festival on cable why have vacant seats over and above your normal requirements when you're not trying to offload the blessed creations?

Outsourcing is your best bet if you're launching a new product or service or testing the market. Outbound telemarketing or driving inbound calls from radio and TV ads, Web banners, e-mail and direct mail are the most common reasons companies use outsourcers. Once the promotion or sale is finished, you don't need the agents or the call center. If you set one up, you would have to go through the hassle of laying people off.

This convenience also applies if you have long running customer service and sales functions and you need to scale your company and marketing back. Service bureaus can shift agents or close up shop, with none of the local heartache and bad press if your company itself laid off or reassigned staff or closed a call center.

Perhaps the most effective use of outsourcer flexibility is as first points of contact for customers in sales and service, such as first level help desk and business and consumer sales lead management. The contact volumes fluctuate, making call center staffing and sizing difficult. The content of these contacts is wheat and chaff. Yet they are sufficiently valuable so as to not force them to be sorted out by self-service. Instead, outsourcers provide a friendly human voice to answer and ask questions. They can escalate appropriate questions and leads to your in-house team, freeing these highly-paid individuals from the productivity-wasting drudgery of answering essential, if low-intelligence calls, like "where is the On button" and sorting unprofitable leads from people and businesses.

Such programs generate results. For example, Interactive Marketing Group (IMG) (Allendale, NJ) has been managing leads for Minolta's corporate and dealership marketing since 1995, including all inbound calls, faxes, e-mails and Web-based contacts. IMG makes outbound followup calls to ensure Minolta's dealers or salespeople have contacted the customer.

"Over the years IMG has provided us with innovative, turnkey dealer programs which have significantly impacted on our business, resulting in more qualified leads and closed sales," says Nancy Gehring, national program administration manager, Minolta Corporation. "IMG's proactive approach, together with a unique understanding of the latest Web-based marketing techniques, continuously enables us to reach more customers and better serve our dealers."

Also, more companies, as they become comfortable working with bureaus, are entrusting them with important customer relations. Monsanto Consumer Foods, now owned by Tabletop Acquisitions and now known as Merisant, discovered outsourcing improved customer service relationships for the company's Equal tabletop sweetener business. Affina has been handling Equal e-mails since 1998.

The Affina contract replaced a small call center: Monsanto/Tabletop kept a three person staff including the Monsanto consumer affairs manager, Susan Jacobsen, plus a dietician and an Affina liaison. Monsanto decided to outsource when it relocated its offices from the Chicago suburbs to downtown; that forced it to look at costs.

"We were worried that by outsourcing, we would lose contact with our customers," recalls Jacobsen, who began the Affina program. "In retrospect, outsourcing was the best decision we ever made. We now know our customers better."

Speed to market

The third key reason to outsource is speed to market. Bureaus get your program set up far quicker, in days rather than weeks or months, with results seen much sooner than if you had undertaken or kept these operations in-house.

The key to their quickness is like that of any contractor: when they make a bid they have to have the people, the place and the equipment lined up and ready to begin delivering on the promised date at the tendered price. They've done the site selection, design and real estate work; the larger companies have on-staff and on-call location teams. They monitor the demand at their centers and expand or open centers if they forecast a shortfall or are bidding on major contracts.

The smart bureaus also have proven, effective call center designs that simplify and speed up set up. Their vendors are only a call, e-mail or fax away. If you need services like creative, direct mail, and fulfillment that they do not provide themselves they usually have partnerships with those that can, giving you one-stop-worry-free service shopping.

Serving international markets

A fourth rationale for looking at outsourcing is serving international markets. If you're expanding your markets internationally and you do not have a strong international presence, outsourcing to a bureau is an excellent first step before investing the considerable time and money in effort, facilities and people. They know the lay of the land and have the right connections, in more ways than one, especially in developing countries.

Non-US centers and those US-owned by locally managed outsourcers are attuned to local cultural nuances that are key to success in these markets. Countries such as Indonesia, Japan and Korea have tough-to-penetrate business and social cultures and setting up centers there can be costly and bureaucratic. Even Canadians, who are immersed in American culture, strongly dislike pushy outbound calls. Quebec consumers often prefer to speak with agents who communicate in their dialect.

Many US bureaus have expanded overseas to better serve their clients. If you are relying on a bureau to handle your US contacts it only makes sense to continue this partnership, if possible, when you grow your business into other countries. Many bureaus have opened up centers or acquired other bureaus overseas to accommodate these needs.

There are also some specialized service bureaus that are experts at serving non-English speakers. Prestige International (New York, NY), owned by a Japanese company made its name by providing Japanese-language concierge services for clients. For example, if a Japanese businessman (most Japanese business travelers are still overwhelmingly male) is staying at New York City's Waldorf Astoria and wants theatre reservations to see the ninth life of *Cats*, a Prestige agent thousands of miles away will handle the request.

"If it's your first time into those foreign markets, you probably are better off outsourcing unless you have experience in setting up international operations," advises Oetting's Gantman. "One would expect the outsourcer to be more savvy internally and externally. Internally when it comes to staffing, and externally in such matters as the marketplace. The downside is the same as outsourcing in the US: you're not building your own internal core competency in that country. Also, you should have a local presence, such as a sales office, in the country or market you're targeting, making outsourcing much easier to manage than if you attempted to do it from the US."

▶ Outsourcing Downsides

There are also some downsides to outsourcing. The key ones are loss of control over agents and customer information. You also risk sharing your information with a competitor that is using the same outsourcer, though the bureaus do take steps to prevent this from happening. I've seen agents working on competing credit card accounts, denoted by signs at their workstations, sitting across from each other but it caused no apparent problems for either client.

Your customer contact and relationship-building skills could also atrophy, yet their value depends on how important customer relationships are to your business. Some functions, such as outbound calling, have less impact on this factor, where the called party is being pressed to buy, rather than inbound customer service where the caller is more engaged and wants something from you. Consultants tend to say that small / medium enterprises, and larger firms seeking a competitive advantage by stressing customer "touch" should not outsource.

Another related issue is that outsourced agents and staff do not have the same responsiveness to your needs as those of an in-house center. They have other clients to satisfy.

There is also a lack of efficiency incentives on the inbound side. E-Satisfy points out that bureaus have little reason to prevent misdirected inbound calls; it says up to 35% of all calls received should not have gone to those numbers. Because the bureau gets paid for them it has little reason to flag them.

Additionally, turnover tends to be greater in an outsourcer than in an in-house center, leading to higher training costs, greater error percentage and lesser quality. There is less likelihood that you will detect problems until large numbers of customers and leads have been burned. That could lead to contract disputes and possible litigation to resolve them. Outsourcer agents do not have the same promotional incentives to perform for you as do in-house agents. E-Satisfy points out that Sony and Toyota draw up from call center agents because they provide the most skilled customer-attuned marketing and management staff.

Outsourcing may also be more costly than opening and running your own center, over the long term. Part of your fee goes to the outsourcer's profits — that's money you could keep in-house. Consultants estimate the tradeoff at the three-year mark. If your project length exceeds that then you may be better off opening your own center.

Service bureaus usually charge by the hour, with a minimum numbers of hours, plus set-up fees. The rule is — the fewer the hours the higher the cost per hour. A smaller bureau can do business with you at 500 hours a month minimum for six months, while a larger firm will consent to talk to you only if you're looking to buy 1,500 hours a month for a year. The bigger firms can charge $20 to $25 per agent hour while the smaller firm must bid at the high 20s to low 30s because of economies of scale. Some bureaus are dropping the set-up charges if you sign up for a huge, "mega-hour" multiyear contract.

Keep in mind that like any business, service bureaus expand, contract, change names, add or delete services, merge or are merged or go out of business entirely. Chances are by the time you read this some of the bureaus mentioned in this book may have branched into other markets, are going under another name or be out of business. The company you start partnering with now may be a quite different firm two or three years later. They may or may not want your business, depending on what is best for their profitability. Therefore you need to keep a fairly close eye on your service bureau and ask what the impacts will be on your business relationship from any change.

It may not be a good idea to split the live agent handling of your phone and the live agent handling of the online traffic for the same function-type between in-house call centers and service bureaus, or between different service bureaus. You will many times run into numerous integration problems meshing different systems. However, as long as the technologies can work together, it makes sense to have two or three vendors sharing the same contract; it can keep them competitive.

"The outsourcing choice makes sense if the business application is relatively simple and does not require extensive training, product knowledge, or cross or upselling skills, and when it is important to develop a call center in zero time with a very small capital investment," points out Bob Engel, principal of consultancy Engel Picasso (Albuquerque, NM). "The owned center choice makes the most sense where the product or service is proprietary, requires heavy agent training investment and where your development strategy employs strong cultural integration and loyalty amongst employees."

This is especially true if you plan to outsource customer relationship management (CRM) applications to a bureau that will take care of initial calls and contacts and, if necessary, then escalate them to account representatives and help desk professionals at your center. To make this work you have to connect your internal system to the outsourcers' CRM package, which can be nightmarish.

"My sense is that if you have a call center with more than 200 seats the cons of outsourcing your CRM outweigh the pros," says Paul Kowal. "You're better off installing CRM and handling the customer contacts yourself. If you have fewer than 200 seats then you should consider outsourcing."

e-Satisfy recommends that you take the following steps to ensure a successful outsourcing relationship and thereby making sure *your* customers are happy. e-satisfy has the background to make the advice; it is owned by outsourcer TeleSpectrum Worldwide.

- **Survey callers.** Require the bureau to continuously and directly measure customer satisfaction by a mail survey to a random sample of callers;

- **Don't emphasize speed.** Limit the percentage of calls answered in more than 60 seconds. Average speed of measurement should *not* be a productivity standard.

- **Get regular and direct feedback.** Make sure the bureau's agents send input to you regularly, like weekly or monthly, not filtered by bureau management. For example, USAA uses e-mail while Fidelity Investments relies on voice mail.

- **Analyze problem calls.** Require the bureau to capture detailed data on repeat and unproductive calls, including causes and calls not resolved on first contact.

- **Supply the tools.** Stipulate that the bureau give its agents all the authority and tools to assure that calls and contacts can be taken care of on first contact and that they be permitted to move into a soft cross-sell when appropriate.

- **Provide customer information.** Give your bureau the customer information files so that agents know who the customers are, their value and enough about their circumstances to cross-sell intelligently.

- **Avoid burnout.** Have your bureau vendor install initiatives and career paths for agents.

- **Stress training.** Assure that the price they quote you includes continuous training to your standards and reinforcement of skills, as well as satisfaction measurement and adequate analysis and reporting of call and contact content.

▶ Remote Agent Contracting, Pros and Cons

One new variant of outsourcing is *remote agent contracting* where you hire agents who work from home as independent contractors, using a third party firm as matchmaker, putting you and the agents together, and then running the network. Examples of such firms are Netmommies (Chicago, IL) and Willow CSN (Miami, FL).

This method has the same facility-saving benefits of outsourcing to service bureaus, but gives you more control over your agents. You hire them for short periods of time, such as call peaks, and terminate the individual contracts when not needed or when they don't perform to your satisfaction.

Willow claims its CyberAgents can slice as much as 50% over your existing operating costs, without sacrificing performance. The agents answer all calls in 15 seconds or less.

Willow's clients, including well-known firms such as Alamo Rent-a-Car, 1-800-Flowers, The Home Shopping Network, Staples, SkyMall and Ticketmaster, and service bureaus such as GE Financial report an 8% average turnover or less.

"Our concerns with remote agent contracting are how well do these agencies screen applicants, do they do any kind of job analysis that defines the specific competencies to screen for and what is their turnover?" asks Kathryn Jackson, associate with Response Design Corporation (Ocean City, NJ). "How does a company know if the agent has been screened for the job's specific competencies and do companies that contract for remote agents know the best applications to consider for this type of outsourcing?"

CHAPTER FOUR

Laws and Trends that Shape Call Center Functions

If you are thinking about setting up or expanding a call center and deciding what functions to include, you should closely examine several key trends that can affect whether you need a call center, or what programs and services it should handle. The same goes for any existing call center services. Some of these trends and developments also shape, and are shaped by legislation governing call center functions. Elected officials, because they want to get into and stay in power, generally follow what their vocal electorate wants.

After examining these trends and the laws you may consider altering your call center functions, which in turn will affect the size, location and costs of your center. Or you may decide to seek different channels to reach and stay in touch with your customers.

The four key trends this chapter will look at are the apparent decline in and growing consumer and nascent business

The Direct Marketing Association's Privacy Promise helps the marketing industry regulate itself, and attempts to forestall harmful laws by having business to consumer marketers comply with fair practices and with federal and state laws.

resistance to outbound telesales, the growing specter of unwanted unsolicited commercial e-mail (UCE) a.k.a. "spam," the rise of customer relationship management (CRM), consumer privacy, and reports of bad service. Consequently, there is a growing number of passed and proposed laws in the US and other countries affecting outbound calling, UCE and the information that call centers collect as part of a CRM strategy and deployment.

This book does not deal with day-to-day call center operations. What is critical is that these trends and consequent regulations will shape the future of call center services, and their acceptance by customers. If the problems continue uncorrected they may drag down your center with them. You may end up literally pouring millions of dollars and priceless time into setting up a center that won't be allowed to make or take calls or e-mails or that has people hang up and complain about them. The end result is a call center not pulling in the profits you need.

▶ Is Outbound Still Worthwhile?

You should think very carefully before incorporating into your business strategy outbound market surveys, outbound live agent calls, OVM/fax and e-mail telemarketing, whether it's cold calling or aimed at your existing customers. While these methods are useful in acquiring new customers, selling to existing ones, and for market research, you may get less sales and more unwanted publicity than you had bargained for.

No, this doesn't mean "no telemarketers" – though that is the wish held by many privacy advocates and others who don't want to be disturbed by them. This is the logo for PhoneBusters, a Canadian police-based effort to stamp out destructive, fraudulent Canadian and US telemarketers. Most companies practice lawful, ethical telemarketing, informing potential customers about products and services they may wish to obtain.

Of all the call center functions it is outbound telemarketing that appears to be most hated by consumers. People appear to like and trust such calls from such faceless agents less and less with each passing day. Many members of the public, especially the elderly and middle to upper class, fear fraud when buying a product or service solicited over the phone. *DM News* is a great source for finding who got nailed and for what. So are, increasingly, the local, daily newspapers.

To cite one of many examples: the Associated Press reported August 5, 2000 that BrandDirect Marketing of Shelton, CT agreed to pay about $2 million to the states of Connecticut and Washington and to shell out another $11 million in restitution, in a case that affected some two million consumers. In a story carried in the Torrington, CT *Register-Citizen*, Washington State Attorney General Christine Gregoire found that BrandDirect failed to cancel memberships in continuity clubs - where people buy items like subscriptions and must tell the company they want to cancel — and it had also shaved weeks off its membership club programs. It also failed to clearly disclose that credit cards could be charged for fees and renewals without consumers providing the credit card numbers and without notice.

BrandDirect denied the allegations. Judging from the press report it is not clear whether BrandDirect's top executives had acted deliberately (which, I think is unlikely because the firm's owners, Readers Digest and Federated Department Stores, are not boiler room operators); or whether the actions were due to carelessness on the executive's part by not realizing that many consumers don't fully understand how continuity clubs work; or because BrandDirect's managers and supervisors were cutting corners on scripting to make quotas.

The point is that the damage has been done — another telemarketing firm locked into the public stocks. Not only are there 2 million more Americans who have just become leery about dealing with a company over the phone but also millions more who read the wire service article. By the time this book appears in print there will be, in all likelihood, many more similar stories that add to the crescendo of bad news for telemarketing.

Even so, fraud is less of an issue with telemarketing thanks to such vigorous enforcement of laws and regulations. What is becoming more important is the "bugging" factor. Americans hate telemarketing with a passion. And, not just because they're worried that someone will rip them off, but because telemarketers interrupt their activities, most notably dinner. This is reflected in today's culture. Rarely a day goes by without an article, comic strip, circulated e-mail, or TV program blasting the practice.

A famous episode of the hit TV series *Ally McBeal* showed actress Calista Flockhart, lifting the agent's head out of the phone, after having her evening interrupted by a telemarketer. "How would you like me to call you at home?!" she yells. Commercial jingle-writer Tom Mabe came out recently with a highly publicized CD called "Revenge on the Telemarketers, Round One," with clever comebacks to telemarketer pitches.

Can you blame people? Especially those who have high-stress jobs, work long hours, and have terrible commutes? Ironically, these individuals are the ones marketers are most likely to target, since they tend to have the highest purchasing power. As traffic worsens around major metropolitan areas, as mall-and-sprawl entangles and strangles smaller cities; all encouraged by land use policies that do not assess price tags for incurred environmental, social and transportation costs, commuting times for *everyone* is growing. There is never enough time anymore to spend with your loved ones, or with doing activities you love and can de-stress with.

Think of the calls *you* get at home. Admit it, haven't you ever told poor, innocent agents trying to do their job to take diving instructions or suggest where to insert their "Dead Kennedys Spirituals CD of the Month Club," "Miracle-Sharp Knives" and "Oligopoly Metropolitan Barium Cards"?

This hatred of telemarketers and other callers is not a media invention. NBC investigative reporter, Liz Crenshaw, told delegates at the 1999 American Teleservices Association (ATA) legislative conference in Washington, DC that if people were not so consistently calling her to complain about telemarketers intruding on their lives, she would not be doing stories on the industry. The ATA, based in Washington, DC, is a trade organization that represents companies that make and take in-house and service bureau telesale calls.

"What's driving this consumer concern is the high volume of calls," said Crenshaw. "People are upset about telemarketers interfering with their precious family and personal time."

Consumers are also taking matters into their own hands by signing up on do not call (DNC) lists. The federal government requires companies to maintain DNC lists; many states also have DNC lists (more about this later). The laws are proving to be popular. The Associated Press reported, in a story carried in the July 24, 2000 *Staten Island Advance*, that 380,000 Tennessee residents or nearly 18% of the state's 1.9 million residential telephone subscribers signed up for that state's DNC program *before* it went into effect. So popular is the new service that high demand delayed its implementation.

The Direct Marketing Association (DMA) sponsors the Telephone Preference Service (TPS) DNC database for outbound, e-Mail Preference Service (eMPS) (for e-mail) plus the Mail Preference Service (MPS) (for direct mail). The DMA, based in New York, NY, represents direct marketers of all media.

All DMA members who sell to consumers must sign to the *Privacy Promise*, a program that assures the public they will notify them that they can opt-out of information exchanges and then honor opt-out requests. Signators must maintain in-house suppress files of consumers who ask not be contacted and use the MPS, TPS and eMPS suppression files that consumers can have their names placed on.

Consumers are also buying answering machines, Caller ID boxes, and other privacy protecting devices and services. Many of these, ironically, are marketed by telcos who provide service to outbound call centers and are sold by outbound and inbound telesales.

One of the most famous of these blocking services is SBC's *Privacy Manager*, deliberately marketed to stop telemarketers. Other telcos are marketing similar services. Privacy Manager, working with Caller ID, identifies a call before it hits the consumer's phone and asks the consumers whether he or she wants to accept, decline or refuse a sales call and tell the telemarketer to put them on a DNC list.

Consumers have been using Privacy Manager and other similar features to block even the calls from companies they do business with, such as their bank or credit card company. This means a growing number of people don't want to be bothered by sales calls, period.

New Yorkers have a particularly effective technique against telemarketers and other outbound callers: being themselves. In a revealing Nov. 7, 1999 *The New York Times* article, "When New York Is on the End of the Line," it was disclosed that call centers award agents supplementary 'danger pay' and give them special training to cope with the city's harried and streetwise residents' legendary verbal abuse.

"There are times when we've called into New York City we've been told exactly where to put the phone — and a number of people have offered to help put it there," David Johnson, president of polling firm Conquest Communications told the *Times*. "While you get rude people all over, the difference is that you get them with every call in New York instead of every six calls."

Even so, many people do buy over the telephone from outbound cold calling telemarketers, even at dinnertime. Actually, according to the ATA, the greatest volume of telesales are made during those hours.

"If people are turned off by telemarketers, then who's doing the buying?" asks ATA Legislative Affairs Manager, Matt Mattingley. "Are the people voicing those complaints truly representative of the population? I think the sales figures demonstrate they're not."

Telemarketers have been taking steps to reduce the annoyance, which also affects outbound survey calls. Predictive dialers, which are very sophisticated hardware or software-based devices that connect agents with outbound called parties, have become better at identifying devices like answering machines and then not connecting the calls. Predictive dialers help make outbound calling doable by adding 200% more live contacts and increasing agent talk time by 200% to 300% over manual dialing. They are a must in *any* high-volume outbound calling function, sales and customer care.

They rely on powerful complex mathematical algorithims that check to see which lines and agents are free and the probability of not putting the call through. They detect busy signals, answering machines and operator/switchboard intercepts. This has improved response rates so that more calls go through.

But Geri Gantman, senior partner with marketing consultants Oetting and Company (New York, NY) is skeptical about that benefit. "The technology helps you know who you cannot reach, but it does not increase the number of people you can reach," she says. "Moreover, the chances are the consumers you can't reach by phone are those that your company is trying to sell to. Those that you can connect through by phone and who don't have those devices may not be your most profitable prospects."

Also, dialers are not perfect. They will ring the number and drop the call, an event known as an abandoned call because no agent is there to speak to the called party. That's because the software balances the benefit of keeping agents busy against the risk of reaching a live person without having an agent on the line. The closer you bring the abandon rate to zero the less efficient they become, requiring you to have more agents to make the same number of calls.

Do not think for a moment that outsourcing your outbound telesales frees you for these hassles. You are legally responsible for their actions. Their agents are calling *your* customers on *your* behalf. Many outsourcers are ambivalent and reluctant to make outbound telesales calls. Some proclaim themselves as inbound only.

Tom Farrell, chief of solution delivery for outsourcer ClientLogic (Nashville, TN) says that outbound calling is "confrontational" for the customer and the agent: the phone ringing is disturbing the called party, who isn't expecting it, and the agent must listen to the abuse and deal with slam downs. It is also often nonproductive; sometimes there are people who have no intention of buying but will tie up an agent for 20 minutes because they can't bring themselves to saying no.

"Outbound will always exist because there will always be a certain amount of the population that will not be as computer-literate as the rest of the world," adds Farrell. "What you're finding is that those folks who rely more and more on telephone contact are not the kind of folks who are going to wind up as premier customers."

If you do use outbound cold-call telemarketing, you need highly accurate and targeted lists, and an ear for your customers. That's the advice from Teresa Hartshaw, president of Centralized Marketing Company (CMC; Cordova, TN), an outsourcer and direct marketer. "When you call, you should make the consumer feel like they are in charge," recommends Hartsaw. "In your script you should ask the called parties how they would like to be contacted, be it by phone, fax, e-mail, or mail. Also, ask when and if they want more information about your product or service before buying."

To get people interested in receiving your call, or making that call to you, may require meshing calling programs with the rest of your marketing plans. Consider sending direct mail and e-mail before instituting the calling campaign.

Also, when people ask agents to send them information, offer to do so by e-mail or fax, especially if the offer is for a limited time. Nothing tempts people, like myself, to quickly respond with verbal abuse and then tell a company to put me on their DNC list before slamming down a phone, than when an agent won't let me review the fine print.

Customer care calls and calls to existing customers appears to be where outbound is going. Both of these functions utilize the similar kinds of customer service and sales skillsets as inbound, enabling more efficient blended agents who are following up on already-created relationships.

Most, but not all people, who recently had a transaction with a company, be it a sales or service matter, are happy to receive the call, unlike cold sales calls. A person is probably less likely to hang up on a call from their credit card company than one from an issuer that they do not do business with.

If your customer strategy involves making courtesy calls, make them as soon as possible after the last transaction. People deal with many companies; they will remember the ones they talked to or did business with last. A call today from CompUSA, where I bought my Compaq Presario a few years ago, would get me to wonder why they are calling, as opposed to one from American Express or Citibank, which I do business with all the time.

Yet, you can overdo courtesy calls. You may find that people are not at home or just do not want to be disturbed. There are already signs that consumer dislike for outbound cold calling is spreading to outbound customer care for the same reason: people don't like being bugged. In a recent episode of comic strip *Nancy*, the namesake character picks up the phone from an agent making a courtesy call for the head of household. Nancy asks the agent if this is a sales call, angrily informing the person that her house does not accept sales calls. When the agent repeats that this is a courtesy call, Nancy slams down the phone and explains to her aunt who had heard the noise that it was a "courtesy slam."

Keep an ear for the market if you are doing market research. If you are promoting a locally known and recognized product or service and your call center is not local, don't try to pass off your agents as folks in the neighborhood. The New York papers reported in glee about a mayoral campaign call: made from Michigan. Don't even *think* about faking accents. Your customer and surveyees, in New York and elsewhere, will give your agents a thorough lesson on how to pronounce certain unmistakable and unprintable words.

▶ Think Twice About E-Mail, OVM Alternatives

Think twice about alternatives to outbound live agent calls like OVMs. The *New York Times* reported July 22, 2000 that ABC backed away from a proposal to leave 10-second messages on answering machines from sitcom stars to promote shows, fearing viewer backlash.

"If there's any risk with these alternative media forms it's something we're not going to do," ABC executive vice president for marketing, advertising and promotion Alan Cohen told *The Times*.

Be careful if you use outbound UCE as a substitute for outbound cold calling or direct mail. As with most things in life, the innovation's same advantage is its biggest disadvantage. Because UCE can be customized and sent for next to nothing there is little cost penalty for lazy, inconsiderate marketers to shoot them off to people unlikely to buy the products and services and jam their inboxes compared with researching and targeting their lists.

This is counterproductive. It annoys the bejasus out of those who might be your customers in the future and earns the hatred of Internet service providers tired of stuffing the spam through their servers.

Because unwanted UCE is cheap, and because it is also very hard to trace, it has become the refuge of scamsters chased out of their boiler rooms by law enforcement authorities, and of computer virus Typhoid Marys. The practice is also spawning work by software developers and IT departments, and by government authorities worldwide to block it with new laws and regulations and strong enforcement thereof. Don't *you* turn UCE into "spam." Target your offers closely. Make sure, if you are not compelled to already, to use your real e-mail return address and Web site, and add your phone number and white mail address. The more you show your legitimacy the more customers and prospects will trust you. Ask your customers for permission to send e-mail to them and to market their e-mail addresses. Set up your own do not contact list. Frequently scrub your e-mail database against the DMA's and others' DNC lists. The people being deluged with the garbage are exactly the middle-to-upper-class Americans who know how to get the attention of legislators and technology vendors, often by e-mail.

▶ Watch for Business-to-Business Outbound

Also, watch how you use the phone, e-mail and other communications media in business-to-business. Most laws do not cover this medium and there are no commercial DNC lists but that doesn't mean that you can get away with slipshod practices. It will only invite more legislation: from the very businesses and business groups that have been fighting against more regulations.

I hear reports about boiler-room-like calls for toners and other such office related products trying to get past the auto attendant or onto employees' direct lines. The agent quality may be drifting downward too. Rudy Oetting of Oetting and Company recounted how he got a sales call at his business from a nice but inarticulate agent who was reading from a script, and when he asked her some questions she was totally unprepared.

"The number of contacts on the outbound side that are in the bad category run about 80%," Oetting estimates. "What people who make many of these outbound calls did was to turn them into automated pre-recorded message delivery machines, only live."

I see this in my work. Public relations is indirect business-to-business marketing. Companies send or have PR agencies transmit releases, make calls and set up interviews to market their products and services in the hope of receiving free mentions in trade media editorial.

These PR companies make some of the dinner-disturbing telemarketers look good. When a telemarketer calls me, if they have done their list acquisition and data modeling correctly, they know that I have some potential interest in their product or service and the income to buy it. If they are flogging day-glo lawn jockeys mounted on mildly electrified mounts (to deter vandals), it is because they know that I have bought objects of little taste, like lava lamps and pink flamingoes from other companies, which is probably how they got my name — by buying their lists.

The same can't be said for PR agencies. For example, I do not, at least as of this writing, cover carriers, their technology and/or wireless systems. Yet, I get many releases and often calls from people concerning those subjects, who are apparently too lazy to research what the magazine's writers cover. I even got spam from a company flogging trade show displays even though I have nothing to do with trade shows.

Still, when I do get a relevant contact, the information from the person making the contact is, seemingly all too often, content-devoid - just a bunch of buzz words thrown together. Most outbound telesales agents I've dealt with are, by contrast, well trained and informed.

Sorry, but I have no patience with such lack of research and professionalism. I worked as a freelancer for many years and I was told to read the publications before pitching the proposals, which I did. If freelancers can do it, on shoestring budgets, then there is no excuse for PR firms not to. Most service bureaus and telemarketers I know of take pains to do their homework. Why can't flashy PR agencies?

The message here is simply this: Outbound is an excellent way to acquire and reach business and consumer customers. Use them correctly by targeting, listening to and respecting your market. Or lose them for yourself and everyone else through the enactment of more laws and by the contacted parties using every device known to block your contacts and/or give you and your staff highly detailed directions to a *very* warm place (hint: it isn't New Orleans in June).

▶ Is Customer Relationship Management (CRM) Right for You?

The biggest problem with traditional outbound calling and contact and with businesses that abuse these methods is that they do not enable businesses to build profitable long-term relationships with customers. They "fire and forget." The same holds true with basic inbound order taking.

Keep in mind that customers are a finite resource. Sooner or later you will run out of them, especially if you annoy them; bad news is a wildfire while good news is a slow burn.

Therefore, one very powerful sales tool to consider for your call center is CRM. CRM is not so much a product, but a philosophy; the application of it may justify opening and growing your center. While individual-function centers, such as outbound and inbound can be useful for your company, CRM can help you get more out of each customer each time you are in contact with them.

CRM software captures and organizes every customer transaction — including service, sales and account management — and data derived from it, from every transaction type: be it outbound cold calling from targeted lists, inbound ordering, help desk, dealer locator and product inquiries and outbound collections. These inputs can come from every contact media: phones, e-mail, the Web, faxes, white mail, and in person.

The software makes this data available to all channels: from agent to retailer, to give you a complete view of your customer. The data is transported from databases to the users: agents, store clerks, field sales reps, callers through an IVR system and the Web site with its powerful middleware, which also delivers the customer information at the same time the call or online contact is picked up by the agent.

CRM enables better service. By putting everyone on the same page, no matter where they are in the organization, CRM software lets you provide a consistent message and results, avoiding the annoying customer service "well I talked to Agent x and she said y" hassle. There are fewer time-consuming, costly, and customer-aggravating call bounce-arounds. The middleware components put the same information from several different databases, on one agent's desktop. In the past, to provide the same service would have required transfer of the call to another person in another department and many times it would have been necessary for the customer to repeat the same information.

The central notion to CRM is treating each customer as an individual. Your goal, as a company, is to provide products and services tailored to that customer to obtain the maximum lifetime value from them.

With CRM you can find out their buying patterns, and, coupled with personal and demographic data you have on them and acquired from lists, you "see" and understand who your customers are, therefore you can serve them more profitably.

The business rule of thumb is that 20% of customers account for 80% of your sales. You learn who your best, aspiring and least valuable customers are and design and deliver the appropriate service levels. You pamper your top buyers with personalized service, such as assigning agents to their account and give them direct numbers with no IVR menus to go through when they call, and tailor offers to their standing. You give your less-valued customers lower-cost service channels, such as IVR with live-agent opt out to nondedicated agents.

The object of the call center with CRM usually becomes to sell and up-sell products and services to callers rather than getting callers/called parties off the phone quickly to handle more calls. While each agent handles fewer calls each call becomes more profitable.

CRM benefits mass market business-to-business and business-to-consumer firms that sell and contact different channels and need to keep, update and dynamically use data gathered from customers and develop relationships with them, such as catalog, financial services, healthcare, high-tech firms, Internet service providers, telcos and other utilities. CRM software can better coordinate and target your sales and customer acquisition/retention programs.

CRM software is especially valuable to firms that sell to a limited customer base, where the buyer and the product/service has high value and whose sales loss would cause considerable pain to the balance sheet. This is especially important where there is limited or slow growth in the number of customers and prospects.

Essentially CRM technology attempts to duplicate for medium to large businesses what small storefront companies take for granted. I first saw this at work in the mid-1970s when I worked for John Garde and Company. Whenever certain customers opened the creaking wooden door or called in, our eyes lit up. We put on that extra smile, and took more time with them than we would with others.

We also handled multiple functions at the same time, with the same customer. When a customer who owed us money dialed in for a repair, I would remind them after I wrote out the repair ticket. If it was an important caller, someone who insisted that he talk to Mr. Garde, I'd try to find my boss.

When Mr. Garde prepared to leave on a repair call, he would ask me for a copy of all outstanding invoices (if the customer owed him money), grab a couple of blank invoices, plus his tools, parts, and his cheap, foul-smelling cigars. With a smile through his stogie, he flung open the wooden door, and waved. A few hours later, he'd come back with a bigger grin. He'd have an order for me to process and a check, which I would write up in the musty black bindered ledgers, and deposit at the Royal Bank.

What Mr. Garde and I had done single-handedly was customer service/help desk, sales and collections, with a literal three-dimensional 360-degree view of the customer. As the owner he had the authority to try and meet the customer needs. I escalated calls and customers to him for special treatment.

Done right, CRM will do the same for you.

▶ CRM Risks

Yet, CRM is not for every company. If you still have a natural monopoly, depend on walk-in traffic, do not have multiple sales and service channels and/or low customer acquisition costs you are wasting your money on CRM. This is especially true for smaller consumer products firms. CRM software is also not worth your while if you have little contact with end-customers or sell low-value products to a small customer base and have a tiny number of contacts.

Chances are you won't receive much payoff from CRM software if you do not have repeat business from customers, or if your product/service market is customers that primarily buy based on the lowest price or the firm that has the sharpest cutting edge technology. If your business functions in islands, designated by product line or function and not connected by fixed links, you will also not benefit from CRM.

"If maintaining long-term customer relationships is not a priority for your company then you're wasting your time and resources by investing in CRM software," says Jeff Kaplan, a principal with management consultancy Pittiglio Rabin Todd & McGrath (PRTM) (Waltham, MA and

Mountain View, CA).

The investment and time involved in making CRM live is considerable; it can be almost as expensive as setting up the call center to use it. You must have the patience and the pocketbook for it. The investment ranges from the tens of thousands to millions of dollars. Depending on the installation, it can take up to two years of hair-pulling and headaches to implement a CRM system, tying up IT and management resources. Especially if your data resides on older, but still powerful legacy mainframes not designed to communicate with each other and with new mini- and PC-based servers.

Even then the CRM deployment might not work right. You may need separate call center agent teams for phone and online media handling, which cataloger/retailer Eddie Bauer has, until everything is in place.

As a story "Online Customer Support Doesn't Come in a Wrapper" in the June 5, 2000 issue of CMP publication *Internet Week* put it: "Customer relationship management is less a packaged software solution than a massive systems integration challenge, experts said. The result: the view of the customer is still less than panoramic."

To get the full benefit from CRM, your firm must also be organized across the different channels and functions to utilize it. The software becomes a difficult value proposition if there is no communication between each department. While you can buy the package and re-engineer the process later, just as consumers like me reorganize their lives or routines once they buy a car or a cell phone that opens more possibilities, it is usually more effective to create sound communication lines and consistent business processes first. "CRM software by itself is not going to do you a lot of good unless your company has the discipline to use it," PRTM's Kaplan says. "There are many more cases where companies buy the software with the hopes of solving problems, establishing a CRM strategy and the foundations for it, and the application fails to deliver results."

Few companies realize the CRM benefits overnight and not all companies see payback. The return on investment (ROI) comes from several sources, again depending on your installation, the package selected and your market. Some companies will see payback in as little as three to four months. And some may never see it because it is difficult to isolate and quantify some of your business results due solely to CRM implementation.

CRM ROI and justification often comes from call center cost savings achieved by directing the least profitable customers to the least expensive media like IVR and Web-based self service, thereby improving profit per customer and increasing up-selling and cross-selling. By presenting that customer record, including any special offers or messages up front to the agent there is no wait time while each screen loads. You can increase the number of calls per agent ratio by shortening the call handling time, hence the cost per call decreases.

Both results: IVR/Web self-service and data-rich screens create greater productivity. You either use fewer agents or handle the same growth with your existing crew, which also saves associated costs such as facilities and equipment.

Consumer sales data collected by agents with CRM software can go into better, more targeted direct marketing campaigns. One company, Community Playthings, saved $600,000 in catalog mailings yet increased sales by 10% by analyzing who their best customers were and sending targeted mailings to them.

Determining ROI can be difficult, especially if the principal reason for investing in CRM is maintaining customer relationships, particularly through sales force automation. While some firms have seen dramatic sales increase due to up-selling, others have not had any measurable results. There are many variables to track, such as market prices, competitors launching new products, flaws in your own products and services that make it difficult to attribute the benefits or assign blame to CRM.

► Segmentation and Privacy Concerns

Whether you have a multimillion-dollar CRM platform or a simple telemarketing list, be particularly careful in how you collect and use customer data. Consumers are becoming very distrustful about how "big companies" as well as "big government" gather and utilize information on them. They want a say in how their information is obtained and used.

Consumers also want to control how a company builds a marketing profile on them, especially on the Web. When a person surfs the Web, Web sites will often place "cookies": specialized software that is stored on the surfer's computer, which can, for example, save information such as passwords and preferences. There are firms that can match a person's Web surfing habits with personally identifiable information. The problem is that companies can easily misinfer a person's behavior and patterns from their Web site activity.

Let's look at one example. How many of you, and let's be honest here, have wandered into, sniffed around, and walked out of a sex shop without buying anything,

QVC Privacy Statement
Your Privacy is our Priority

When you buy from QVC, either via our show or the Internet, we protect your privacy. We do not sell, rent, or exchange customer information. We share identifiable information only with those parties entrusted with the processing of your account and the fulfillment of your order. We've established procedures to protect your privacy, which we vigorously uphold. Of course, this policy does not apply to information we are required to disclose by law.

Customer information is gathered so we can better serve you, and we make every effort to ensure its security and to treat your information responsibly. When you become a QVC Member, we ask for your name, address, e-mail address, and phone number. We also ask for your credit card number and its expiration date, should you select that method for payment. Once we have your credit card information, we will not ask for it again unless a change is required, or you are shipping to another address. Your order history information is maintained in order to service your account.

From time to time, you may receive mail, e-mail or telephone calls from QVC in order to update your account or communicate information which we hope might be of interest to you. At any time, you may request your name be removed from any of these methods of communication. Simply relay your request to a Customer Service Representative and your name will be removed from the appropriate list. We want your experiences with QVC to be based upon your preferences – always.

QVC markets jewelry and other products via phone and IVR and Web self-service. It offers a fine example of a privacy policy and accompanying explanation about the information a company collects.

just to see what all the stuff is about. Does that mean that you're into the studded and vinyl variations that the merchandise enables? Yet, if you did that on a Web site and a marketer knows who you are, you might begin to receive catalogs, calls and spam from people that, if you were not into it, you wished would drop off the face of the earth.

Every company should watch how they handle customer privacy. Post the company's privacy policies on its Web site outlining how it treats its customers' data and interactions with the Web site. Ask callers, e-mailers and surfers for permission to market their lists. If you and your colleagues do not institute these procedures, don't be surprised if some government agency orders you to do it at some point in the very near future.

You can also take what you know about your customers, especially those in the mid and lower levels and deliver a service level so mediocre or demand surcharges that are high enough to drive them to competitors. This has reportedly happened in the financial services industry. Today's marginal customer that you always route to an IVR menu may shut *you* off when they grow, or keep their larger accounts elsewhere. They might also tell their colleagues, friends, and contacts to do the same.

To prevent this scenario, you need to find out as much as possible about each customer and treat each one with care and respect. You should survey your mid to lower level customers to find out what service levels and types are acceptable to them. Your agents should talk to each caller as if he or she is a potentially important client, no matter how small the current order.

In a letter published in the February 8, 2000 *Financial Times*, the author, Don Cook of State College, PA, says that while customer segmentation tools are excellent for providing personalized service to top-level customers, they are not yet sharp enough to chop bottom-ranking customers. He cited a bank (that will go unnamed) that has made that mistake. "Companies that use it as such do so at their peril," says Cook.

Don't Annoy the Customers

Another trend to ignore at your peril is increasing customer annoyance at bad service, delivered by live agents and by IVR and Web self-service technologies. Just as telemarketing fraud makes headlines so does customer service stupidity. *The New York Times* ran an article July 20, 2000 "Is the Customer Ever Right" on the decline of customer service, pushed in part by terrible call handling systems, but often by employees with an up-yours attitude. Just as bad outbound practices threaten to junk a media so will terrible customer service, risking more consumer protection laws.

This isn't a recent phenomena. One August morning in 1997 I was listening to WCBS radio and I heard a story quoting the *Wall Street Journal* on an audit of leading software makers such as Adobe, Cortel and Microsoft by Service Intelligence (Seattle, WA). The reports said that Service Intelligence found many help desk agents had the wrong answers or were not able to solve the problem or, even worse, stated the problem was unsolvable. Service Intelligence had pulled the questions from the companies' own Web site FAQs. I got a copy of the audit and used it in an October 1997 *Call Center* article "Keeping Your Support Center Afloat."

I groaned as I listed to the radio. It seems common sense for a help desk agent to have access to the same information that is on their corporate Web site, *especially* the FAQs. They should see what their customers see. Yet my wife, a programmer who is on her company's Web team is not at all surprised. "Of course, the help desks don't have access to the Web," she told me. "It's not uncommon." And, from both talking to her and what I read today, not that much has changed from 1997 to this writing. No wonder, it seems that the image of this industry is going into the toilet. Head first.

Companies have long abused IVR by creating long, impossible to navigate menus, conveniently forgetting that people forget information told orally after the first few minutes, and not giving zero-outs to live agents when they can't find what they want. As a result people loathe such IVR systems with a passion.

Web self-service is becoming another nightmare. As with telemarketing fraud, rarely a day goes by without some study showing how ticked off surfers are and how many abandoned their online shopping carts. Scamsters and young logic-impaired programmers have infested this medium like plagues of parasitic wasps on tarantulas, injecting their malicious or badly written code that grows and destroys sites. As a result badly designed and hellish-to-navigate sites proliferate, as do broken links and Javascript errors, sometimes with fraudulent information. Nevertheless, one of the top complaints is, guess what, lousy customer service.

Unfortunately, many companies do not provide phone numbers for frustrated surfers. The classic example of this idiocy are when there are problems with the Web site or the Internet connection and the company tells customers to send them an e-mail...

The best resource to guide you through what you can, cannot, should and should not do with your call center in marketing and sales are industry trade associations like the ATA, DMA and the ICSA. Some, but not all, fight unnecessary restrictive legislation but at the same time they educate their members on legal and ethical compliance through conferences, seminars, books, newsletters, releases and notifications. Many have codes of ethics and standards that members must abide by, or face sanctions. They also produce operation guidelines to help you stay in the spirit and the letter of the law. They help combat fraud and help consumers maintain privacy.

There are also similar organizations in other countries, which are becoming important as consumers and businesses buy via phone and online worldwide. The Federation of European Direct Marketing (FEDMA, Brussels, Belgium) monitors and lobbies the European Commission for its member national DM organizations, which track and follows up on their governments and individual members. Developments in Australia, a leading Asia Pacific call center location, are followed by the Australian Teleservices Association (Sydney, Australia).

In some nations the associations' codes of conducts have the *de facto* force of law; if a company does not belong to or worse yet gets thrown out of an industry trade association, that company may have a difficult time obtaining customers. For example, the US limits hours that telemarketers can call but Canada currently has no such blanket restrictions. However, the Canadian Marketing Association (CMA, Toronto, ON), which represents the industry there, including US companies that sell to Canadians, requires its members to limit calling to between 9:00 am and 9:30 pm weekdays, 10:00 am to 6:00 pm weekends and bans it on government-designated statutory holidays.

At the same time these associations are a superb networking resource. They often have trade shows and exhibitions, as well as meetings. These are great venues to find an outsourcing partner, a list broker, lists, a database management firm, e-commerce, telemarketing, site selection and training consultants, and other products and services to help your call center, including attorneys.

▶ Legislation and Regulations

The best way to keep your call center regulatorily clean and help the direct marketing industry survive is to comply with all laws and regulations. It is not in your corporate and personal interest to have your name blackened amongst the public, your trade colleagues and with regulators. There are attorneys-generals and other lawmakers that thrive by taking aim at call center lawbreakers. There are also consumer and privacy advocates that have call centers and e-commerce firms in their laser sights and want to see outbound and opt-out data collection outlawed. Don't give them the ammunition and don't point out to them your weak spot.

The nasty political reality is that despite call centers being big job creators, the numbers of those who are employed making calls and sending e-mails, and who obtain data from callers and pull it from Web sites, are the politically "invisible." They count for little compared to ticked off and vocal consumers, especially the 50-plusers who belong to and are well represented by active, vocal groups such as the American Association of Retired Persons.

The following is a general overview of just some of the key laws and regulations that will and could impact on call center costs, operations and functions. Your trade association will also update and keep you informed on new laws and regulations and offer compliance advice. But, because things change rapidly, I strongly recommend that you contact and stay in touch with the governments in whose jurisdictions you sell and service customers and/or have your call centers. You should consult with an attorney, particularly one that specializes in telemarketing and privacy laws, before planning your teleservices.

▶ Outbound Telesales

At present most of the US federal and state laws restrict outbound telesales, chiefly by hours, the technology used, and regulate what telesales agents must say and do. They also let consumers opt out of telemarketing by placing their names on DNC lists.

The two key US regulations are the *Telephone Consumer Protection Act (TCPA)*, administered by the Federal Communications Commission (FCC) and the *Telemarketing Sales Rule*, under the jurisdiction of the Federal Trade Commission (FTC). These laws are intended to protect consumer privacy and prevent fraud. Note that neither governs telesales to business.

The TCPA requires call centers making outbound sales calls, both to prospects and existing customers, to place anyone on the DNC lists if so requested. Companies must also have a DNC policy. The law exempts legitimate registered tax-free charities from this provision. It limits the hours that all outbound telesales agents can place call — 8am to 9pm. Companies must also disclose a telephone number and address where they may be contacted and have a training program for its agents.

The law prohibits cold unsolicited faxing and OVMs for sales purposes; charities are exempt from this OVM provision. And you can't send OVMs to numbers, like pagers and cellphones where the called party pays to receive it. Anyway, people hate this with a passion, especially if they're driving or in a meeting.

Be careful how you use an OVM; it must release a called party's line within five seconds of calling. Also, if you are using these devises for business-to-business they can't tie up two or more lines of a customer/prospect's multi-line business phone system.

And never, *ever* load it with emergency phone numbers. Scrub those lists as if your life depends on it. It just may. You could have a heart attack but the 911 lines are tied up with your company's machines. Too bad. Also, what an experienced, skilled and fully equipped emergency personnel like my paramedic son would enjoy doing to some fool who misuses an OVM, would make the FCC penalties seem very mild, indeed!

If you send faxes to existing customers either off a separate machine or through a modem, the fax must identify the company or individual creating it, not just the party transmitting it, such as a service bureau. The fax must also identify the creator and the sender if you use a third party.

The TCPA provides consumers with several options to enforce limitations against unwanted unsolicited telesales. Consumers can and will ask the FCC and state officials to go after you if they feel you violated the law. Absent state law to the contrary, they can sue you in state court. The states may bring civil action on behalf of its residents against you. State attorney generals have shown great zeal in going after violators. It makes good press.

The Telemarketing Sales Rule (TSR) goes after outbound consumer fraud. The FTC created the TSR as the result of Congress passing the Telemarketing and Consumer Fraud and Abuse Prevention Act in 1994.

The TSR contains the TCPA's calling hours restrictions and DNC requirements, with similar federal and state law enforcement heft; states can and will prosecute fraudsters who operate across state lines. Here are just a few of the TSR provisions.

Telesales agents must tell consumers the call is a sales call and who's doing the selling *before* they start selling. For prize promotions they must tell consumers that no purchase or payment is needed to win.

Telemarketers can't lie about any of the information in the promotion, including about the product or service; they must tell consumers what are the total costs and about any restrictions on getting or using them or that a sale is final or non-refundable. For sweepstakes and other such promotions they must tell the consumer the odds of winning, that no purchase or payment is necessary to win, and any restrictions or conditions of receiving the prize.

Telesales agents cannot withdraw money from a consumer's checking account without their express verifiable authorization. Consumers do not have to pay for credit repair, recovery room, or advance-fee loan/credit services until these services have been delivered.

The TSR also has provisions seeking to stop abusive telemarketing practices, such as foul language and threats. That an agent may not make their quota because the person at the other end is hemming and hawing on the offer is not the called party's problem. Also, while customers and prospects can be infuriating at times there is no reason why your agents should sink to their level.

The TSR exempts inbound calls except those responding to ads for investment opportunities, credit repair services, recovery room services, or advance-fee loans. Sales that are not completed, and payment or authorization for payment is not required, until there is a face-to-face sales presentation.

There are other important federal regulations. The *900 Number Rule*, the result of Congress passing the Telephone Disclosure and Dispute Resolution Act and governed by the FCC, bans most use of toll-free numbers if they lead to charges to callers. This rule is becoming important as companies seek to shift customers to less costly IVR and Web self-service and away from more expensive live agent handling.

The rule requires, for example, that companies disclose the cost of the call and about parental permission. It does not cover prepaid plans such as tech support. However, if you offer a 900 plan you must disclose the terms and conditions up front including the cost of the call and your name, address and business number. You must also notify customers of cost changes and give them a PIN or other such number to prevent access by nonsubscribers.

States also have laws that limit telemarketing. For example, many states, ranging from Alabama to West Virginia require companies to register if they are performing telemarketing, except for established businesses, tax-exempt charities, political and religious organizations — on First Amendment grounds, and those who are governed and must register under other laws, such as for securities dealers. Some states, such as Arkansas and Utah, prohibit agents to rebut offer declines from consumers.

Several states further restrict calling hours beyond federal requirements. For example you can't call into Alabama on a Sunday or holiday; you can do so in Texas but only between 12 noon and 9pm. You can't bother their breakfast before 9am on other days in Texas and seven days a week in Connecticut, Michigan, Minnesota or New Mexico.

Kansas has restrictions on predictive dialers used in outbound. Kansas requires an outbound call to be put through to a live agent on a dialer or answered by an OVM within 5 seconds of the beginning of the call. The law addresses consumer complaints about dead air when a telemarketer rings using a dialer.

Many states have created their own databases. Consumers register with them, usually for a small fee, and marketers must scrub their databases against these names.

The direct marketing and telesales industry supports the federal TCPA and the TSR, saying it is important to protect privacy while permitting telesales and preventing fraud. It is the states' DNC laws that have drawn the most fire from the industry, followed by no rebuttals and dialer restrictions.

What telesales firms hate the most about state DNC laws is that they impose unnecessary and costly restrictions while all have exemptions that permit charity, political, polling firms and calls from companies that con-

How to Keep Your Dialer (and Your Outbound Calling) Compliant and Less Annoying

The American Teleservices Association (ATA) and the Direct Marketing Association (DMA) recommend that you follow these practices to keep your predictive dialer customer/prospect and lawfully acceptable:

- Set a company-wide standard to encourage agents to speak promptly to consumers, keep abandons/hangups to the lowest level and release the line within two seconds if an agent is not available to take a dialer-made call;

- Let the dialer ring at least four times or 12 seconds before hanging up;

- Do not abandon the same number more than twice during the same month of a campaign and ensure that any future calls to that number are connected to an agent;

- Do not knowingly call anyone with an unlisted or unpublished number;

- Screen numbers against all DNC lists, including the DMA's TPS.

sumers have existing business relationships with to call them. This still means consumers will get called at dinner: a frequent complaint.

ATA state legislative counsel, Tyler Prochnow, points out that people who sign onto state DNC lists could have placed their name on the marketers' DNC lists required under federal law, if they had not already done so. The issue is not whether telemarketers want to reach them. Rather, Prochnow argues marketers are incurring high administrative expenses that do little to protect consumers. He knows of a couple of marketers who had to hire additional technical staff to handle DNC lists.

"You're talking about paying $250+ per quarter, or $1,000 per year," he points out. Then multiply that by the number of states that have these laws. On top of that, you have administrative and IT expenses coping with all these different databases, with many different computer languages and you probably have to integrate them all into one single DNC database that fits into your own DNC database. And then you have to run that against your own calling database. This creates a huge headache just to please a minority of the population."

▶ Outbound E-Mail and Privacy

Many states have passed bills to put spam into the can and curb fraud by regulating UCE. Rhode Island has gone so far as to require UCE to have toll-free numbers and valid return addresses. Expect to see federal laws governing spam with DNC list requirements and with legitimate address requirements. The DMA's eMPS is already in place for consumers who don't want spam.

These bills have been supported by the DMA. The only exception has been where bills require marketers to insert "ADV" in the subject line, which the association opposes. And, for good reason. There is no easier way to block legitimate UCE than by inserting ADV into your e-mail program's automatic remove feature. Such laws are like going after drug dealers on tax charges; of course, the crooks aren't going to paste in ADV but it gives fire-breathing assistant attorney generals another club to hit them with.

There are new consumer privacy protection laws and more on the way. The trend appears to give consumers more authority to deny companies access to information collected on them — including by phone, e-mail and the Internet — and tell them how they cannot use the data including sale and transfer.

For example, The Financial Services Moderation Act permits financial institutions to share customer data with other marketers except for account numbers and similar information, but only after they notify consumers and give them the right to opt-out. Similar measures covering medical records are in the works. Congress also attached riders to a transportation bill that requires states to ask consumers to opt-in, i.e., give their permission before states can market their drivers' license lists.

The direct marketing and teleservices industry has supported the right of consumers to opt-out but they see troubling signs that such provisions are now becoming opt-in. This they say is counterproductive both for business and for consumers. The ATA and the DMA contend that data collection permits more desirable, targeted offers and less "junk mail" and unwanted calls and e-mails. By restricting data access, the ATA and DMA warn that just to market their products, companies may be forced to send "junk mail," spam and make more "telemarketing" calls.

The FTC approved in July, 2000 a self-regulation plan by Internet companies, called the Network Advertising Initiative, which represents about 90% of the industry. Reported by the Associated Press it requires member Web advertising companies to tell consumers that they are creating profiles of them and allow them to choose whether they want to have their Web site visiting activities kept anonymous. Participants who violate it can be sued for deceptive practice.

The move may forestall future legislation but at this writing there are signs that it will not. Expect to see state if not federal laws during the lifespan of this book. A July 28, 2000 AP story quoted a spokesperson for the Minnesota attorney general's office saying: "The DMA tried industry regulation with direct mail and it was a miserable failure. No one complies and there's no way to check compliance."

▶ Laws and Regulations in Other Countries

Many countries also have or are considering laws that restrict telesales, combat fraud and protect consumer privacy that will affect your call centers in those markets. These laws and regulations are usually, but not always, more stringent than American legislation.

For example, Germany bans outbound cold call telesales. The country also prohibits US-accepted practices such as money-back guarantees but there is movement to allow that on the grounds of greater consumer choice. Many, but not all, German states require you to seek permission from authorities to operate 7x24 for all call types though this too is being changed as these governments recognize the job creating benefits of call centers, and as consumers and business demand more call-center-delivered services.

The European Union (EU) regulates business communications and data used for commercial purposes by companies operating in its member states to permit trade-encouraging harmonization and uniformity. The European Commission (EC) devise directives that must be passed by the democratically elected European Parliament, subject to final passage by member states' legislatures.

The EU and member states have passed into law several key directives that affect customer service and sales in Europe. The most important of these new acts is the *Data Protection Directive*. In effect since October 24, 1998, it guarantees the free flow of information across European borders.

The Data Protection Directive also protects business and consumer privacy by giving them the right to opt-out of commercial data (e.g., names/address/telephone numbers on lists) and opt-in to sensitive data (e.g., political preferences, health information, religion and trade union activities).

Consumers must be told about the purposes of data collection (e.g., in telephone surveys) and are given the right to object, and to access and rectify incorrect data. Outsourcing companies that collect data are acting as the clients' agents. If they are acquiring data on behalf of a firm, it is as if the client itself was collecting the information. The law does permit consumer profiling as long as it is not harmful.

Marketers are responsible for blocking and erasing names. Each company operating in the EU must appoint a data controller to manage the data and comply with the laws. The information gatekeepers are nationally appointed Data Commissioners (or The Data Registrar in the UK).

Companies must tell national Data Commissioners if they wish to send their files to a non-EU country; the Data Commissioner can permit or refuse the shift. But the non-EU country must have what the EU refers to as "adequate protection" on consumer privacy. This may be guaranteed by law, self-regulation, contracts or by company security systems.

Where the directive risked causing problems to call centers and Internet firms is in collected data transfers to the US, such as from a branch office or an outsourcer to an American head office. There were worries that US laws and practices may not pass the EU's "adequacy" test on commercial data.

Europeans are very sensitive about this issue. In early July 2000 the European Parliament shelled but did not sink a long-negotiated "safe harbor" agreement between the EC and the US to permit such data transfers in exchange for American firms swearing they will comply with the directive's provisions, which US privacy advocates have argued give Europeans better protection than Americans. At this writing a deal is in the works to permit some modified data transfer rights between the EU and the US, driven by the mounting importance of data in global customer service and marketing, expect to see some deal during the life expectancy of this book.

Another EU law, the *Telecommunications Data Protection Directive*, formerly known as the "ISDN Directive" prohibits telcos from profiling subscribers' personal data, which is erased or made anonymous once service is cancelled. Consumers must give permission before telcos can solicit them by automatic dialers and fax. Telcos must also set up lists of those who do not wish to be contacted: akin to the DMA's TPS.

Canada also has laws that affect US firms who sell and service Canadians. For example the *Personal Information and Electronic Documents Act* governs privacy and is reportedly stricter than current US regulations. Under this act Canadian consumers must give consent before information on them is collected, used or transferred to a third party, such as for outbound and inbound telesales. They also have the right to find out what data is kept on file about them and to change false information. Canada has a privacy commissioner to gather, investigate and act on complaints, which could lead to legal action, fines and data management audits.

The law requires provinces to enact similar or stronger laws within three years or be forced to adopt the federal regulations. Quebec has long had stringent privacy laws.

Canada is an excellent example of how the marketing industry got ahead of the game and took a positive pro-active stance that limited harmful legislation; instead of waiting for consumers and businesses to get angry as is happening in the US. In 1991 the CMA, then known as the Canadian Direct Marketing Association helped create privacy standards that became the basis of Canada's new privacy law. In 1993 the association created and implemented a mandatory Privacy Code for its members to give consumers control over how their personal information is used by the marketing industry. CMA amended its Privacy Code in 1996 to require members to obtain opt-in from consumers before transferring any sensitive information.

The CMA then changed its standards of practice to accommodate online consumer data collection and e-mail marketing in 1997 and again in 1999 to cover marketing to children, including the concerns over collection of children's personal information.

"A senior federal government official told me that if the privacy legislation had been drafted now it would have been far more stringent than what we're getting," explains CMA president John Gustavson.

CHAPTER FIVE

Designing Your Call Center

Now that you've decided that you need a new or expanded call center including what functions it will have, but excluding those handled by self-service and outsourcing, you need to figure out how big the center will be and what it should look like. And have it ready yesterday and under budget.

Effective call center design is critical if your call center is to be a success. A sound, attractive and functional work environment almost always encourages employees to be productive, and helps to keep productive employees. Workers who sit in chairs that support their body, a workstation that they adjust for comfort and without eye-squinting glare, whose surroundings are pleasant, yet interesting, and isn't too warm or cold, will focus more on their tasks than a worker who experiences hassle and discomfort. The agent who doesn't have to wait in line to use the washroom, who can grab a sandwich or salad, pick up the dry cleaning and check up on their kid at the child care will likely stay with you longer than the one who feels they've been drafted and confined to barracks.

You certainly don't want to follow the call center building advice in a series of *Dilbert* comic strips that ran in late 1999. The strip's pointy-haired boss, in league with his firm's evil HR director, Catbert, cynically recommended keeping costs down by making the working conditions "inhumane" with tiny cubicles, six minutes of bathroom breaks per shift and creating "incompatible" goals such as speed and customer service.

If the Dilbert strip touched a nerve, it was meant to. Too many call centers have been built and are operated that way, which could lead to poor customer service and relations, high turnover, and ultimately higher costs and lower profits. In a boom economy your employees, especially your top performers, can tell you to "take this job and shove it!" and get another one easily. That could cause customer acquisition, retention and sales hassles for your company. If the only agents that will tolerate your poor working conditions are lazy, smart-alecky or stupid that's not the customers' problem, its *yours.*

In their efforts to curb turnover many companies will throw money at employees without thinking that the cause may literally lie at their feet. Making the work environment employee-friendly is cost-effective. According to Roger Kingsland, principal with KSBA Architects (Pittsburgh, PA), investing as much as $25 additional per square foot (sf) or $2,750 per seat is equivalent only to an additional 16 cents per hour or a 1.61% hourly wage increase.

Unfortunately, justifying many of the higher costs to senior management may be difficult. Kingsland points out that although you can prove that some hard improvements, such as sound masking, can increase performance; conceptual improvements, such as having nice surroundings, are much more difficult to quantify and show to top executives.

"The difficulty is that the link between good design and employee savings is not direct," he explains. "With few exceptions, it is also hard to peg actual productivity improvements and lower turnover to improved facilities and design. There are many other variables that come into play such as staffing, training, supervision, wages and benefits."

Herman Miller (Zeeland, MI), a leading furniture maker, and now a call center consultancy has found practicing what it preaches pays off. *Business Week* reported June 5, 2000 that Miller witnessed a 1.5% productivity increase when it opened a factory that had 100% fresh air and daylight — enough to repay the structure's mortgage. Also, employees that had left the firm returned.

"If CEOs have half a brain they would start to pay attention to the fact that their employees are their main cost-and-benefit center," the magazine quoted architectural expert and consultant William McDonough.

You may find that senior management is quite willing to make such an investment if they see the call centers as key to their business not only in function but as a showcase to customers, directors, investors and analysts. As more companies integrate call center activities with sales, marketing and product development, call centers are being dragged from the basements and the broom closets and closer to the executive suite.

No longer are functions as customer service and help desk "peripheral" to the corporate bottom line. As you see in nearly every TV ad there is a segment showing a smiling agent with a headset — customer service is the bottom line in this new retain-the-customer one-to-one marketing era. If this is your call center, its design reflects its higher, more central status, according to John Francis, vice president of worldwide architectural firm Hellmuth, Obata+Kassabaum (HOK) (St. Louis, MO)'s consulting division.

"Such centers will have to look more corporate," Francis points out. "They will need higher quality materials and they will have to look more showy and dramatic now that senior management is in control because they are now part of the corporate tour. You can, for example, put in large screens that show activity, say over an agent amphitheater or install raised supervisory stations where an executive

Attractive design turns high volume outbound and inbound call centers such those owned by service bureaus into interesting yet productive facilities, even those with standard "cube row" workstations. For example, TeleSpectrum Worldwide's Stevensville, MD call center, designed by Young, Bickley, Geiger (Boston, MA) features non-glaring indirect lighting and transparent top partitions that let in light and permits easy supervision while helping to cut down on noise. The colors are vibrant without being overpowering, lending the right amount of eye-catching interest.

can look out over the call center."

Bob Stinson, president of architectural firm, Stinson Design (Houston, TX), agrees. "Because call centers are becoming central to companies' business strategies, as we've seen in advertising, they're now showing them off," he says, "They must have modular flexible furniture, and larger workstations that reflect corporate standards."

Now, as more companies contract with service bureaus to serve their customers and establish relationships on their behalf they want their bureaus to recruit higher quality agents and have them stay. This is especially true if these clients are competing with others on service.

"The design, functionality and feel of the office has a direct impact on your ability to attract and retain high caliber customers and people," points out Roy Young, president of the design firm Young, Bickley, Geiger (Boston, MA). "This is especially true in service bureaus. We have clients who compete with big name firms such as AOL for people, they had us redo their facilities because they didn't want to lose agents. Also, being able to attract top-name clients is a selling point to agents. They like to work for hot well-known customers."

▶ Pre-Planned Sound Design Saves Time

Well, you might say: "That's nice but I don't have the time. I need to get butts in seats yesterday! "

You're not alone. Call center site selection consultants say they've seen the site selection window shrink: from the day a company chooses to open a center to when the agents take or make their first calls has gone from 18 months to 3 months.

Yet, if you want your call center to be a success in attracting and keeping your new employees and keep them productive you can't make them unhappy. Especially when they can get a job at the local WalMart or at the insurance company call center down the road, the one with the neat gym.

What you need to do is pre-plan and prove out your designs, including workstation and furniture ahead of time, and have the RFPs and quotes in hand along with the local dealers' addresses and numbers so that when you need to expand you can literally roll them into place. You already have enough to contend with, such as staffing and training, building quirks and inevitable hardware and software bugs.

When you do pre-plan and pre-design involve your employees. Don't leave it all up to the architects, the interior designers, upper management and the bean counters. *They* don't have to work in your call center.

Ask your agents and supervisors how you can make their existing call center more comfortable. Bring in different chairs and workstations and study their reaction. Try new lighting and noise reduction techniques in portions of your call center. If the innovations work out, consider retro-fitting your present call centers. As well as providing you with advice, you also empower your staff, making them feel better about working at your call center. The more agents feel valued as employees and the more empowered they feel about their immediate environment, the more likely they'll be willing to stay and recommend your call center to others.

Space planner Laura Sikorski of Sikorski-Tuerpe and Associates (Centerport, NY) says, "Remember, the workplace is the employee's home away from home."

Roger Kingsland is a big proponent of pre-planning. He points out that much time can be saved by discussing and settling all design issues up front, instead of planning and making changes on the fly as the project gets underway.

"If the design firm doesn't give the information up front, including costs, then your executives may want to revisit initial decisions later," he says.

You can also fine-tune your design and specification to prototype blue-prints to save time. Many call centers, especially outsourcers, have such blueprints. Kingsland says prototyping shaves four to eight weeks off a 14- to 20-week schedule for a 300- to 500-seat call center.

"You'll begin to experience the benefits of blueprinting after the second or third center," he points out. "You're proving out the prototype in the first one or two centers."

Remember that despite the call center's newfound status in many com-panies, top management still wants to keep costs down — there are design innovations that may help to achieve that goal. For example, Rick Burkett, president of burkettdesign (Denver, CO), has seen steel indirect lighting fixtures that are about one third less expensive than the cost of conventional aluminum fixtures.

"The steel fixtures have very good illumination and quicker ship times," says Burkett "The process to produce aluminum fixtures is much more time-consuming: eight weeks compared two weeks for steel."

▶ Size of Call Center

How big your call center should be is shaped by what types of calls you want it to handle, the call and contact load it needs to carry and by the optimum number of agent workstations. I call the latter factor "agent/seats" (a/s) for supervision, management and economies of scale.

The agent/seat, a.k.a workstation a.k.a. seat is your basic unit of production in a call center. Your maximum output is based on how many you have. Just like the number of sewing machines in a garment firm or buses with a bus company or transit authority; one worker per each seat or station, machine or vehicle.

I devised and prefer the agent/seat measurement because I think it is a more accurate descriptor for call center size and design needs than just plain "workstations" or "seats"; only one agent can sit in a seat at any one time. If you have a 200-a/s call center and you're running full eight-hour shifts you can have up to 600 agents occupying the same seats but at different times. The a/s value recognizes the physical demands people place on call centers. "Seats" and "workstations" don't go the bathroom, smoke, nuke leftover Chinese in the lunch room, wear out the carpet or discuss with the day care supervisor about their sweet little girl who insists on pummeling the boys in the day care.

And, just like making clothes and providing transportation, the demand on and for your call center a/s-es varies in volume, complexity and in occurrence according to market needs. Figuring out your call load and staffing demand, especially for inbound is a very complicated exercise best worked out between you and your experts, based on your experience. Architects and site selection planners say their clients come to them with this figured out; most know how many seats they want their call centers to have. Also, if you choose to outsource or telework part of your call load (see Chapter 3) you must also calculate how much and when those solutions will drain the demand, leaving a net load to handle and the number of a/s-es required.

There are call center benchmarks to help guide you. For example, according to Dr. Jon Anton, of Purdue University's Center for Customer Driven Quality (Lafayette, IN), the benchmarked average call handle time at this writing for general customer service is 3.45 minutes while for help desks this jumps to 9.75 minutes.

When planning err on the side of allowing for more a/s-es than your calculations state that you need. One of the worst decisions you can make is grossly underestimating the number of a/s-es for your call center. Although, you don't want to waste money buying space that you don't need, or on oversized hardware and software or paying for agents who will spend most of the day playing solitaire on the Web, buying swampland in Florida or looking for more challenging jobs elsewhere.

You also can't afford to put people on hold for long periods of time or wait forever to respond to their e-mails, or hurry them through the customer service litany when their matters have not been resolved. While most people understand that they have to wait there are limits to their patience, *especially* if they contacted your live agents after trying to order or solve their problem through your IVR or Web site. After all, it's not the customers' problem that you don't have enough agents and workstations. They paid you for it, in a portion of your product or service's price or service contract or paid technical support.

Usually the less sophisticated the call type, such as outbound sales or inbound order-taking, especially direct response, the more control you have over it, therefore, the easier it is to calculate call load. You know from experience how long it will take for each agent to pitch and the customer to ignore or swing back in an outbound call; you can set your predictive dialer to throw a set number of calls, say 10 to 15 each hour to your agents. In inbound order sales and response you will have some idea from your records the average call length; if you use infomercials, you will know precisely when the volume spike will hit your centers.

The challenge with many other inbound calls, such as customer service is that not all of them are the same length and they often don't occur at predictable regular intervals. You are at the mercy of your customers. Some are quick with what they want and have simple requests, other take their time or have complicated problems. If your company has adopted the service-oriented customer relationship management (CRM) philosophy where the objective is to retain and sell more to customers over their lifetime by determining and understanding their needs, you can't easily shove them off the phones.

Complicating these matters further is if you plan to have blended agents: inbound agents that make outbound calls when inbound demand is slack and vice-versa — you will need to train the agents in both skillsets.

If your call center will also be handling e-mail and text chat, as many increasingly are, you must account for the fact that it takes longer to receive and reply in writing than by voice, which means that each contact will have longer handle times than with voice. Though there are e-mail response templates to speed answers to where it could surpass voice, according to Brad Cleveland, president of the Incoming Calls Management Institute (ICMI), (Annapolis, MD), chat and escorted transactions can be two or three times as long or more than voice. This depends on the nature of the dialog, the customer's equipment and typing proficiency, the quality and speed of the voice and Web connection, the tools and resources available to the agent, and the proficiency of both the customer and agent in handling these dialogs.

On the other hand in many instances you can set aside e-mail responses or pre-arrange for chat at less busy periods. But don't be too long. Nothing annoys a customer who is e-mailing or chatting more than a company that will not respond promptly; e-commerce researchers report that the lack of timely response to e-mails ranks in the top tier of customer complaints. That defeats your CRM philosophy and wastes the millions of dollars you've spent to CRM-enable your business including adding and integrating online communications to your call center.

Brad Cleveland and Julia Mayben are the authors of one of the best books on the market to help you: *"Call Center Management on Fast Forward,"* published by the ICMI. It will help you understand the dynamics of inbound and offers advice on forecasting call load and determining base staff and voice/data trunks required from your local exchange carrier.

To help you determine how many workstations or seats your call center needs Brad Cleveland has outlined this seven-step process:

1. Establish the call center's mission: This critical first step is to define the call center's role in the organization and the responsibilities it will assume. For example, what types of contacts will it handle? What channels, e.g., telephone, e-mail, text chat, Web collaboration, video, etc., does the organization plan to provide? How will the call center leverage contacts into improved customer loyalty and information that can improve the innovation of quality and services? The answers to these questions form the basis of good resource planning.

2. Forecast the work load: The forecast must include all channels of contact, and anticipate which contacts will require the assistance of agents versus those that will be fully automated. It must predict volume, average talk time and average after call wrap-up for future time periods, usually down to half-hours. For determining workstation requirements, the forecast needs to look well into the future (e.g., 3 to 5 years) and anticipate the workload for the busy time of day, on a busy day of week, during the busiest season of the year. That becomes the basis for calculations. (If you are uncertain about the forecast, see step 6.)

3. Establish service level objectives: Accessibility — expressed as service level or response time, depending on the type of contact — is at the heart of effective call center planning. The faster you respond to customers, the more resources you will need. Consequently, accessibility objectives are essential in defining staff and system requirements, along with associated costs.

4. Calculate base staff requirements: The moment-to-moment arrival of contacts will be random, ultimately the result of countless decisions made by customers, based on a myriad of individual habits and motivations. Accordingly, it is simply not possible to determine staff or workstation requirements for a call center the way you would plan work in other parts of the organization. Instead, required resources should be determined using either a queuing formula that takes random call arrival into account (e.g., the widely-used Erlang C formula) or computer simulation, which is more adept to analyzing complex, contingency-based environments, such as skills based routing.

5. Calculate workstation requirements: Workstation requirements are a derivative of base staff requirements. At the busiest point in time anticipated, how many agents will need to be at workstations handling the workload? That is how many workstations will be required.

6. Repeat the forecast and calculations for alternative scenarios: Until somebody invents a crystal ball, forecasting for a new or expanding call center will be a challenge. This step involves running some alternative "what if" scenarios, calculating the resources required to handle different possible workloads, and determining the range of resources at stake when making these decisions. You should also illustrate what will happen to customers if you *don't* have the required resources in place for each scenario.

7. Determine final requirements: Since workstation requirements are ultimately based on the workload forecast, which will never be perfect, you need to mix the art of good business judgement in with the science of resource calculations. What is the most likely scenario? What are the consequences if the workload is more or less than expected? How fast can you adjust if necessary, e.g., is it possible to add workstations later on, and what's the associated lead time? These questions will enable you to specify the workstations and other resources required.

▶ Do You Need a Big Call Center?

There are substantial economies in scale when designing and constructing a call center. Finding, renovating, leasing, building and outfitting one facility is less expensive and complicated than two or three for the same number of a/s-es. One PBX/ACD, with IVR/CTI and contact management and CRM apps can support thousands of agents. There is less money spent in cabling and wiring.

The size of your call center is shaped by its function. If your call center is to provide technical support, say for Asian-speaking callers in the US chances are that you will need fewer a/s-es than for inbound sales for a large telco. If you make cereal you will need educated, cheerful, helpful individuals who can handle customer service but have a far less need of college-trained computer techies. Ergo, a center in a locale where you can tap the workforce that you need to assist your customers.

Also, as with so many other things in life a bigger call center doesn't often mean better. These economies of scale are worthless if you cannot staff your center to the desired levels over its lifespan or you don't get the volume to justify it. There are many fewer communities and buildings in most countries that can support a 1,000-a/s call center compared with a 100-a/s operation. Moreover, if you have a call center that has high turnover, such as outbound cold calling, you will burn through that labor supply far faster than customer service or help desk.

Further, should you need to downsize, such as dropping sales, canceled product lines and contract terminations, disposing of a bigger center and its employees becomes much more difficult than if you had a smaller center. The negative impact on the community and the resulting bad publicity will be less. More about that in Chapter 10.

You may be better off designing and opening smaller but networked call centers in two different labor markets, e.g., a pair of 300-a/s centers instead of one 600-a/s facility. You have other benefits by distributing your centers. They are: more location choices, enabling you to tap into markets with certain skills such as language proficiency, freedom to dedicate centers to certain products or clients, disaster recovery and a promotion and retention ladder for managers, i.e., a "regional supervisor" overseeing two or more call centers and their managers.

HOK's John Francis goes one further. Prompted by tight labor markets and new technologies he believes that call centers, as we know them, may disappear. Instead they will emerge as smaller, discrete units attached to individual departments as these functions become integrated with other corporate functions, such as, engineering, marketing and sales, and as improving self-service technologies answer high-volume low-value contacts. Individuals in these "mini-centers" will be cross-trained on sales, service and help desk: acting as true "account representatives" for each customer.

Francis made some valid points that you should seriously consider. You may not need a barn for your call center when back rooms will do. The call center technologies are becoming so versatile and at lower costs to make these mini-centers viable. There are now fully functional PBX/ACDs that can handle as few as 20 to 25 a/s-es.

This vision avoids the need for expensive and challenge-to-locate-and-staff separate medium to large call centers. You will have less trouble finding 20 people in 20 locations, and the room to put them in, than 400 in 1. These mini-centers do not have to be in the same physical premises as their attached departments. They can be linked by voice/data and, if necessary, Internet or dedicated video links. You could have an engineering department in San Jose, CA and the attached mini-desk in Port Townsend, WA. You can keep your center(s) in your own country, without planting the operation in India, Jamaica or The Philippines and having to deal with the complex bureaucratic, cultural, managerial and access issues of running an offshore call center.

More importantly, there is logical and important time-saving and profit enhancing synergy between customer service/sales and marketing and product development. This can shorten new item lead times, improve design and delivery and solve problems faster. Your customer service and sales agents are your company's front lines. The quicker it takes for the real-time information they gather to reach the colonels and generals usually the more accurate your company's response will be. Can you make or refine a product or service well if you don't hear what your customers are saying about it? This technique also provides a career ladder, the near absence of which is a major problem in call center agent retention. A person starts on the sales/service/help desk and moves up, with additional education and training, to reach each level. They get to see on the job what such development and marketing entails.

▶ Effective Design Elements

Here are the major physical characteristics and features for your call center that you will need to consider and ask about when working with your architect and designers:

Call center floors and space

Whether your center will need 30 or 3,000 workstations you will have to plan for their space and for the needs of the employees who will work in them. A good rough calculation, provided by KSBA Architects, for figuring out how much total room you will need for the actual call center plus hallways, training, break and administrative space is to multiply the number of *productive* (non-supervisory) workstations by 90-140 sf per workstation. Each workstation, say a conventional 6'x6'x 1.5' cube and including circulation takes up about 60 sf, or about half of the total area required.

There is enough margin in the math to provide for supervisory stations. Agent/supervisor ratios range from 8:1, such as for help desk where agents may need to consult with their bosses to solve difficult problems to 20:1 for simple, straightforward catalog sales, with the mean around 10:1 to 12:1. The actual rate you select is based on your experience.

Call centers work best on single floors or floorplates. This makes for much more efficient supervision. You don't want your supervisors running up and down stairs or playing elevator tag. A single floorplate design provides installation economies of scale. You don't have to run wire between different floors, which can be a headache. If you need to expand you can build outward, if your center is on the ground floor.

You can make nearly every space into a great looking call center. For example, you wouldn't know from this photo that this center, designed by Whitney, Inc and belonging to ABN-AMRO is actually in a renovated downtown Chicago building erected in 1906.

There are functions such as outbound calling, selling insurance and real estate that do not need to be mixed in with other call center activities. If your center also sells securities you may need to separate those agents to help comply with regulations. Also, if you are a service bureau you can dedicate floors to clients, giving them greater service exclusivity. You do not need your administration and training on the same floor as your center.

Building codes and laws such as the Americans with Disabilities Act (ADA) govern facilities issues such as how many washrooms you need and accessibility. There are also private voluntary standards for how much heating ventilating and air conditioning (HVAC) you need for your call center. The American Society of Heating, Refrigerating and Air-

Conditioning Engineers (ASHRAE), recommends that you provide 20 cubic feet of outside air per minute, per employee.

Yet most of these laws and standards are minimum requirements. To attract and keep employees and maintain their performance you may wish to exceed them, as permitted.

David Meermans, senior manager of professional services with switch-maker Intecom (Addison, TX), recommends that you have an HVAC engineer determine an appropriate air rate for your facility. He advises that you plan cooling so that you have one "extra" cooling unit.

"This n+1 arrangement, where n is the number you need, allows one unit to fail with the rest able to maintain the temperature," says Meermans. "It also means that you do not have a crisis requiring emergency service — just get it fixed soon."

Also, when sizing your cooling systems keep in mind that how much you need depends greatly on where you locate your center, plus how much direct sunlight you plan to have pour through your building. A hot, humid climate requires more chilling capacity than a cold dry, one, which needs more heating. A call center that is bathed in direct sunlight, even one in more temperate climes will place more load on a cooling system than one that is not.

Meermans also suggests having a humidifier if your call center is located in desert or cold areas. Each unit, which costs about $4000 to cover a space of 7,000 to 8,000 sf, can address bad air, dry throat, and static problems. They work by injecting steam into the air ducts; they do require annual maintenance.

Another good tip is to provide, when agents ask, for fans or small supplemental electric floor heaters, where permitted by code and law, to help accommodate individual temperature preferences: from the killer whale lookalikes to the fashionably tubercular. Some offices I've worked at have locks on the thermostats: to prevent "temp wars" that give an HVAC system fits, and ultimately breakdowns. Having fans or heaters are also handy when the HVAC system goes down for repairs or squeezes its last cubic feet of coolant. I worked in one office where the building management shut their system off on weekends; it took half the week for the work areas to cool down or warm up (depending on the season) to adequate levels.

Another irritant, especially in public places, are not enough and inadequately sized washrooms. Women use the restrooms more often and for longer periods of time than men. If your workforce is predominantly female you have to accommodate that. Meermans points out that adding them during construction is economical compared to the cost of an operation with too few.

Also, too often the stalls are too tiny for women *and* men. Not everybody is built like an Olympic athlete, a jockey or a heroin addict. Ask your architect to see how your center can accommodate *real* agents. If you will be running 24x7 Meermans advises that you arrange for weekend janitorial service and install the giant-roll toilet paper dispensers, and oversized (or several) towel and soap dispensers.

"The single greatest and most easily resolved source of complaints you are likely to observe is inadequate restroom accommodations," he points out. "This sounds simple, but it is amazing how easily such simple things can get out of hand."

When planning your space don't forget to include provisions for the seemingly little items that are very big to agent convenience and comfort. One of them is where they can put their coats, umbrellas and other personal items.

Meermans suggests that if you don't have or want workstation storage, then provide small lockers, about a 12" cube, for headsets, handbags, and other small articles. Agents tend to want to keep their coats with them, so include a coat-hook in each workstation.

"A coat closet should be included in the center, but do not be surprised if no one ever uses it for coats," he says.

Lighting

Your call center needs to see the light. KSBA recommends 30 foot-candles of light at each workstation. But where you place lighting is as important as the quantity. Call centers benefit greatly from glare-free indirect lighting, where you place or suspend fixtures to bounce light off ceilings or walls.

Alan Hedge, professor of human factors and ergonomics at Cornell University, conducted a study on lighting at Xerox from 1989-1992 that tested direct and indirect lighting and found that indirect lighting caused less eyestrain and increased productivity by 2% to 3%. In an article "How to Design an Ergonomic Call Center" written by Randy Hayman and published in the April 1998 *Call Center*, Hedge found out that the lighting system costs about 1% of salary costs. The article reported that office space designers said the Hedge/Xerox study ranked among the top in the field.

"If you can boost productivity by 1% you've covered the cost of the system in a year," said Hedge.

Meermans advises that you arrange the lighting fixtures to keep the light off the monitor screens. Generally this is with the long axis perpendicular to the screen. You should also locate the fixtures in conjunction with the furniture, not just "every third grid."

He also suggests that if you are buying new fixtures, install parabolic diffusers. If you are using existing fixtures throw away prismatic diffusers: the flat, white or clear plastic ones with the bumpy surface. They only scatter light, filling the top of the room with white fog and glaring on monitor screens. Instead, replace them with egg-crate diffusers. These look like a grid of small squares and direct the light down.

You may find, however, from consulting with your agents that they may prefer less light, such as technical help desk where your employees spend a lot of time concentrating on information presented on-screen. A gloomier office or section may be less distracting than one that is brightly lit. On the other hand, older agents may require more light than their younger counterparts.

You should consider having adjustable lighting at the desktop, especially if your agents are reading manuals or doing paperwork, which require more light than staring at computer screens. While your employees can't control the indirect lighting, they can customize desktop lighting to compensate.

On the subject of windows, be careful how and where you place natural lighting. It makes a big difference in your call center's look and mood. Many studies have shown that people simply feel better when they receive natural rather than artificial light. How much natural light your center needs also varies by location.

Says Rick Burkett: "If your call center is in St. Paul, MN your day shift agents won't see sunlight at all during winter. If your call center is in Jacksonville, FL agents will see it on their way in or going home."

Natural light presents two problems: glare and heat load, even in winter, making your air system work overtime, adding to costs. I once worked in a black-clad Manhattan office where my supervisors had the misfortune of having south-facing windows. It might be 20 degrees outside but to them it felt like 200.

The expression "Go where the sun don't shine" easily applies to the Pacific Northwest, with its long, gloomy and damp fall, winter and spring months. That makes adding natural lighting even more important. LiveBridge's Wilsonville, OR call center features plenty of windows, with lush rain-soaked greenery surrounding the building. The center is also separated into smaller, quieter and more collegial spaces.

The key is to figure out where and how to use natural lighting. Burkett suggests having work areas placed where there are north facing windows that provide indirect light and your break areas where there are south facing windows. You should also consider adding skylights if the building permits because they provide light without overloading the air system; exhaust fans can remove any heat pockets generated from the skylights.

Color

Color, like light, sets the mood in any business; color reflects light in different amounts. You use color in walls, ceiling, carpet and furniture. The closer to white the more light they bounce off. Entire books have been written on how to use color to excite or calm people down. The stronger the color the more eye-distracting, which is not good for workstations but fine for everywhere else.

Meermans says color is a good way to break up the design uniformity in a open "big box" call center. Color, like windows, also compensates for dreary climates. You can also put color on walls if you do not have a lot of windows or the view from them is drab, like another building or parking lot.

"Paint is relatively cheap," says Meermans. "If you can do things with color then work it into your plan."

The April 1998 *Call Center* ergonomics article cited the advice of Marilyn Joyce, founder and director of The Joyce Institute, a unit of Arthur D. Little (Seattle, WA). She recommended that color should be neutral or muted in work areas whereas it can be livelier in break areas and hallways.

Noise

Noise is a major issue in office environments like call centers. Sometimes the level can be so high that agents have a hard time understanding the person at the other end of the line and can't think. According to the KSBA's Kingsland, when the overall noise level rises above 50 decibels, people compensate by speaking louder, setting up a vicious cycle.

To cope with noise levels Kingsland recommends that you specify noise-absorbing furniture panels and ceiling tiles. High workstation partitions also cut down on noise. White noise, also known as sound masking can lower the noise of voices that employees hear by as much as 2/3 by masking the frequency of human speech. The sound is generated and distributed through ceiling speakers. One study he had seen, of a telemarketing call center, showed a 20% productivity increase over the same months in the previous year.

Meermans recommends specifying moderately high (10 to 15 feet) ceilings as these can control sound significantly. He also advocates sound absorbing ceiling and sound-blocking furniture panels, carpeting, more room between agents and white-noise generators.

"You can also design out noise sources," he says. "For example, locate the time clock and doors to the work floor away from agent workstations. You can put copiers, shared printers, shredders, and busy fax machines in a separate room. The constant traffic and mechanical noises are very distracting."

Kingsland points out that for the method to work you need high-absorption ceiling panels and high partitions. "If you go into a space that has open desks and hard ceilings," he told *Call Center* in the April 1998 ergonomics article, "you're wasting your money."

Another, much less expensive way to keep noise down is monitoring your agents for the bigmouths. If you hear agents whose voices boom or sound like blackboards being scraped tell them to lower the volume: customers don't like to be yelled at either. Or as one middle-aged woman once sweetly told me when I was talking too loudly on a train: "Excuse me, but do you have a broadcast license?"

Flooring

How you design your floors affects where your power, voice/data lines and/or HVAC is fed to your workstations. This will also affect the center's appearance and the ease by which you change the floor layout, and your costs.

There are two competing methods, with their pros and cons. The conventional technique has been to have plain carpeted floors and run HVAC and cabling from ceiling ducts, dropping the wires to workstations in poles. This has been challenged by a new system, raised access flooring. This is a skeletal floor that takes cabling and/or HVAC to the work areas underneath the walkway. Cable-only floors are about six inches high; those with HVAC ducts are 12 to 16 inches high.

Raised access flooring, with the utilities underneath, such as at CompUSA's Plano, TX call center permits you to move workstations around more easily than conventional flooring that feeds voice/data and power from above-ceiling spaces. You must decide whether the flexibility and arguably improved appearance provided by this method is worth the extra cost.

The proponents of raised access flooring, such as KSBA's Roger Kingsland, cite its improved air distribution (air rises past workstations to vents, instead of staying at the top as in forced air-heating buildings with above-ceiling distribution) and ease of utility access (enabling easier workstation shifting). Raised access floors provide better esthetics by not having and working around ugly poles.

"One of the myths about raised access flooring is that it is very expensive and ugly," Kingsland points out. "People also think of the heavy plastic laminated flooring in computer rooms [that are at least 18 inches high]. In reality, office raised access flooring is carpeted, lighter weight and about half the price."

Raised floor panels can also be taken with you, like furniture, if you move your call center. Since raised floors are an asset, like furniture, you can depreciate them, which offsets costs.

But raised access floors also add about 25% to 35% to the leasing price, according to Dan Frasca, The Alter Group's (Lincolnwood, IL) VP of development. "Companies that get the most out of raised access flooring are those that frequently change their floor layouts," says Frasca. "It gives them quick access to the underfloor cabling and duct work."

Opponents such as Laura Sikorski say that raised access flooring is not necessary. She also doesn't like the feel when walking across them. How often do you move around workstations, which requires an electrician to come in - at up to $100/hour — to change the cabling.

burkettdesign's Rick Burkett adds that raised floors require you to add ramps to access closets, elevators, stairwells and washrooms built on the structure's slab. Building codes mandate handrails if the elevation change exceeds six inches. Other designers, such as Roy Young, point out that you can make the transitions gradual or incorporate them as design elements.

Instead, Burkett points out that there are ways to drop utilities from ceiling spaces so they improve the look of the call center space. Partitions and closets that mask the wires yet allow access to these services break up the monotonous open appearance of many call centers.

"You can also go for exposed cable trays, making the wiring a design feature, giving a fun industrial look that works in many call centers, like help desk or where it serves young trendy industries like the Internet," says Burkett. "Such designs can help you recruit people by making them think 'hey, this is a cool place to work.'"

Workstations

Workstations are your call center's "bottom line." They are where your agents produce. How you set them up will affect how efficiently they produce. And that depends on what the agents will be doing and how aggressively you need to supervise them. Are they working individually or in teams? Are they self-motivated and disciplined or do you have to watch them like a hawk?

When you are setting up in labor-short areas be very precise about how much supervision you provide and to whom. You may be forced to hire less-than-ideal people that need more supervision than you had planned. On the other hand good agents may hate to be micromanaged and may go elsewhere where they are "treated like an adult."

Call center agents have traditionally worked alone: in outbound or inbound order taking, with little need for interaction except with a supervisor. They have sat in stereotypical rectilinear "cube rows," in straight or more contemporary curved or zig-zag patterns with supervisor stations at each end. More agents are now sitting around cores, also known as 'hub-and-spokes' or pods where they face central cores separated by partitions. This high-density design helps reduce noise.

Unfortunately these designs — especially the cores — are the workplace equivalent of the dreaded hospital gown: with the agents' backs exposed. They provide no privacy, permitting the supervisor to sneak up at any time. To check this some call center agents have reportedly fitted rear view mirrors at their stations.

"If you need more aggressive supervision then rectilinear rows, hub and spokes work fine," says Kingsland. "If your supervision is less aggressive then more conventional cubes, with 3 or 3 /1/2 panels, offer more privacy."

If your call center works in teams you should consider either a workbench design where more than one agent and desktop/phone share the same primary work surface, or conventional cubes arranged around a supervisors' station. This way they can focus on individual and group tasks as need be.

Herman Miller's Resolve design not only accommodates conventional floor and cable tray wiring but it adds a contemporary, classy look for call centers.

Some workstation designs try to bridge the raised-versus-conventional floor debate. Herman Miller's Resolve style, which features utility-carrying vertical stanchions that extends from floor to ceiling, unlike conventional core designs that stop at partition level. Resolve is also highly flexible, allowing delta, single and multiple hexagonal, half-hexagonal, shell and zigzag seating patterns and workgroups. It also has rolling screens, tables and mobile bins.

"This clever design provides a very high-tech core appearance without the ugly power pole look," says Stinson.

When planning for workstations look at buying those that permit agents to adjust them, to fit their needs and change positions to prevent getting stiff. Some models even allow agents to stand while they are working. For example, Mode Office Systems' (San Leandro, CA) SMART workstation is a sit/stand two-part table. Mounted to the front of the primary work area is an infinitely adjustable tiltable keyboard platform. Herman Miller's Passage line of freestanding furniture combine modular desks with storage, and have height-adjustable work surfaces. It can also be reconfigured without disrupting other workstations. Individual stations are completely independent from each other.

Roy Young, of Young Bickley Geiger, likes adjustable workstations because they make the work environment more adaptable and flexible. They can also save you money.

"By letting your agents move a workstation up and stand up at the same time they get the benefit from a fatigue-relieving change of position while still being productive," he points out. "It also lowers your facilities costs by avoiding customizing workstations for each employee."

There is an equally wide range of options for accommodating your supervisors and managers. Managers at Centralized Marketing Company's (Cordova, TN) call center work out of a four-turret raised tower.

Chairs

Chairs are the literal backbone of call center design. If they don't fit or cannot be easily adjusted your agents and your call center suffers. The chairs must provide adequate back and shoulder support; the armrests should support the arms while agents are keyboarding. Yet because the chairs receive heavy use they must be strong, durable and wear-resistant.

Fortunately, there are many new innovative ergonomically sound and highly durable chairs on the market. For example, Cramer (Kansas City, MO), *Interfaces* is a combination workstation and chair that features fully adjustable integrated armrest keyboards and seat.

Because everyone is built differently, some manufacturers offer chairs designed to seat people who are bigger and taller than average. Cramer's TritonMax is scaled up for these users. Domore (Elkhart, IN) Big &Tall Series

Ergonomically-designed furniture comes in many shapes and sizes, such as this strange-looking but very comfortable is Grahl's Duo-Back chair. Its split back supports the spine without putting pressure on the spinal column.

covers chair models from executive to task and intensive use. BodyBuilt also offers chairs in larger dimensions.

Flat Screens Versus Conventional Screens

One increasingly popular feature that can influence call center design is flat panel monitors (FPMs). They are becoming increasingly affordable while providing a snazzy high-tech look.

More importantly, as KSBA Architects notes, they can allow you to shrink your workstation size by 10% to 20% without giving up functional room. They are also much more energy-efficient, and they require less wiring than conventional cathode ray tube (CRT) screens.

But are FPMs worth the added cost? Laura Sikorski doesn't think so. She points out that in most cubicles, the CRT back occupies the dead corner space; most people like to sit at an angle to the cubicle partition so that their elbows don't hit the sides.

"Instead, call centers should invest in larger 24-inch monitors and get away from the smaller 15- to 18-inch screens," says Sikorsky. "They are easier to see and they can accommodate more workflow, such as drop down quadrants and windows."

Rick Burkett says that flat screens are essential in some environments, such as help desks and in high tech call centers. FPM can also be used in place of corkboards or the traditional readerboards.

"FPMs are high tech and cool," says Burkett. "They're high tech and they attract high-tech people you want working for you. They're eye-candy and they're functional."

Amenities

Amenities make and keep your center livable and productive. They give your hard-working stressed-out human production means, i.e., your agents, space and time to relax, eat, satisfy cravings for toxic, if legal and still-socially-acceptable substances, and re-energize. They provide room for them to become human, to network with co-workers and blow off a little steam.

At the very least you need some kind of break and meal-eating facility. Agents and supervisors alike need to get out of the workfloor pressure vessel. You can let them unwind, say on video games, foosball and by reading.

Allowing them to eat at the workstations should be a no-no. Spilled food and sticky beverages, like coffee and soda, can ruin costly keyboards and chairs in an instant, while attracting real, live, creepy, crawling bugs and mice into your computer system.

When planning your lunch space David Meermans offers some good advice. Size it to accommodate the maximum number of agents who will eat at

Break rooms should be appealing to employees and close to their workstations, as is the one at MediaOne's Jacksonville, FL call center, designed by burkettdesign.

any one time. He also recommends having water filters or a reverse osmosis unit, serviced by the supplier to ensure old dirty filters are replaced, which are less hassle to fiddle with than bottled water. For ice he advocates commercial icemakers because domestic models cannot keep up with demand. In keeping food cold a domestic frost-free unit works well and is far cheaper than sub-zero units.

One of the biggest lunchroom nuisances, which can cause health problems, are filthy dishes. Piles of them lying in a sink provide a buffet for bacteria, germs, and their carriers, i.e., flies, roaches and rodents. Yum-yum. While employees should wash up after themselves, many do not. Meermans advises that you hire and pay someone, a surrogate Mom or Dad, whose responsibility includes cleaning the lunchroom (and the fridge). You should also consider buying a dishwasher — Mom or Dad can run it.

"This may mean the end of microbiology experiments in the coffee cups, but you are running a call center, not a pharmaceutical lab," he says.

Smoking areas

You have to find some way to accommodate those employees that are smoking-addicted. Many people who work in call centers are. Under *no* circumstances should you permit smoking indoors, especially at workstations and in the offices, even if you are allowed to. The health risks to occupants, directly and secondhand, the very real possibility of fire and damage to furnishings, plus the hard-to-eradicate stench, not to mention the additional trash is not worth permitting the so-called 'right' to smoke. Many companies actively discourage employees from smoking and building codes often limit where one can smoke.

The best way to accommodate smokers is to create outdoor, sheltered and easy to clean "butt pads," with neat-looking and easy-to-clean ashtrays and chairs. The smokers should be responsible for cleanup. Install your pads away from building entrances or from intake vents to prevent the toxins from being drawn into buildings and to keep the entrances tidy and presentable.

Call center agents and supervisors like the little things too: like groceries and personal items. If you locate your call center some distance away from stores, such as in suburban office parks, having them on site as Convergys has contracted for with Goodings, a local chain at its Heathrow, FL call center, north of Orlando, makes life easier for your agents and for you. The convenience store records about 900 transactions a day from the center, which has over 600 workstations.

Supplemental amenities

There is also a supplemental group of amenities, whose availability depend on your workforce and their interests. Chief among them is childcare. Ask any working parent what is the toughest, most problematic thing to find and they'll tell you a good, safe, convenient, available and affordable childcare provider. Once signed up for one it is a chore, a hassle and an all round pain in the !#$%^&(*())_+ backside to run your cute if troublemaking carrier of your DNA to the center in between work trips and shopping trips, and is even more so if there if the off-spring is hurt and sick, requiring a rescue....

On the other hand your call center may appeal to other employees, such as college students, which in most cases do not have children. Or the workers do not bring their kids with them under any circumstances.

Other popular supplemental amenities include gyms, cafeteria and restaurants. Some call centers even have picnic areas and grocery stores.

Whether you provide these on-site depends on where you locate your call center. Some companies that prefer to be in isolated office parks or similar facilities remote from restaurants and shopping will have to be self-contained: with all of the supplemental amenities company-paid or arranged on-site. Other firms prefer to be on main shopping strips where their employees are in easy access of these services, provided by others.

Be prepared for employee gripes with any employer-provided amenity, no matter how good it is: the service becomes a focal point for complaints of all kinds, rightly or wrongly. Many people are not comfortable with an Army-like lack of choice, doled out by the boss.

▶ Ergonomics Regulations

According to my old but trusty *Concise Oxford Dictionary*, ergonomics is the "study of efficiency of persons in their working environment." The federal Occupational Safety and Health Administration (OSHA) and individual states have been devising ergonomics standards to reduce workplace injuries such as those caused by repetitive movements like keyboarding in call centers. One such injury is carpal tunnel syndrome where agents experience pain in their hands and wrists.

Carpal tunnel is a musculoskeletal disorder (MSD) that these standards govern. According to OSHA, about 300,000 workers and $9 billion can be saved annually if the standard goes into effect. The median days away from work for MSDs is seven, compared with four for other serious injuries.

Women workers will especially benefit from the standard. OSHA says they comprise 70% of carpal tunnel and 62% of tendinitis, a related injury, in part because women are more likely to perform repetitive tasks like keyboarding. The standard would protect up to 12 million women at risk from experiencing MSDs.

Although call centers are not directly singled out in the regulations, which would immediately cover manual handling and manufacturing jobs, if an employee at your center became inflicted with an MSD you have to comply with the regulations. While controversial, there is strong likelihood that some form of ergonomics standard will go into effect. This will either be by law or by practice by employers who want their workers to stay and be productive, and save on health insurance, sick leave and temporary replacement costs. And, in a competitive labor market, don't be surprised if your employees make that decision for you.

There are 23 OSHA-approved "state plan states" (see listings and more information under www.osha.gov) whose regulations are as effective as and can be stricter than OSHA's regulations. In two of those states, Connecticut and New York State, their plans apply only to local and state employees. Private sector employees come under the federal regulations. The OSHA Web site page that covers state plan states has links to those states and jurisdictions.

For example, Washington State has proposed its own ergonomics rules. Employers with what the state defines as "caution zone jobs" are covered by the regulations. A caution zone job is a job or task where an employee's typical work includes physical risk factors such as awkward postures and highly repetitive motion.

Two awkward posture risk factors cited in the proposal are working with the hand(s) above the head or the elbow(s) above the shoulder, and working with the neck, back or wrist(s) bent more than 30 degrees, both for more than a total of two hours per workday.

There are two highly repetitive motion risk factors. One is performing intensive keying (defined as keying with the hands or fingers in a rapid, steady motion with few opportunities for temporary work pauses) for more than four hours per workday. The other is repeating the same motion with the neck, shoulders, elbows, wrists or hands (except for keying) with little or no variation every few seconds for more than two hours per day.

"These risk factors are often combined," explains state industrial

Stretching and Sitting For Performance

It isn't enough for you to provide excellent ergonomically designed chairs and workstations to keep your agents and supervisors comfortable. They have to offer their share by stretching and sitting correctly.

The August 7, 2000 *New York Daily News* had a great article on how to stay limber while on the job, citing a new book "Stretching at Your Computer or Desk" written by Bob Anderson. The exercises include hand-wrist-arm stretch, shoulder-arm stretch, shoulder shrug, neck stretch, neck-upper-shoulder stretch, upper-body stretch, lower-back stretch and hamstring-lower back stretch.

Anderson also recommends that you and your employees should stand up and move around as much as possible, counting breaks and washroom trips. He suggests that you stretch every 45 minutes,

"To me the most difficult job in the world is to sit in front of a computer for hours and hours and hours," Anderson told The Daily News. "Your body atrophies, circulation decreases and muscles get tight."

The news story also had a box on how to sit right. According to Kell Roberts, owner of Real Fitness (Los Angeles, CA) and spokesperson for the American Council on Exercise, you should have a light but natural arch in the lower back. Shoulders should be directly above the seat and pulled down and back. The chest should be open and the head should be directly above the shoulders, not in front of them. If you're working at a keyboard, elbows should hang straight down from the shoulders.

"Sitting is one the hardest things to do correctly," said Roberts. "When you don't do it correctly you end up with back, shoulder and neck pain."

hygienist John Peard. "If you have no awkward postures, you can have intensive keyboarding for seven hours."

Fixing MSD hazards do not have to be expensive. A company where agents were complaining about wrist pain, particularly in the "mouse hand," installed adjustable height keyboard and mouse trays that sit atop desks and lower into position. The cost was $40 per employee. Simply training agents to use the adjustments in their chairs, desks and monitors, coupled with proper phone use, printer and in-box placement, and encouraging them to take breaks can reduce or eliminate pain.

Workplace furniture maker Cramer offers these suggestions for your agents to reduce the risk of these ailments:

- Keep and use a soft squeeze ball at the workstation to break up the keyboarding hand and wrist position;

- Take a break, ideally every hour or so, by getting up from your workstation and walking around;

- Avoid leaning on desk edges and armrests;

- At the keyboard try to keep the hand, wrist and forearm in a straight line. Don't bend your wrist up, down or to the side dramatically;

- If agents use their hands and wrists off as well as on the job, they should avoid off-duty activities that overuse the wrist such as bicycling, rowing, weight lifting, racquet sports, prolonged writing, holding a steering wheel and certain crafts;

- Pay attention to hand and wrist symptoms. Tingling, numbness, burning and pain don't have to come with the job.

CHAPTER SIX

Call Center Technology

When putting together a call center don't forget the tools the agents need to do their jobs: the voice and data supporting hardware and software that connects them to your customers, and the carrier services that enable it. Figuring out, planning and specifying the right products beforehand saves you time, money and hassle.

This chapter will not delve into the intricate details of the technology and services you need. Other tomes like Keith Dawson's *Call Center Handbook*, Jane Laino's *The Telephony Book — Understanding Systems and Services*, Kerstin Peterson's *Business Telecom Systems* and Richard "Zippy" Grigonis's *Computer Telephony Encyclopedia* do that very well. What it will focus on is what you need and how to avoid common problems in researching, specifying and installing these increasingly complex systems.

The key to determining what your call center needs is the same as what you need a call center for: present and future customer demands and requirements, especially communication channels. You must know this before you decide to add and fit out call centers.

When you are researching, specifying, buying and installing any kind of hardware or software avoid going to the two extremes: (1) buy cheap or (2) go out on the town and coax the vendors with money for the latest and greatest. You'll lose flexibility, in the first instance; and waste money on goodies that you don't need or that will be obsolete by the time you do need them, in the second. The best course is to source what you need; but make sure what you buy has room to grow, and can be adapted to new technologies.

Also, avoid buying at the last moment. Know what you want ahead of time. It is like grocery shopping on an empty stomach: you'll buy more than what you need and not what you need because you're hungry.

Here's a general look at the technologies and options you'll need for your call center, some application tips and what to watch out for:

Switching calls has progressed considerably from the manual plug-and-connect days; sophisticated computers now handle the function but the principle remains the same: routing calls arriving on outside lines to the phones belonging to the intended parties.

▶ Switching and Routing

The most essential set of equipment you need for a call center, besides the phones themselves, is a means to connect the calls and contacts from your customers to your agents, and your agents to your customers. You can have separate direct inward dial (DID) telephone numbers for each person, say for an inside sales agent responsible for a given product line or territory; but this is only practical in a small office.

Or you can have all calls come through one number and have them switched to different people or departments. This can be handled off-premises on a switch owned by the incumbent local exchange carrier (ILEC), known generically as *Centrex*, leased by you; or on-premises in a switch owned by you, the most popular type is known as a *private branch exchange (PBX)*. You can also make Centrex and PBX systems work together. PBXes are usually more flexible than Centrex units, and come with their own phones.

There is another, newer, and less common type of on-premise owned switch known as a communications server or *"comm server"*, a.k.a. "PC-based PBX" or "unPBX". Comm servers use highly flexible and customizable open-architecture computer platforms to switch calls (unlike conventional PBXes that rely on highly specialized closed-architecture computers). However, comm servers are less expandable and reliable than PBXes, and the good ones are almost as expensive. Comm server owners often attach their devices to a conventional PBX for backup, have a second or third unit for backup and spare computer cards on hand to swap in for dead ones.

Far more common for call centers is third type of on-premises switching equipment: *automatic call distributors (ACDs)*. ACDs not only switch calls but they route them as per your instructions, usually to the first available agent but increasingly to agents that have special skills, such as language, e.g., "numero deux pour Francais," service, or help desk or product offerings, like "Palladium Club Members." This is known as skills based routing.

ACDs also provide vital information about your call center activity. They let you know exactly what is happening with your call flow, such as volume, flow peaks and valleys, where the calls are coming from and going to and hold times and abandoned calls. This information helps you maintain your basic service levels. If the hold times, say on the "Silver Club" queue are too long and customers are becoming annoyed and are dropping out you can direct those calls to "Palladium Club" agents for prompt attention. Some systems will also let priority callers "queue jump."

There are also ACD systems and offerings that can provide the expected time until the next agent is available, which customers very much appreciate — as well as those that let them leave a phone number for callback without losing their place in line. Many systems let you play recordings; but, if you employ the latter option please be careful about hitting callers with "elevator music" or promos on how wonderful you are. Customers get very irritated when forced to listen to promos. Then, depending on the issues they're calling about, like how come they can't get a flight out of Newark on a windless sunny day, those promos might prompt *them* to hit your hapless agents with mean, disgusting and likely illegal suggestions about what you can do with your company, its service and phones. Give them an opportunity to vent, like an e-mail address, and have agents with ears equipped with heat shields to answer them *promptly*, and let your Web site become a fount of knowledge with *frequently* updated information.

ACDs come in many different sizes and devices. There are standalone ACDs that handle switching as well as routing. There are PBX/ACDs: PBXes with ACD functions, often on an open-platform computer where you need the business phone functionality of the PBX and Centrex ACDs. Comm servers, such as Interactive Intelligence's EIC have ACD functions.

When shopping for a switch you should also look for one that can handle, with special software, online contacts and integrate them into your call flow. If your business is expanding chances are your online contact volumes will rise to a point where depository addresses such as sales@... or "service @..." are not enough to handle them. Find a system that can also handle faxes. You can tie in your Web site by installing Web callback where surfers can request a live agent to call them back — either immediately, which puts them in a queue, or at a specified time.

Be careful how you set up such integrated queues. E-mails and chats can take longer to handle than the same service request or sales in voice because they must be read and then responded to by keyboarding. This could drag your service level down, especially during peak calling. If the service level is sagging you should set up, in advance, a signal for agents who are handling e-mail inquiries to put them aside to answer calls. But make sure e-mails get answered promptly, since poor turnaround time is one of the top customer complaints.

Also, you have to pick and assign your online-handling agents carefully. Those that are great on the phone may not have the written language skills to communicate effectively (see Chapter 9). Your best bet is to have online-qualified agents placed in a separate online queue that can answer phone calls, but only when needed.

▶ IVR and Speech Rec

At some point your call volume will grow to the point where live agents cannot handle everything, if your call center isn't already at that point. You then have a choice: hire more agents, and perhaps open another call center for them, or introduce some form of automated self-service, such as IVR, discussed in Chapter 3.

You may consciously decide to have live-agent-only handling as a customer service and market differentiator, as most people don't like talking to or playing with machines, but it will be at the risk of adding costs that you may or may not be able to pass on. Most companies prefer the pen-

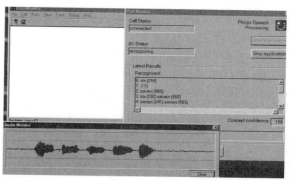

Speech rec systems are growing in power and viability. Philips Speech Processing SpeechPearl speech rec application can understand spoken words with acoustic, language and lexicon modes. These methods slice speech by minimum sound units, comparison to words in the system's vocabulary and to specific terms in a list.

nies per transaction costs of IVR for basic calls like "where is the nearest dealer" or buying a product they already have the order number, specifications and price for" compared with the dollars per transaction cost for a live agent.

The main factor when considering and planning an IVR system is to make it user-friendly. The better the ease of use, the less likely callers will want to zero out and speak to a live agent, defeating its purpose. That means simple, easy-to-use menus; people can't remember more than a few words at a time.

You should look for an IVR system that has speech recognition; but you can also buy this software separately. Speech recognition is a great but very complex technology that permits people to "converse" with a machine "naturally" compared with fiddling about with a touchpad menu — which isn't advisable for cell phone users in situations like driving a car. Also, believe it or not, many home phones are still rotary-dial pulse, not touch-tone.

Speech rec relies on artificial intelligence to "understand" and respond to words, phrases and sentences. This isn't easy. Software engineers must code for dialect and cope with colloquialisms and callers answering with questions. With my mutt-like intermingled mix of American,

British and Canadian accents, dialects and phrases, I give low-voltage fits to speech rec apps.

"You want to design an application so that when a caller calls, it can respond in a way that makes sense," Bruce Balentine, director of speech recognition with the Enterprise Integration Group (San Ramon, CA) told *Call Center,* in the November 1999 speech recognition/IVR buyer's guide article.

▶ Computer Telephony Integration

At some point you will need to mesh your voice and other media customer contacts with the data you have on them. That is the function of computer telephony integration (CTI) the so-called "screen pop." In essence CTI takes who is contacting your company and matches them with the file or record you have on that customer or prospect residing in your database(s) and transmits them to your agent. It saves them from hanging your customers on hold while they key it up. There are a vast range of CTI products and variations. You cannot have an effective call center without it.

CTI is easier said than done, especially if your firm is big and established. Don't expect it to be "plug-and-play." Let's look at a banking application. A customer who lives in San Diego just got a big raise and decides to move their money and calls your 800 number. You may have their checking account on a Unix server in a Tampa data center, their savings account on an IBM 390 mainframe in the bowels of a regional office in downtown L.A., their IRA on a Windows NT machine in Las Vegas while their credit card accounts reside on a Compaq/Digital mini in Ottawa, Kansas. And your call center is in Port Angeles, Washington. Somehow all of these computers have to be made to "talk" to each other.

▶ Contact Management and CRM Software

Every business that uses call centers needs some form of contact management software, to record the transaction, wherever and whatever media it is coming in on and make the information available for others in your business. Few events are more embarrassing for both parties than a customer calling a company complaining why haven't they received their order and the poor agent at the other end not being able to find out what happened to it. Except, maybe, for a field sales rep walking into a client's premises only to be blasted because the hardware or software they bought isn't working.

Companies also need to connect their online and call center operations. It is a good idea for your sales, service and help desk agents to have access to the same information your surfers can tap into, including the site's FAQs (frequently asked questions). This applies to large and small call centers alike. A few years ago Service Intelligence (Seattle, WA) publicly embarrassed such leading edge firms as Intuit and Microsoft by auditing their external help desks. They found that too often — 25% of the time — the agents gave the wrong answer or said the problem could not be solved — to the questions SI's auditors posed even though the answers were on their Web site FAQs.

The same goes for customer relationship management (CRM) software, discussed in Chapter 4. These complex software packages pull the entire customer interaction together: on the phone and on the Web with your database. They let you set the rules for dealing with your customers. Yet they are not all things to all people. Some are better at problem management and problem resolution, others at sales force automation. And they can take 18 to 24 months to implement and cost hundreds of thousands if not millions of dollars in the process and probably drive you and your IT staff into early retirement, long vacations, or to the hair loss wizards.

▶ Outbound Dialing

If your call center is handling a medium to large volume of outbound sales and customer care calls you will probably need a predictive dialer. Predictive dialers check to see if the to-be-called lines are not busy and free of answering machines before connecting the agents, using complex algorithims to determine when to "throw" the calls at agents. These dialers pull the numbers up from calling lists of prospects and existing customers that you want to sell or follow up with. Predictive dialing can cause abandons, where it hangs up a called line, leaving annoying "dead air." Because of this tendency some states are passing laws to regulate dialer use.

There will be occasions when the outbound agents are trying to beat the dialer, like hamsters on amphetamines, while those taking the calls are seeing by how many points their favorite tech stocks are tanking on the Nisei. And there will be moments, such as when your scratch-off-the-activation-strip-and-win a vacation for two cruising on the Staten Island Ferry turned out to be too popular for your inbound staff and you'll have to tow in your outbound agents.

To balance these loads you can hook your ACD and dialer, or ACD and dialer functions to send inbound calls to outbound agents, and vice-versa turning them into *blended agents*. But before you invest in them you should cross-train your staff in customer service and sales. More about this in Chapter 9.

▶ Network Routing

Finally, you may have or need additional call centers, which is probably why you're reading this book. You probably need to integrate them into a network, thus creating a "virtual call center." This is called network ACD or *network routing*, you can get away with dedicating individual call centers and numbers to certain functions, i.e., customer service, outbound, help desk, but not for long. You'll find that there are too many periods for your liking when one call center has callers on hold for 15 to 20 minutes while in the others the agents are playing "Mime Hunt" only with your silhouette in the crosshairs. Or you can have management staff manually juggling which call goes where, like a railroad or subway signal tower. "Oops, I sent the 5:15 Babylon Express on the same track as the 5:10 Huntington local! Hope the brakes work!"

Network routing works like this: inbound calls handled by your carrier hit a routing device, such as Cisco Systems' ICM and sends them to available agents in any of your call centers. You set the routing parameters. If callers are dialing from the east coast you may want them handled by east coast centers only; however, if they're calling from Quebec and the only call center that has French-speaking agents is there, you had better be sure they go to that location. If not, your customer service department may hear from them (and from the provincial government and the French-speaking media) with words that you weren't taught when you took French lessons in high school.

Professional Tips on Buying and Installing Technology

Robert Vilsoet, systems integration director for SBC Call Center Solutions Group, offers these suggestions:

- Avoid rigid requests for proposals (RFPs). Many vendors feel that customers don't read the replies anyway. Instead, they believe they have more chance to win your business if they are talking to you rather than if you're scanning price sheets. Most companies say they are selling value, which doesn't always come through in an RFP response. It is also difficult to ask the right questions in an RFP process to minimize the reading and maximize the value gained from it. Ask vendors to differentiate their products from others.

- Always have at least two product vendors vying against each other to drive hardware and software prices down.

- Choose a reputable vendor. Research their financial stability so they can deliver what they promise. (Ed. Note: many companies are publicly traded, which means you can obtain copies of their financial statements and prospectuses. News services such as Bloomberg and the leading financial media like the Wall Street Journal carry stories about them. Also, see what your broker says about these companies.)

- Ensure the app you buy can be supported by help desks, with one number to call.

- Pick a vendor that can provide systems training. Every supplier can train people on their product or service but in many instances theirs works with someone else's. You need a company that can work with the complete installed application, and provide adequate training for your people.

- Consider hiring a consultant. Because there are so many companies providing call center products and services a consultant can help you sift through them. An experienced consultant will know market prices and can lower the cost of ownership.

- Check references for every product and service, including consultants and integrators. Find those that you can trust.

- Ensure that you pay enough to your project management team to get the level and skill that will directly correspond to your level of customer satisfaction. Don't blame the vendor because you skimped on the project team.

- Involve yourself in system testing. Have input into the acceptance test plan. Don't rely on the vendor to say 'all done'. You need to ensure that all testing levels — unit, system, integration, load and compatibility — is completed. But don't shrink the testing cycle. If you get to that phase late — still do not stint on time; the support costs and aggravation are too high.

▶ What to Watch Out For

There are many fine new and existing companies supplying highly useful products for call centers. The technologies, their products and their vendors change rapidly. You can attend CT Expo in March of one year and March the next or Call Center Demo from May to May and the same hardware or software could have a new name, new modules and new owners or new names of owners. For example, at this writing, the maker of the Definity series PBX/ACD is no longer "Lucent" (which once was "AT&T") but "Avaya". "Teknekron Infoswitch" which makes call monitoring equipment, is now "e-talk".

Never before have call centers been so flexible, adaptable and functional, yet efficient. The imaginative engineers and developers who created these products and the entrepreneurs who financed their efforts have made life easier for callers and call center managers. For example, the auto-attendant feature on PBXes quickens the call, and permits you to deploy those individuals who had been operators more productively by serving callers directly with their issues and orders. Auto-attendants have now been generally accepted by the public. IVRs, for self-service, and CTI functions and predictive dialers have made a big difference in controlling contact handling costs and in improving service. CRM software keeps everybody on the same page. It is truly the best of times for the call center business.

At the same time there is a lot of hype in the marketplace, much of it seemingly written by people who could not explain the difference between an electron from a proton let alone what their employers and clients make. For example, Aspect

Internet Telecom Revolution

Through in-booth theatres, live demos, and hands-on activities you will see product categories including:

Don't miss the chance to be a part of the first ever Internet Telecom Expo. Register today and join us on the exhibit floor!

- Convergence and IP Solutions
- Computer telephony
- M-commerce
- Telecommunications and network infrastructure hardware
- Unified messaging
- Web-enabled call centers
- E-commerce
- CRM applications
- Wireless internet services
- Server/LAN- based telecommunications platforms
- And much more...

Exhibitor List
(continued)

NYIT	Sound Advantage
NYNMA	Symon
eGain Communications	Talkingweb, Inc.
Opto Teleinks LTD	Teknnr Applicom
Parity	Tekurdia Common
Periphonics	Language Prod.
Phonetic Systems	Telephony@Work
PriceInteractive	Telera
Prima	Teltone
Quicknet Technologies Inc	Teltronics
Rave Computer Association, Inc.	ThinkLink
Rizal	Tundo Corporation
SBS Technologies Inc	Vocal Technologies Ltd
Seagull	VoiceGenie Technologies
Sencommunications Inc	w-Trade Technologies
Shoreline Communications	Wall Street Technology
Silcontras-Sliger	Association WSTA
Softinis	Websiteforfree.com
SOSINC Communications	WHEREVER.net Holding Corp

As of July 17, 2000

Trade shows are fine venues to see what's new in technology and network with your colleagues. But before you buy down the road make sure what a company displays on the stand is more than smoke-and-mirrors.

no longer makes ACDs, it's now "portals." Suppliers make products and services not for companies but for "e"businesses. As if businesses don't have "e" as in t"e"l"e"phon"e"s or "e"l"e"ctricity.

That's the downside of being in this business. There is something about the word "technology" that makes eyes glaze over and consequently brings out the snake oil dealers and their pleasant-sounding fashion-molded flacks as well as the geniuses and entrepreneurs. A good reporter has, by experience and training, a finely tuned internal 'b.s. meter.' Mine goes off the scale when I read the press releases issued by so many technology vendors or visit their booths at trade shows. The more buzzwords I see and hear and the more flash and smoke at shows, the more I become skeptical whether the product has any value.

I'm glad I don't have to buy this stuff. My sister-in-law, who is an office manager for a healthcare company has had to. What she would like to do to the salespeople and installers is not fit for a family trade book. But I'll give you a hint. It involves someone calling my son. He is a paramedic.... It is probably a good thing that I don't buy and specify call center technologies. I am bad enough as it is on big-ticket personal items, like cars and computers. I am every salesperson's nightmare because I research what I want to buy and bug the bejeebers out of them, like Peter Falk's Lieutenant Colombo, with "one more question." And then if there is the slightest problem I annoy them again until I'm satisfied everything is working as it should.

It probably isn't a bad idea to be your own Lt. Colombo. Ask around. Read the professionally written-and-edited trade magazines, such as *Call Center, Computer Telephony, Tele.com* and *Teleconnect*, which feature product overviews, buyers' guides and case histories.

It may be worth your while to work with consultants and systems integrators. They have hands-on experience with hardware and software installation; they can act as your "personal shoppers" when sourcing technology. Integrators will also design and create applications and software to mesh systems together. They usually offer post-installation support.

Be careful with these individuals. Find out who they're representing and to what depth. Many of them have strong ties to vendors that they've often picked because they are good companies and make fine products. The good ones will give you a straight line whether the product and technology from a particular vendor will meet your needs and budget.

Remember, you're looking at filling someone else's pocket with five to seven digits of dollars that are your own or your company's. If you make the wrong buying decision someone is going to give you the 'Mr. Dithers' treatment': in your backside.

Here is some other common sense advice when buying complicated products:

Make sure it works. Will the hardware or software perform reliably, under all conditions? Is it engineered to the KISS (keep it simple, stupid) principle?

There are amazing cool products that work surprisingly well, in unexpected ways. For example, hooking one maker's PBX to another can be a nightmare because of their proprietary designs. However, I like Iwatsu's ADIX PBX and its add-on ACD software because it provides this functionality. I heard about this from talking and meeting with an outsourcer, Interactive Marketing Group (Allendale, NJ), who found and appreciated this feature because it lets them design call escalation hookups to their clients.

Watch out when you see the prefix "smart-". When I see this I come up with my own three letters that together form an unprintable suffix. I don't want a "smart product. " I want a stupid product. One that will function reliably and automatically *without* thinking. Smart items can have glitches caused by 'thinking'; stupid items can't because they're dumb. It takes one or two lines of badly written code to make a "smart product" a useless space-wasting but budget-draining "vegetable product."

If you're responsible for a call center you can't play around with developers' and engineers' toys. Your standards are closer to 911 call centers than to typical offices. Your supervisors and staff don't have time to play with complicated user-hostile junk. The products must work close to perfect or else you're going to have angry customers that you risk losing; for them to redial or resend e-mail costs you money and escalates their annoyance.

To find out if it works, check out the demo or better yet, the real thing. Get references from resellers and suppliers and contact them but don't just take their word for it. Amazing how people can change their tune when change goes into their pockets. Therefore you should ask others that you know in your industry about their experience with the "MegACD 7.6" or call them at random and make some new friends.

The second key fact about a product that you need to establish is *does it really exist?* You'd be surprised how much stuff that is promoted at shows and in magazines that is months away - if ever — from being tangible or "live." There is too much "vaporware" in various "alpha" or "beta" stages. There are also products that change for change's sake, what I call the "4.125" phenomenon, an upgrade from "4.121" with too few substantive changes, and not worth tossing the old software out for.

My favorite "4.125" example, one from a few years ago, was when every vendor was proclaiming that the 4.125 version of their software had a 'gooey' (GUI or graphical user interface, or click instead of keyboard commands). Wow. You mean we can chuck the keyboards altogether? Now that would be something....

I'm also always suspicious when vendors wants to meet with trade magazines to show off product demos with no definite release dates, or just to chit-chat at the end of the month, especially when the request comes in at the last moment. It makes me want to reach for the phone and find an analyst and grab my paws on their financial statement pronto. Gee, and when do their earnings come out? You mean they're going public? What a coincidence!

If you're looking to buy any big ticket item, like a PBX/ACD or CRM software or to create a business relationship with an outsourcer, it is not a bad idea to poke into their financials so that you know the company is solid and can deliver on what they promise. When one firm, which need not be mentioned, went public in 1996 I reported in *DM News* that the investment was risky. When the company called to complain I cited the report on them.

▶ Online-enabling Your Call Center: Owning or Leasing the Technology

Sooner or later, your call center will have to be fitted to handle online contacts between customers and your agents. E-mail and the Internet are here to stay. People like using e-mail and going online: by landline and increasingly, from their cellphones. They find out much more information about a product or service far more quickly than they ever could by phone or buy thumbing through a catalog.

Beware of Buzzwords (and Buzzletters)!

When I read a press release about a new product or service, or come across their vendors at a trade show, I look out for the buzzwords or 'buzzletters'. There is almost always an inverse ratio between the amount of hype around a product or service and their value, quality and the stability of the firm peddling them.

There are two notorious overused "buzzes" that get my internal b.s. meter bouncing off the red zone: "e" anything and "solution".

"E" as in "eCRM" means nothing and is completely useless. Why? Because the "e" stands for "electronic". Well, how else does software like CRM operate? With air, animal, hydraulic, mechanical, thermal or thermonuclear energy?

Similarly, "e-commerce" referring only to the Internet is a misused term. People buying and selling by telegraph, Telex, fax and by telephone are also forms of electronic or e-commerce. Why? Because the communications are made by electronic means, i.e., the transmission of electrical energy from point A to point B, are they not?

A better term is direct commerce because the products and services are being sold directly by the seller to the buyer without the buyer acquiring them through a reseller or retailer. Direct commerce applies to all media, including direct mail.

Another annoying term is "solution". Too often I hear companies bleat that they do not make products they make "solutions".

Nonsense. My trusty Concise Oxford Dictionary lists, as the second definition (the first applying to dissolving materials of one state of matter into another) as "Resolution, solving, explanation, method for the solving of, for, to a problem, puzzle, question, doubt, difficulty, etc."

Ergo, vendors make equipment and electronically encoded instruction sets to computers, i.e., hardware and software. They don't make "solutions". A vendor can hope that their hardware or software will be a solution once purchased and applied; but by itself, it is *not* a solution. There could be flaws in the product or on the customer's system that could make the application of the technology a *problem*, rather than a *solution*, as anyone who has installed hardware and software knows all too well.

What should a call center watch for when seeking and negotiating with a carrier? This is what author and expert Jane Laino recommends:

- Unrealistic minimum commitments for call volumes
- Rates that can go up within the life of a contract
- Useful and accurate management reports on call volumes and costs
- Toll Fraud protection
- Avoid long contracts (no more than 2 years)
- Ability to renegotiate rates within the term of the contract, particularly if volume increases.
- References in the contract to tariffs without providing the actual tariff
- A "business downturn clause" can protect you if your business changes and you cannot meet the volume you've committed to.
- To get the lowest rates always create a competitive bidding environment.

I like buying products/services and asking questions through e-mail. I have an instant text confirmation of each interaction and transaction. No guesswork. No misunderstanding.

Yet, e-mail and Web self-service is not enough. Nearly every e-commerce study says that the top priority of online users is getting a living human being when they need one; the absence of such personal customer service is why they hate buying on the Web and will abandon their shopping carts in some binary back lot.

To meet this burgeoning need for online live agent service there are a wide range of applications and tools from many vendors to connect your online customers to your call center. These include e-mail handling, Web callback, escorted browsing and IP telephony, where customers and agents can talk through the Internet. There are also tools to route and manage these contacts.

There are also powerful CRM packages that pull all your customer contacts-by phone, online, fax and self-service and enable you to decide how you want certain classes of customers handled and route them to the most profitable channel. The software yanks the data together and lets you see what your customers are doing: buying, complaining or just seeking information and what, where, for how much, in which channel and when.

▶ Buying Alternatives

Don't be cajoled into buying the latest gadget on the market, even if it does work and it exists. You may not need it or when you do, it may be out of date and no longer supported by the manufacturer. Even when you do find what you need or determine that you do require it down the line, there are two options to outright purchasing the equipment out of the box: *used* and *applications hosted*.

Used equipment, such as PBX/ACDs, IVRs, and predictive dialers can be had for substantially less than new gear and will still have some years left on it. Although anything older than five years tends to be obsolete there are still some huge "iron box" PBXes and standalone ACDs that are older than that and are still clicking. You can buy used equipment 'as is' or refurbished and remanufactured.

If your call center is mainly inbound but makes a few outbound calls, a secondhand dialer is worth it, as long as it keeps the abandons low. The same goes for outbound centers; a simple PBX may be all that is required to answer inbound. If you're looking to set up a new call center the building you pick may already have a PBX/ACD installed.

As with buying any other high ticket and complicated product, like a car or high-end computer system make sure you deal with an authorized and reliable dealer. Many of them will offer training and support. Check the articles and advertisements in *Call Center* and *Teleconnect*. If you're leasing a building that has the systems in situ have your tech people or an integrator check everything out and make any changes so it can be meshed in with yours.

Applications hosted is where another company, owns/buys the product, installs them on their hardware, or yours, and is responsible for maintaining and upgrading them. Instead of purchasing the product you in effect lease it; you pay a setup fee and user charges. Applications hosting has long been common on IVR (see Chapter 3) where IVR service bureaus lease thousands of ports for, say short time periods, like contests and disaster recovery, whose purchase/upgrade costs you could rarely justify. The long-offered Centrex switching from the telcos is a form of application hosting.

As wonderful as these technologies are, the reality is that they are not cheap nor are these systems "plug-and-play." You may have to upgrade and modify your computer hardware and software to support them. Complex interactive e-mail/Internet applications and CRM software can take cost tens to hundreds of thousands to in some cases millions of dollars to buy, the same if not more to install and integrate, over many months, if not years. You are looking sometimes at spending months, spreading into the years, before these new tools begin to pay back your considerable time and money investment, which is up front.

App hosting is usually supplied by specialized technology-only firms, known as application service providers and by traditional live agent service bureaus. Some systems integrators, such as eLoyalty (Lake Forest, IL), also offer app hosting. Service bureaus can also handle some of your live agent phone and online handling. They bring to the table experience in installing and running the apps at their call centers. System integrators are also experienced at putting the technologies in at many different call centers, so they have a good idea what works and what doesn't.

The most important benefit of app/hosting is that it saves time to market. According to Chris Fletcher, vice president and managing director, CRM Aberdeen Group (Boston, MA), app hosting for, says an enterprise-wide CRM application can save approximately 3 months to 9 months off buying and owning. This translates to 12 months to 18 months from 18 months to 24 months for a large application like a Siebel, and to as little as 30 days from 3 months to 9 months for a mid-size CRM package such as Onyx or Pivotal. You also avoid buying additional hardware and arranging for more networks and applications.

Another big advantage of app hosting is that it reduces IT resources. Much of this software is complicated. Many IT departments do not have the time to handle the grunt applications, coding, programming and integration work for call centers. And from the seemingly endless meetings with every affected department to sort out how the technology will be set up and by whom before a single line is written. Also, with app/hosting the IT department is responsible for overall system design and performance but they would not have to execute the project.

Last, but not least, app/hosting offers lower up-front costs. Most applications are priced from the hundreds of dollars to the thousands of dollars by seat. Vendors then usually charge for applications and installation services on top of that.

In contrast, app hosters charge a monthly fee, usually based on software licensing costs and attributed overhead expenses and profits spread out over 36 months, plus setup charges. This means you can keep your capital in the bank; your income, including the benefits will hopefully cover the added costs.

On the other hand the lower initial costs leads to one of the downsides of app/hosting: higher long-term costs. If you keep, say a CRM platform longer than 36 months you may be better off buying.

This segues into a second liability with app/hosting: less flexibility. In doing so you may not have the best components or packages for your needs and budget. You are dependent on the hoster to pick and design the package. To keep costs down and profits up hosters like to standardize platforms and features for all clients, though some are now beginning to offer tailored services for specific markets such as financial services, if not for particular companies.

This leads into another downside, loss of control. When you outsource anything, you give up a measure of management. It is no different with app/hosting. The question that you must answer is how comfortable you are with this, and how receptive potential partners to providing you with real-time information and input, without micromanaging the contract.

If you do decide to have your apps hosted watch carefully how the vendors handle your data privacy. Make sure you know where it is and how it is being protected from unauthorized use.

"No one suggests that there is widespread data theft among hosting providers, and many top carriers hold strong views that hosted data is the sole property of the customer," Marbie Semilof wrote in "The Darker Side of Hosting," the lead story in the May 8, 2000 issue of *Computer Reseller News*. "Still, some solutions providers and analysts said honesty and integrity are the only things stopping such theft - certainly not the vague language common in today's customer contracts."

When weighing up the pros and cons of buying versus app/hosting the best way to think of them: it's like deciding whether to buy or lease a car. You pay more up front when you buy a car and you're responsible for it but it's yours, even if you finance it. You also get the features and options you want, add or take them away at your convenience, run the car for as many miles and when as you wish and if you get a big dent or even a tiny scratch that's a matter between you and your insurance carrier.

When you lease a car you pay less up front and when you turn it in at the end of the lease period you can get a new one, with improvements and new features. Though you don't own it you're not using your capital and savings; you save your money for other purposes, such as expanding your business.

For these reasons, capital short but fast growing small-medium-sized businesses benefit the most from using app/hosting. They get the advantages of the online and CRM technologies without the capital drain.

Larger firms can also benefit from app/hosting. If your company is gradually rolling out online/CRM services to a division at a time, paying as you go, you save money and hassle compared with a potentially hellish one-shot enterprise-wide implementation.

Therefore, you have to look at your needs and your wallet. When I was in the market for a car I did not have much money budgeted. However, my wife and I like to drop off the face of the earth on weekends; we would exhaust the "free" miles on a lease in no time. So we bought used, from a reasonably reputable Chrysler dealer in New Jersey, a 1993 Dodge Intrepid that was in fairly good shape. The car has quite a few miles, some wear and tear and while it is not the state of the art it has power to spare, ease of handling and is very comfortable. I don't like the "new" style Intrepids because you can't see out of the rear window. I look after our car and it keeps going...knock on wood or reasonable substitute.

You can apply the same lessons to call center technology. What matters is that it works reliably, new or used. Keep that in mind as you kick the tires at the resellers' and at trade shows.

▶ Does the Technology Pass The "Spit-Broiler" Test?

When I was growing up, my father, a mechanical engineer, used to bring home all sorts of weird gadgets. One day he unveiled a tiny ceramic tray with a wire rim. My mother, after unrolling her eyes, watched him plug it in and describe its advantages, like warming cup of coffee. I was 12 then, and I tested the device out in a way that 12 year olds are wont to do: I spat on it.

As the substance sizzled on the once-white surface my mother's eyes lit up and she proclaimed: "I know what it is! It's a spit broiler!"

The kitchen aid disappeared into some dark recess of an obscure cabinet, emerging to be sold (I think unsuccessfully) at a garage sale. And today people warm their cold cups of coffee in the far more practical and versatile microwave oven.

When sorting new technology, ask yourself, is it something truly of value or is it a "spit broiler": a seemingly valuable but, in reality, worthless tool. Do you have a true use for it, or do you have to engineer your life around it, in unacceptable ways?

An example of one such "spit broiler" in call centers and in telephony may well be picture or video phones either at homes or in public kiosks connected to call centers. There's been plenty of talk about businesses and consumers buying and using them and, in anticipation, a few firms have geared up their call centers for this media including selecting and training good-looking agents for video communications and fitting workstations with mirrors.

Fancy and space-agey, video phones promise to be the ultimate in communications. Yet they been around for years but have never been widely adopted or accepted, like monorails, another "spit-broiler" technology. Both were featured on the hit 1960s cartoon "The Jetsons".

AT&T tried to flog video phones at and following the 1964 World's Fair. According to an Associated Press wire article written by Bruce Meyerson and carried in the September 8, 2000 *Staten Island Advance* the carrier first demonstrated it in one-way communication in 1927, by future president Herbert Hoover. The article reported that AT&T, Panasonic and Kyocera have taken swipes promoting them in the 1990s but despite technology advancements and dropping costs, still no luck. In the new millennium Talk Visual began marketing one that uses ISDN lines, joined in by Aethra, an Italian firm.

And at least one bank, which will go unnamed, no longer has video kiosks. After a flurry of reports about such applications they seemed to have disappeared from whence they came. Instead the "big thing" is the Internet, with live chat and escorted browsing.

Here's the spit broiler test. Do *you* have or plan to buy a video phone? Do you use the IP video software that came pre-packaged with your home PC and if so, how often do you use it and for what purposes? And if the makers of your PC or your Internet carrier "gave" them away, like wireless operators do with cellphones, would you sign the service contract?

If not, you probably have good reasons and they in likelihood boil down to is *why*. Why do you want to see someone's mug shot, like that of a call center agent? With the lack of quality in picture resolution and not being able to reproduce color exactly, showing items like swatches of fabric is a waste of time. I could care less what my sources looks like and I'm sure they feel the same way about me.

The *Advance* article pointed to another reason: people wander mentally and physically while on the phone. Busy people are usually doing two or three tasks at once, like working on a computer. A call center agent that is staring at a customer's file on screen can't fully look at the customer.

Anxious grandparents will probably use video phones. So will consenting adults. So far, it seems those uses have not generated the necessary demand to get the technology rolling.

This is not to say that they don't have uses. Video phones are excellent for conferences and for managing teleworkers. They save a bundle on travel and transportation costs and hassle. CustomerAssistance.com, a subsidiary of outsourcer APAC Customer Services (Deerfield, IL), has fitted its call center to let you visually visit agents working for you.

Just don't rush out to buy the tools to "video-enable" your call center for your customers unless you have a client or customer set that definitely wants them. Otherwise they'll be taking up memory-gathering dust like my father's 'spit broiler'—for quite some time to come.

Installation Advice

When you purchase your hardware and software new or used, or even if it is app hosted you have to make sure everything works together, which can be nightmarish; the so-called "open standards" are anything but. The process of integrating phone switches with other systems — including systems that enable your center to communicate with on-line customers and CRM software that gathers information about customers from multiple data sources — can be far more complex than simply designing rules for routing calls. You may not know what works until you go live, and have to learn the hard way.

"It's a jungle out there for call center managers," reports Robert Vilsoet, director of systems SBC Call Center Solutions (Chicago, IL). "It is not enough to simply list which versions of vendors' software products work with each other. We've found no matter how much lab testing you do, a production environment sometimes causes unusual situations that were never thought of in the test environment."

"When routing used to be only in the switch, it was easy to design," he adds. "Now, with IVR and computer telephony middleware assisting in routing decisions because of access into the customer databases, the design logic has to take into consideration more components than before. And you have to account for backup routing when components are unavailable."

Here's some good advice from system integrators when deploying technology:

First, you should have sound reasons and objectives for installing new systems. Fully understand your needs and know what systems can and cannot do to help you meet your objectives. Ensure that you have a blueprint that shows how systems support each other to provide consistent customer service. Don't expect tools such as IVR systems, CRM packages or e-mail management software to magically handle calls or on-line inquiries.

"You can have the best IVR system or call center technology, but if you don't design it where the customer's experience is the same across all channels, you'll have to go back and retrofit, wasting 30% to 40% of your investment and time," points out Greg Stack, senior vice president, eLoyalty.

Second, don't underestimate your needs. Avoid buying products whose capabilities you will quickly exceed.

Cary O'Brien, director, Call Center/Data Products Williams Communications Solutions (Houston, TX), says that companies do not always save a lot of time when they purchase and install smaller or less expensive equipment because these systems can require as much integration effort and time as more robust systems.

"If a customer is looking for an advanced call center, our first step is to analyze and evaluate that customer's business objectives and growth patterns before we make a recommendation," says O'Brien. "We conduct extensive studies of their customer base and discuss their short- and long-term business goals. It's just not cost-effective to buy low-end call center products that will be out of date in two years if a client's annual growth rate is 10% to 20%. It is our goal to recommend a call center product that will help that business meet its goals today and tomorrow."

Third, system integrators strongly advise that you maintain redundant systems. Although comm server systems are becoming more reliable, they're still not always as dependable as phone switches, which explains why most call centers still entrust call routing to PBXes or ACDs.

"If you decided to go with a PC-based IVR system, and you had it on only one server and it crashed, you lost the system," explains Dave Clancey, chief technical officer at systems integrator Edgewater Technology (Wakefield, MA). "Why not instead have the IVR platform on two or more PCs so that if one server crashes you have backup?"

Fourth, you should budget enough time to get your new or updated center up and running. "Let's say you have to implement a system by a certain date," explains SBC's Vilsoet. "And the implementation cycle should be six months for the complex integration. What ends up happening is that the contract talks and your approval of the funds end up taking the lion's share of the time, so that approval of the contract doesn't happen until three months before the deadline, but the cutover must still occur on the deadline. As a result of the squeezed implementation, something is missed, and you end up unhappy."

▶ Buying Carrier Services

Whatever technology you buy, you need carriers to supply your voice and data. Yet buying and specifying them also depends on the needs of other voice/data users, such as your head office. If you are a service bureau, in all likelihood your call center(s) form the bulk of the voice/data demand.

However, if your call center is only part of a large enterprise, the other users' specifications and preference may dominate yours.

To help you in your carrier sourcing decisionmaking I asked a leading authority, author and consultant on telephone systems, Jane Laino, founder of Digby4 Group (New York, NY), to contribute information for this section.

According to Laino a call center typically needs both local and long distance service for voice communications; only the smallest of companies need only local service. Local may be used for incoming calls from the nearby surrounding area and for placing outgoing local area calls. All other calls may be classified as "long distance" whether they are within the state, to another state or to another country.

There are both outgoing and incoming long distance services. Incoming may be called 800 or toll free service. Connections to the outside world, for all calls, can be via individual circuits (one pair of copper wires per outside line) or by high capacity circuits, known as T-1 or PRI (primary rate interface — a more sophisticated version of T-1). They handle the equivalent of up to 24 outside lines. The T-1 handles incoming and outgoing calls.

To figure out capacity requirements, Laino says you must remember that there must be a separate outside line for each call in progress (either incoming or outgoing) so, for example, if you have two T-1s (24 calls each) you can have 48 simultaneous telephone calls in progress.

For an existing operation, you determine the number of calls handled in the busiest hour of the day and refer to a statistical "traffic engineering" table to identify the number of outside lines needed to handle that call volume. To use the tables, you must convert the call volume into a total number of minutes or seconds in the busiest hour of the day. See *"The Traffic Engineering Handbook"* by Jerry Harder.

"For new call centers make your best guess of the number of simultaneous calls and double it. It is better to have excess than to have callers reach a busy signal," advises Laino. "Excess capacity may be absorbed or turned back in if not used."

The data circuits needed for a call center depend upon what business is being transacted there. There may be a need for Internet access, which can be via a T-1 circuit as well. As with voice communications, there are statistics that consider the amount of information that needs to be transmitted and the speed requirements. This dictates the "bandwidth" (capacity) of any data communications circuit.

If the call center is Web-enabled then the volume of people clicking a button on the Internet site to speak to a representative must also be considered. If the call center must connect with another division of the organization at a different address, there may be a need for a data circuit connecting the two.

The types of voice and data circuits and the capacities are not as much a function of the type of activity as how the callers reach you and the call volume. There is a type of incoming toll-free service known as DNIS (dialed number identification service) that enables you to have many different 800 numbers without having the equivalent number of connections to the outside world. This may have an application for inside sales, for example, where you may want each salesperson to have his own unique 800 number. This capability can be purchased from your long distance company.

"Since the lines are blurring between local and long distance telephone companies, you may also buy both services from the same company and access the services over the same T-1 circuit," she recommends. "Most of these companies also sell Internet access, so if the volume is not great, the Internet access can share the same T-1."

Long distance services may be purchased from the major providers such as Sprint, AT&T and Worldcom or from the many resellers of long distance service. Many resellers sell local *and* long distance service as well as Internet access and other data communications services. The distinction of local vs. long distance telephone companies is blurring. Some traditional long distance companies sell local telephone service while the local companies are moving into the long distance arena.

When buying and specifying voice/data services she suggests that call centers prepare a request for proposal (RFP) for carrier services. This provides any carrier wishing to respond with an understanding of the call center's business, the objectives, the growth, the total minutes for each type of call (inbound, outbound, intra-state, interstate, international, etc.) and other requirements such as service levels, support, billing, management reports, etc. The RFP should be prepared in such a way that the responses can be easily compared.

If your company is going out to bid for carrier services and there is a call center as part of the operations, the needs of the call center should be carefully considered and described in the RFP. It is common for others in the organization to purchase the carrier services for the call center. This may be someone from the telecommunications or IT department, a facilities manager, an office manager or perhaps a committee representing several departments. No two organizations handle this in exactly the same manner. The "grounds" are whatever selection criteria have been developed such as price, billing and management reporting capabilities, etc.

The call center may not have its own separate facilities connecting it to the outside world, but may share circuits with others within the organization.

A well-run call center can provide statistics on the call volumes and business times of day. Passing this information along to the people who are doing the purchasing can help them to order the appropriate number of outside lines to handle the calls.

"Since carrier services are somewhat of a commodity, there are truly few advantages of one carrier over another, unless you have a complex multi-site network or require specialized services," Laino points out. "If you do, these can be described in the RFP and you may find differences in the carriers' capabilities to provide exactly what you're looking for. Each carrier network is put together somewhat differently and each do have strengths and weaknesses, but this is not apparent if you are purchasing straightforward capability to place and receive calls."

You and your company should also look very carefully at the value-add services carriers provide. They may include capabilities such as having a single 800 number that is routed to the nearest call center (assuming more than one). The carrier network recognizes the caller's location by the calling telephone number and routes the call accordingly. Carriers also provide an automated announcement offering callers a menu of options — "If you're calling for a repair problem press 1, for technical help press 2, etc." The carrier then sends the call to the appropriate call center. Carriers also offer the ability to use their networks to transfer a caller from one call center to another.

She is skeptical about Centrex switching. Most call centers prefer to have the switching equipment that handles their incoming and outgoing calls on their premises.

"Using Centrex ACD capability for a call center telephone system was never widely accepted," Laino points out. "In general the reporting is not as complete as with an on-site ACD and some measure of control is given up."

Voice over IP, another carrier service, may be appropriate for a group of call centers needing to communicate and move callers from one location to another if they have a network connecting them for data communications.

"One would need to look at the application and the costs vs. using the public switched telephone network," she advises.

▶ When Considering Technology, Remember the Customer!

Call center customer service and sales technology like auto-attendants, IVR, Web self-service and CRM are cool to play with if costly to buy. Unfortunately, you run the risk of being so mesmerized with their alleged benefits to the point where you forget what call centers are for: **the customers**. Which means you run the risk of having them curse you out, do less business with you, leave you or have you regulated.

Remember people by and large prefer talking to people. They hate, but to differing degrees tolerate, talking to machines, especially ones that don't let them talk to live people. Especially stupid live people.

During the summer of 2000 *The New York Times* ran two scathing articles and op-eds about foolish and hostile customer service technology applications that imply today's so-called 'customer service revolution' is a crock. The article, "Is the Customer Ever Right-The Decline and Fall of Customer Service, With a Technological Push" that appeared July 20 reported that customer service satisfaction, as measured by the American Customer Satisfaction Index compiled by the University of Michigan, has *dropped* since 1994.

The Times reports that experts and sources blame technological advances like automated phone systems and the Web. But it also points to labor shortages forcing companies to hire less qualified people.

The Times quoted Forrester Research analyst Bob Chatham: "Would you look forward to coming to work if you had to spend the day talking to irate customers?"

Horst Schultze, president and chief operating officer of the Ritz-Carlton Hotel cited the same University of Michigan survey in an August 27 op-ed where he called "'customer management' is in fact anti-customer" citing the difficulty of getting intelligent customer service competently and quickly. He blames overmanagement of call center agents, not giving them the power to quickly solve problems and overreliance on technology as "proxies for real service".

"Imagine walking into a fine restaurant and being told: 'Foie gras is over here, truffles are over here and sorry but our bread is on back order, but you can check the status of your bread order online and don't forget your express service tag when confirming your entrée,'" wrote Schultze, whose employer knows a thing or two about customer service, and fine restaurants.

He believes that companies should pay more attention to hiring and training people, to examine their own glitches seriously and entrusting employees with their own judgement. I agree. Hopefully you will pick up some tips in the next few chapters on site selection and staffing and training, as well as in preceding ones.

As Mr. Schultze pointed out, referring to the dot-coms but applicable everywhere: "Never mind that these enterprises are offering innovative products and services. Their common failing is they haven't learned to treat their customers the way they themselves would like to be treated."

CHAPTER SEVEN

Site Selection

You're now ready to begin site selection. You know what functions you want your center to carry out.

You've taken a hard look at alternative strategies such as outsourcing and teleworking. You've either contracted out what you could without losing your corporate identity, have several top agents working from home, or decided these methods would not work well for your firm. You have your designs and technologies worked out.

Now you are ready to look for a new home for your call center, either in the US or in other countries. You face tough competition for labor and facilities. Meanwhile, senior management wants to keep your firm's clients and/or impatient investors happy and wants this new center up and running today.

"Without question, our call center clients tend to present us with the most demanding timelines to fulfill," reports John Boyd, principal with The Boyd Company (Princeton, NJ), a site selection consultancy with over 25 years of domestic and international site selection experience. "Our industrial projects and major corporate office assignments usually take four to six months, if not longer, to carry out. In contrast, our work period for call centers is half that — typically two months, sometimes less."

You may have few problems finding a floor for between 25 or 50 seats that are connected by a tie line to your PBX/ACD. But consultants say when your need is above that number of seats, the site and property choices get more complex. At this point you may need to either develop in-house expertise or call on a site selection expert.

"When you're siting a call center with 50 seats or more, finding employees and space becomes more challenging," points out Ron Cariola, senior VP with Equis (Chicago, IL), a global site selection and real estate consultancy. "When you are this size, you begin to have an impact on local labor markets."

▶ **The Lifespan of Your Center**

Before shopping for your new call center home, you should project its life span, including its size. By doing so, you can estimate the size of your center's labor pool, which, in turn, depends on your turnover. That will help winnow down your location choices. How many employees do you go through every year? In a mature economy with low-unemployment and slow population growth, there are limits to your labor force and the percentage of workers interested in jobs at call centers.

Different types of call centers consume labor at varying rates. Outbound telemarketing centers have high turnover because the work

Annual operating costs in the Boyd study are based on a corporate call center facility employing 150 workers, oc 15 million minutes of toll-free telecommunications service.

	Chicago, IL	Omaha, NE	Sioux Falls, SD	Dallas, T
Nonexempt Labor				
Weighted Average Weekly Earnings	$531	$478	$445	$520
Annual Base Payroll Costs	$4,141,800	$3,728,400	$3,471,000	$4,056,00
Fringe Benefits	$1,449,630	$1,304,940	$1,214,850	$1,419,6(
Total Annual Labor costs	$5,591,430	$5,033,340	$4,685,850	$5,475,6(
Electric Power Costs	$50,400	$34,376	$34,828	$42,684
Office Rent Costs	$488,125	$446,875	$350,625	$508,75(
Equipment Amortization Costs	$960,000	$960,000	$960,000	$960,00(
Heating and Air Conditioning	$36,025	$27,100	$29,421	$32,523
Telecommunications Costs	$1,578,123	$1,508,188	$1,474,898	$1,470,75
Total Annual Geographically-Variable	$8,704,103	$8,009,879	$7,535,622	$8,490,3(

Operating Costs

Notes:
(1) Includes all major geographically-variable operating costs
Source: The Boyd Company, Inc., Princeton, NJ

This call center simulation study, prepared by The Boyd Company (Princeton, NJ) gives you some idea how operating costs vary from city to city involves a lot of stress and the pay is lower. A help desk usually has low turnover and higher pay.

At the same time, the labor pool for minimally skilled workers, such as outbound sales and inbound order taking, is usually larger than that for help desks, which require people with better education. There are also regions with such sufficiently high numbers of unemployed and/or strong population growth that your center's life span may be over before the labor pool is drained.

Too often, firms underestimate a community's population size, labor supply and the skills that are most in demand, Susan Arledge, principal with Arledge/Power (Dallas, TX), a real estate consultancy points out. Although, firms are well aware of their turnover rates, they are often unaware of the impact turnover has on the available workforce. "You may have many people working for you when you open up, but when you need to replace them, there may be too few skilled workers to take their place," she warns.

roximately 30,000 sq. ft. of office space, and having an annual inbound customer service call volume of

Santa Clara, CA	Boston, MA	Fairfield Co, CT	Princeton, NJ	Washington/Fairfax Co, DC/VA	Orlando, FL
$568	$539	$555	$528	$575	$470
$4,430,400	$4,204,200	$4,329,000	$4,118,400	$4,485,000	$3,666,000
$1,550,640	$1,471,470	$1,515,150	$1,441,440	$1,569,750	$1,283,100
$5,981,0401	$5,675,670	$5,844,150	$5,559,840	$6,054,750	$4,949,100
$64,975	$87,220	$59,172	$69,621	$50,542	$42,936
$756,250	$577,500	$529,375	$508,750	$646,250	$536,250
$960,000	$960,000	$960,000	$960,000	$960,000	$960,000
$19,144	$55,532	$37,786	$44,789	$37,577	$32,334
$1,478,516	$1,543,003	$1,562,778	$1,557,700	$1,626,363	$1,566,121
$9,259,925	$8,898,925	$8,993,261	$8,700,700	$9,375,482	$8,086,741

Your call center's lifespan also helps determine your real estate and facilities needs and costs. How much room do you need to start and how much will you need at your center's peak? You can lease and renovate existing structures or discuss build-to-suit options with real estate developers. A renovation lease typically runs five years compared to roughly 10 years for a build-to-suit. Consultants recommend that you negotiate exit and expansion options and tenant improvement givebacks.

How long you plan to be in a particular labor market also helps you choose which type of property you need. If your company plans to locate a call center with the goal of eventually adding to it, you should look for room where the building can expand, preferably next to the space your center will initially occupy, and put your intentions in writing. Your options include insisting upon a right of first refusal on adjacent spaces; renting or building more than you need and retrofitting later; or agreeing to a "must take" arrangement where you pay rent on a certain amount of additional space within a year or so after you sign your initial lease.

"If you are not sure about negotiating and signing what your space needs will be, then you might want the right of first refusal," advises Arledge. "If you know that you are going to need the space, then a 'must take' might be better deal."

▶ Understand Time and Monetary Costs

Location experts recommend allocating no fewer than three months (preferably more) to research and seek sites. They suggest you start looking during the period between your initial decision to seek a new call center and your decision to identify a new place for your center. The timeframe for adding a new center varies with the type of real estate deal you're considering. For example, you can expect to open a new center within two to three months for existing property and within five months to a year for a build-to-suit. If you choose to locate a center in a region with a wintry climate, you have to factor in more time to open your center than you would for a warmer area.

Cariola estimates that costs for real estate and for facilities associated with renovations, build-to-suits or leases can range between $2,500 and $5,000 per seat, assuming 100 square feet (sf) per workstation. The cost of IT infrastructure (e.g., telecom, data, power) often ranges between $1,500 per seat to $2,500 per seat. (Higher amounts typically apply to knowledge-intensive help desks.) Call center hardware and software usually costs between $1,000 and $2,200 per seat.

"Your IT costs depend on how densely populated you want your space," Cariola points out. "If you move to a less dense environment, say 125 sf per agent, it may cost you more, but you may achieve a better working environment. Also, your IT costs depend on whether your center works with line-of-sight management or with technology like workforce management software. If you rely on line-of-sight management, typically in outbound centers, you pay more for supervisory labor. If you depend on technology, such as for help desks, you pay more for management hardware and software."

Be careful that you don't become penny-wise but pound-foolish in your evaluation of costs related to site selection and property. Robert Engel, principal of Engel, Picasso (Albuquerque, NM), says that call center building costs can greatly vary between $45 to $120 per sf depending on the type of building, location and finishes. He advises that the key to affordability is improved productivity, sales and customer retention.

"For example, better lighting or a higher resolution terminal costs $15 per month extra, yet it reduces fatigue to the agent so that, in the fifth or eighth hour of a shift, that person is 30% more productive," he points out. "The return on your investment is huge. Likewise, if the workstations are so tightly packed that most agents can't hear their customers due to the ambient noise, the overall facility cost savings will be more than spent in lost customer satisfaction."

▶ Site Selection Steps

Once you decide that you need a new call center, decide on its function and what its requirements are, including costs and timeframes, then you can begin your search for a new site. The people you should have on your team include your human resources department, as well as people from your company's operations, IT, property and finance departments.

Arledge and Cariola recommend that you bring on board senior management, such as marketing and business development VPs, which customer service and sales call centers usually work under. This way you have buy-in from top managers in your company on your site selection project. In some firms, such as service bureaus, final site selection reviews and decisions are made by the COO, CEO or the president.

"Senior management should buy in from the start because they have to ultimately sign off on the project," explains Cariola. "You don't want a situation where they find out some details they didn't like after you started the process. They may hold up the project because they weren't provided with enough information to make a prudent decision."

You also need to be aware of what you offer. You are going into geographic markets where you are competing with other employers for labor and space. You have to convince the labor force to work for you and do business with you rather than work for and do business with your competition. Andrew Shapiro, site selection consultant with Deloitte and Touche Fantus Consulting (New York, NY), recommends that you look at the "three Cs": culture, careers and compensation. You also have to consider the physical environment that you will offer, your firm's image and your recruiting capabilities.

If your company is well-known and respected and it has a reputation for being a good place to work, then you have more choice of locations open to you. Highly regarded firms that enter new regions can attract workers from other employers.

"If your firm is less well-known and has a lower compensation package, you have to look at other ways to be more competitive, such as your firm's location, career paths and work environment," advises Shapiro.

Site selection consultants recommend that your team devise checklists, establish criteria such as your desired cost and labor availability, weigh each item in importance and create a scoring system. You should gather data about each locale and run it through a matrix (see box). Then you should rank your priorities and narrow down your choices to the three or four sites that most closely satisfy your requirements.

If you have closely defined what you want your new call center to accomplish, you should have already sifted out many locations. You may have excluded others based on the views of your clients and members of senior management in your company, as well as your own opinion of a locale. You may also have eliminated some possible sites because you do not want to be too close to other call centers. If you locate your center near another company's center, you run the risk of having to contend with more competition for labor and perhaps greater turnover.

Consultants recommend that you always keep your primary objectives in mind as you establish your criteria for choosing locations. "Ask yourself what you are trying to accomplish," Shapiro says. "If you don't tie your criteria back to your objectives, then how can you be assured of success?"

Once you identify the locations that meet your criteria, you should then conduct a more intensive evaluation that includes site visits and meetings with local officials. Shapiro recommends that you interview comparable employers (e.g., branch banks and retailers) about their recruiting experiences, compensation levels, turnover and the quality of their workforce. He suggests that you then test a new labor market by placing blind ads and attending job fairs.

"You then draw your own conclusions and make a choice," says Shapiro. "You pick the best overall community, identify the most desirable neighborhoods to open your center in, find the most competitive property, secure any available incentives, plan your recruiting and staffing strategy, create a communications program, choose a transition team and secure your resources to open the center."

▶ The Three Key Site Selection Criteria: Labor, Labor, Labor

Let's look at some of these key criteria. I have split locations from real estate, which will be covered in Chapter 8. While the availability of property in relation to where your expected workforce lives is a key consideration in your final site selection, it *should not be* the deciding factor in why you picked a particular community for your center. You *should not* choose a location because its real estate is less expensive *if* the labor cost is greater than that of other communities you're considering.

The reason is very simple: to twist the old real estate adage, the three most important attributes to look for in call center site selection is **labor,**

labor, labor. Labor is *why* you have a call center. Your call center houses people, which account for 60% + of your operating costs. Nearly all of the space in a center is designed to accommodate the agents who work there: the workstations, training rooms, washrooms, lunch/break room and butt pads. The hardware and software that transmits the calls and contacts take up a very small portion of the call center.

You can find the fanciest, least cost, wow-isn't-it-a-fantastic-deal building, with acres of free parking, Jacuzzi, gym, child care and a 7x24 supermarket in the basement, a three year lease and available now. Yet, if the city or metro area doesn't have the people you need, at your budgeted cost, the property is worthless. You are much better off financially and in your customer service and sales goals if you pay more for real estate to get the labor you want.

Experts say that real estate should represent no more than 10% of your total costs. Susan Arledge illustrated why call centers have to factor labor costs into their real estate planning at the Direct Marketing Association's Telephone Marketing Council conference in June 1999.

In her example, Arledge described a fictitious outsourcer that had a choice between two facilities in two different cities. The outsourcer intended to select one of the facilities only on the basis of real estate costs and labor costs. It planned to provide 150 sf of space per agent and planned to pay each agent for 2,080 hours of work per year. Each center was to house 300 employees.

Building 1 offered a rental rate of one dollar per sf below the rate for Building 2. Building 2 offered a labor rate of one dollar below that of Building 1. Building 1 therefore cost $150 less in real estate per employee per year, given the difference of one dollar in rental rates between the two buildings and given the 150 sf allotted to each agent.

But if the outsourcer occupied Building 2, it would save **$2,239 per employee per year** in labor costs. The outsourcer determined its savings from the difference of one dollar in labor rates between the two buildings; from the number of work hours per year for which it would pay each agent; and from the lower employment taxes it would incur as the result of its lesser labor costs.

The savings that the occupant of Building 2 experienced from the lower labor costs would be significantly greater than the additional amount of money it spent on real estate. Since each building employed 300 agents, the company that bought space in Building 2 would spend a total of $626,700 less than an occupant of Building 1 over the course of a year.

In the above example, a difference of a dollar per hour in labor savings in Building 2 offsets a difference of $14.93/sf in rent in Building 1. In other words, the rental rates in Building 2 could have been far above those in Building 1, yet, because the occupant of Building 2 paid lower labor rates, it still would have had lower total operating costs than the company that bought space in Building 1.

"Usually when you think of site selection, you think real estate costs," says Arledge. "However site selection for the teleservices industry is real-

UNEMPLOYMENT IN CANADA		
Province	Unemployment Rates	Size of Available Labor Force (in thousands)
Newfoundland and Labrador	15.4%	37.5
Prince Edward Island	11.5%	8.3
Nova Scotia	8.4%	38.7
New Brunswick	10.2%	37.6
Quebec	8.4%	316.4
Ontario	5.4%	334.2
Manitoba	4.4%	25.8
Saskatchewan	5.6%	28.6
Alberta	5.0%	83.3
British Columbia	6.7%	140.9
Canada-wide	6.6%	1,051.2

One of many quotes attributed to the late Sir Winston Churchill is "there are lies, damned lies and then there are statistics!" Unemployment data falls into that category. As this chart comparing Canada's seasonally adjusted unemployed for June 2000 indicates, three provinces with double-digit unemployment percentages actually have fewer available workers than two out of three provinces that had rates below 5.5%.

ly about labor, its quality and the quantity of the people who staff the site."

There are several key factors that you must consider when looking over your labor requirements. The challenge is to match your preferences as closely to what is available within your site selection timeframe.

Supply

In order to staff your call center you need to find places that have the people who are willing to work for you for as long as possible at the wage/benefit packages that you offer. Most call center jobs are entry- or semi-entry level requiring customer service and sales aptitudes and preferably experience, say in retail. These general skills give you access to the largest labor pool.

Governments track labor supply by measuring the number and percentage of workers who are employed and unemployed. Don't be dazzled by high percentages: while they may be indicators of plentiful labor in some jurisdictions the raw numbers of workers available may be less than in others with lower unemployment rates (see page 165). Also be aware that many governments adjust their data to reflect seasonal fluctuations, such as agriculture and fishing where large volumes of people work for very short periods of time.

Be cognizant of the reality that unemployment statistics tell only part of the labor force story. Governments draw their figures from people who are collecting unemployment insurance, who are actively seeking work and who are working. They do not include individuals who are not officially in the work force, such as those on long-term disability, students, those who never held a job, people who had given up seeking employment, stay-at-home spouses and retirees. Also, statistics count one person holding one job as their primary income source. They do not account for multiple jobs, such as a call center agent working for two different companies, one a call center and the other, say, in retail or as an agent on evenings/weekends to supplement their income at another job.

Yet many of the "unofficial" labor pool may wish to work or are working in a call center. For example, when male-dominated highly-paid jobs such as in heavy manufacturing, resource extraction and processing and transportation disappear, it is often their spouses (who had been supported by the high incomes), who then go out to work. This has happened in many US, Canadian and European communities, especially those outside the major metropolitan areas; it formed one of the subplots in the hit film *The Full Monty*, about a group of forced-to-be enterprising unemployed steel-workers filmed in and set in Sheffield, UK: a once-thriving steel town.

The statistics also do not measure underemployment. Under-employment occurs when people work at the first available jobs they find, even though they possess skills that would help them get work in other occupations. For example, college-educated people often work in low-paid, part-time jobs, such as in retail stores or restaurants. An underem-ployed workforce may exist in an area that has a high quality of life or because other regions that offer jobs better suited to an educated work-force are less accessible by car or by public transportation.

"Underemployment is very difficult to analyze because you have no data to track," Arledge says. "You can't measure unhappiness. All the unemployment statistics show is the percentage of people who are not working. The only way you can find out if there is underemployment is by researching the local market, including talking to local economic development agencies (EDAs)."

One factor aiding the value of underemployment is the desirability of call center employment compared with other types of service sector jobs. Call centers are usually the service sector employer of choice. The relative sedentary nature of the work means people who have difficulty standing or walking can be call center agents.

"Even in a tight labor market, call centers will always draw people from other service jobs," observes King White, vice president of the site selec-tion group for real estate firm Trammell Crow (Dallas, TX). "They pay higher and provide nice offices, unlike being on your feet in a big store or a restaurant. They are white collar jobs that someone, like a high school graduate, can get."

Be sure when you are examining local labor supplies that you check to see what other call centers are there. They probably will, but may not, compete for the same workers as you. On the other hand, you may offer better than average compensation, have a desirable "cool place to work for" reputation and/or your center may be seeking specialized skills, such as non-English-speakers, superior language skills for online communications, technical training and insurance/securities licensing. Also, the presence of other call centers mean your applicants know what to expect. You may also be successful at attracting agents and supervisors from the other centers.

This leads to another point: you need to make sure that the communities have the *skillsets* you require. Does the area workforce have adequate or better education and training for your needs? As the services senior management wants call centers to provide become more sophisticated and customer targeted, then the more specialized the skills your agents will need.

For example, if you are serving many French- or Spanish-speaking customers you need to have access to potential agents with that ability. You'll probably have more luck finding them in Quebec or south Texas than say, in Staten Island or northern New Hampshire, respectively. If you provide external help desk with minimal escalation you probably need to have customer-service-oriented individuals who have some technical training

Community Call Center Saturation Analysis										
			Saturation Rate*							
Community	Total Labor Force	Estimated Call Center Jobs	1% Low Saturation		2% Moderately Saturated		3% Saturated		4% Very Saturated	
			Max. Employees	Available Positions	Max. Employees	Available Positions	Max. Employees	Available Positions	Max. Employees	Available Positions
City A	198,518	1,800	1,985	185	3,970	2,170	5,956	4,156	7,941	6,141
City B	545,000	11,360	5,450	-5,910	10,900	-460	16,350	4,990	21,800	10,440
City C	63,282	3,450	633	-2,817	1,266	-2,184	1,898	-1,552	2,531	-919
City D	706,000	36,699	7,060	-29,639	14,120	-22,579	21,180	-15,519	28,240	-8,459
City E	371,000	12,820	3,710	-9,110	7,420	-5,400	11,130	-1,690	14,840	2,020
City F	419,000	20,072	4,190	-15,882	8,380	-11,692	12,570	-7,502	16,760	-3,312

* *Saturation Rate* attempts to model the employment potential of call centers in relation to the labor force size. To assist with a market by market evaluation, this analysis has been run whereby each percentage indicates the resulting *Saturation Rate* for a particualr community. As unemployment remains low and call center positions continue to grow, markets throughout the United States have become more saturated and the acceptable saturation rate has increased. As the Saturation Rate is raised, call centers run a greater risk of future recruitment and retainment challenges. The *Max. Employees* indicates maximum number of call center employees acceptable at the particular Saturation Rate. The *Available Positions* indicates the differential between the *Estimated Call Center Jobs* and the *Max. Employees* indicators. A negative number indicates that there are more existing jobs than the market can handle (at the specified Saturation Rate). Likewise, a positive number indicates the number of additional call center jobs that the market sould be able to support (at the specified Saturation Rate).

Source: CB Richard Ellis Information Services, Bureau Labor Statistics, Community Economic Development Organizations.
CB Richard Ellis considers its sources reliable, however accuracy cannot be guaranteed.

This model saturation analysis chart from CB Richard Ellis compares the impact of saturation rates at different call center locations. It shows how many more, if any, new positions that a locale can support.

Labor, labor everywhere...

Just because a location and market has many unemployed people, especially in developing nations and regions such as eastern Europe, Africa, Asia Pacific and Latin America, that does not necessarily mean you can locate large low-cost call centers there. You may face in the labor market, an experience akin to the 'Ancient Mariner' with water, water everywhere but none to drink.

Yet, the need for call center services, especially over the Internet, are increasing in these countries.

Unfortunately, many of these countries' residents lack the literacy required to work in modern call centers. They also often do not have the necessary customer service and sales skills. According to Martin Conboy, director of ACA Research and CEO of Callcentres.net (North Sydney, Australia) many countries, such as China, Indonesia and Thailand do not have a large middle class that call centers draw workers and services demand from. Instead they have a large population of poor illiterate people and a small rich elite. The vast majority of residents lack the reading and writing skills required to work in a modern multimedia call center.

Conboy cites nearly nonexistent mass property ownership — that the owners can leverage for capital to start businesses — as a major reason for such disparity. This limits the market for goods and services, and call centers to provide them and the labor to staff call centers. Many of these countries lack democratic systems of government and rule of law that protects investment.

To cope with these marketplace realities you should plan to open a modern, sophisticated, limited-seat call center with speech-rec-enabled IVR and Web self-service to serve the elite and the small middle class. Conboy reports for example that Philips has a new natural language speech recognition system in Mandarin: the most widespread and important Chinese dialect.

"Call centers are a middle class occupation," he points out. "You have to have a middle class to support them. You need people who can read and write to work in the new call centers that have online communications and they come from the middle class. You can't have uneducated people with no skills work in call centers. But the only people in many countries who are literate are the rich and they don't want to work in call centers. For them that is a low-status job."

and aptitude, usually from a good local college that offers computer science. Communities that have attracted many hardware and software developers and manufacturers are more likely to have such individuals than those cities and towns that have not.

On the other hand, metro areas, such as San Jose, CA and the outskirts of Boston, MA are too costly for call centers. And you may find it easier and less expensive, but with access to workers with the same language skills, if you set up your French-speaking center in New Brunswick or eastern Ontario or your Spanish-speaking facility in Mexico. Many companies have done just that.

Many locations are already saturated with too many positions for the available labor supply, both in total and in different fields, such as call center work. To ensure you have enough labor, no matter the skillsets, Engel recommends that you follow what he calls the 5% rule. He advises that you locate in areas where the number of people who are currently employed in call centers plus those people who have previously worked in call centers does not exceed 5% of the area's total workforce. "If the number is greater than 5%, then it could become increasingly difficult to attract and keep qualified people," he says.

Intimately related to the issue of supply is of course, *cost*. How many employees will you attract and keep at X wages/benefits per annum? What are the prevailing wages and other compensation expenses for call center agents and supervisors in the communities that you want to locate in? How much have they grown by over the past year? What are the packages offered by those employers, including other call centers, that you would be competing for labor with?

Local EDAs should have this cost information. You can also do your own research by studying the help wanted ads, visiting college and government employment offices and dropping into the companies' recruitment offices or passing by their job boards. Good site selection consultants use such practices to gain information before letting the word get out that a company is thinking of coming to town.

If you are new in town, especially if your company is not a brand or name familiar to residents, like that of a service bureau, be prepared to pay somewhat more than what you would in an area you are already established. This will help overcome potential employee skepticism about your value as an employer, especially if you are setting up in an area that has relatively low unemployment. Remember, neither the community nor its workers *know* you as a good company and employer; you do not have a track record that generates word-of-mouth employment.

These employees, who work at a WalMart in Thunder Bay, ON, Canada, may be your call center's agents if you decide to open yours in that northwestern Ontario city. One good way to see if they have the right attitude for your customers is to go inside and be one of theirs.

Labor force traits

Workers are not automatons, no matter how little you pay them. They have attitudes and cultural traits that affect their employment performance. Before you set up your call center in a given community you need to find out what those are, and see if they mesh with your requirements.

The first and the most important trait is *attitude*. Do they have the right mindset for the job? The attitude to have in customer service: friendly, intelligent and helpful is markedly different from the one you need in outbound sales: sharp, aggressive and goal-oriented.

If you want your call center to sell products, such as in outbound, you must locate it in a community that has what site selection consultant John Boyd calls a "sales culture". Where there are aggressive retailers, like car dealers, electronics superstores and furniture dealers, that employ thick-skinned salespeople who think quickly on their feet to find those emotional buttons to press to get you to say "yes".

By the same token if the purpose of your call center is to provide customer service then you need to have it in places where there is a customer service culture. Where in the hotels, restaurants and stores the workers have a calm, patient "may I help you?" demeanor. They are there, but not in your face.

Canada has long been a popular call center location for US companies serving American customers not only because the labor supply is plentiful, low cost and educated but also because Canadian agents are friendly and courteous. Many firms have opened call centers in rural US communities to tap into similar attributes.

Yet many communities that have the right customer service attitudes may not have those for sales, and vice versa. One company, CyberRep.com, formerly Unitel, re-located an outbound call center to Florida from rural western Maryland because the agents there hated making telemarketing calls that would disturb other people, who may be their neighbors. Towns whose dominant employer is the military, with an active base may not make great places for customer service. Those attributes are not the ones you want in service personnel who fight for their country.

However, more companies are converging their attitude requirements as they adopt cross-selling and up-selling practices. A good outbound agent can be trained to use the same investigative skills that tries to find out why a person won't buy and answer their qualms to solving their problems. A fine customer service agent can be taught to regard cross-selling and up-selling as problem solving.

Attitude is also expressed in what kinds of people you can expect to work in a call center. This is a function of the local economy, demographics and culture. Where other employment is scarce, except for at the call center, the local populace will tend to regard such jobs more highly, and appreciate them, and in turn will attract higher-quality applicants.

The opposite is true if there are many other and higher-paying positions available. Then it becomes: "oh, you got a job telemarketing. How nice. When are you going to get a career?" *All* service sector employment suffers from that stigma; I know, I've been a "rent-a-cop" and a telemarketing fundraiser.

In some communities and countries, most notably Japan, call center customer service and sales are still considered "women's work." That cuts out potentially half your potential labor force, i.e., men. Also, many potential women workers who are stay-at-home spouses prefer to be that way. Ireland, whose booming economy has led to labor shortages and rising inflation, has been trying to encourage stay-at-homes to enter the workplace, but is reportedly facing some reluctance in this still Catholic and tradition-bound nation. Only about 48% of working-age Irish women are in the labor force: much less than in other European countries.

A second key trait is *dialect*. You need to set up in locations where the residents speak clearly. If your customers can't understand your agents then you may have customer service and sales problems.

While this has become less of an issue in recent years, with increasing ethnic diversity, greater acceptance of regional accents and paradoxically their fading away through media and mobility that encourage vocal harmonization, some regions residents' twangs are stronger than others. New York City is still notorious for its nasal accent. The province of Newfoundland is noted for its catchy, sing-song but fast "Newfie" dialect, which is more muted (and intelligible) in St. John's, the capital and largest city, but more pronounced in outlying areas. Some ethnic groups, such as immigrants from the Indian subcontinent, speak well but too swiftly for many other people's ears.

These traits cover languages other than English. Many companies reportedly prefer Mexican Spanish speakers to potential employees from other Hispanic countries or regions because they talk slower and the accent is not as harsh.

Also, some people prefer to talk to native speakers of their own language, and in some cases their dialect than to those who learned the tongue in school. This is especially important in Europe, parts of Asia (e.g., Japan, Korea) and to some extent in Quebec where individuals are very sensitive to language differences. For example, *The New York Times* reported on February 23, 2000, of an increase in discrimination against nonwhites and French-speaking immigrants from countries such as Algeria. The story described how one immigrant, who applied for a reporting job, was told that her accent was "not Quebec enough."

"Fluency depends on the expectancy of the person calling," says Philip Cohen, a teleservices consultant and chair of the Federation of European Direct Marketing's (FEDMA)'s Teleservices Council, who is based in

Skelleftea, Sweden. "If the parties calling in are consumers they will likely want to talk to an agent who is fluent in their language and culture. If a Portuguese housewife is annoyed when her vacuum cleaner breaks down and your agent is not conversant in that language she will get even angrier at your firm."

If this is the case with your customers then you have to look for cost-effective locations that have enough of those native speakers, both domestically and recent immigrants or college students from those target countries. Countries like the US, Canada, Australia, Germany, Ireland and The Netherlands have long attracted immigrants and students from other nations. The European Union guarantees labor mobility for residents of its 15-nation members.

This may not be easy. The costs and bureaucracy entailed in setting up and serving the native speaking markets in their countries may be horrendous and the cultures are insular, blocking well-meaning outsiders. This is especially present in Asian countries such as Japan and Korea. Also, their individual markets may be too small to justify locating call centers to serve them.

Other nations' political, economic and telecommunications infrastructures are still developing, requiring a heavy investment in time and resources, and patience. The former Communist East Bloc is struggling to meet Western standards: but at different rates, with the Czech Republic, Hungary and Poland, and the former East Germany emerging faster than the other nations. Russia, whose economy is gradually turning around, has a huge educated population and potential market. There are now call centers being set up there. Some countries, especially in Africa, Asia-Pacific and Latin America are too unstable to risk setting up your own call centers.

Also, the supply of immigrants and students fluctuates. You may not have enough of those speakers. If there are jobs back home or the costs of living in their new home rise dramatically they may not arrive or stay in adequate numbers to support call centers, or they may quit to work in other higher-paying employment in their new countries. These factors, coupled with boom economies have apparently dried up the Irish Republic and parts of the Netherlands for large multilingual "pan-European" call centers.

Keep in mind that labor supply and cost consideration can outweigh some of the reservations you may have about accent. In boom economic times finding an adequate supply of people to work in call centers becomes challenging worldwide. You can train people to speak clearly; one US call center trainer I know of has been contracted to help agents at Indian call centers converse with American customers. The big payoff is that it costs a fraction to operate a call center in India of what it would cost in the US.

Even Canada's Newfie accent has not stopped call centers from taking advantage of the province's available labor force; Newfoundland has long had one of the country's highest unemployment rates.

"Although these dialects may be obvious to Canadians, US customers are more receptive to them," says Gloria Griffin, senior director of planning and site development at Convergys (Cincinnati, OH), an outsourcer that has a 575-seat center in St. John's. "For example, five to ten years ago, outsourcers tried to minimize regional dialects. However, as this industry has grown, the issue has faded. A good example is our operation in Pharr, TX, where all employees have a Spanish accent yet serve English-speaking consumers. Our major client, DBS, is impressed with the results and the high level of customer service."

Dialect had been a concern of Fonemed (Colorado Springs, CO), a new innovative global health care advisory service, which opened a 15-seat center in St. John's in March 1999. Fonemed's president and founder, Kevin Bleakley, cited a 30% cost savings in St. John's compared to similar US cities. The center employs customer service agents and registered nurses to answer calls.

"We haven't found dialect to be an issue in St. John's because the city is more cosmopolitan than the rest of the province," says Bleakley.

You can also hire learned language speakers that will be acceptable to customers. I've listened to an American Xerox help desk agent converse with a French-speaking customer from Quebec. Learned language speakers may also be better at online communications, according to experts, than native speakers because they have had to be formally taught grammar and syntax.

A third labor trait is *lifestyle*. This is especially important if you are examining rural locations for call centers. If you pick a community in a region with lakes, marshes and woodland, and you want to know why your center is suddenly vacant in the late fall and you have a strong fool-hardy somewhat suicidal streak, don a fluorescent and preferably Kevlar-lined vest and take a stroll. Instead of targeting your customers you'll find they're taking aim at deer, geese, ducks, and most anything else living, or sort of, or dead, as well as various inanimate objects like cars, houses, barns and gasoline tankers between their crosshairs.

Employers and school principals know that absentee and truancy rates shoot up when hunting season begins. The same happens when the snow is deep enough for snowmobiling and the ice is thick and strong enough for fishing: both increasingly rare occurrences thanks to global warming. Don't be surprised to find some of your agents limping in like war veterans. That teaches them for thinking wearing fake reindeer antlers would be cute or expecting that the ski-SUV would go over that boulder like the ads showed...

Before anyone thinks this advice is coming from a city slicker you're dead wrong. I did part of my growing up in rural Massachusetts and New Hampshire and once lived in the Canadian Rockies. Last spring my wife and I drove to northern New Hampshire and stayed in a B&B in a small somewhat picturesque town. The owner told me that when some of the local employers tried to crack down on the absenteeism some of the employees responded with bomb threats. Somehow I wasn't that shocked.

If you are considering a location outside of the US keep in mind most countries have more holidays and give more vacation time, at *your* expense. European companies typically give their workers five to six weeks off, usually two weeks at a time. Some countries, such as France, practically shut down for the month of August.

A fourth important trait is *class consciousness*. This is an old Marxian term that describes workers knowing that they *are* workers and are wage slaves to the bosses that hire and fire them and treat them as they wish, rather as an independent free agents who are equal to them. Employees think in "us versus them" terms.

The existence of class consciousness is usually but not always a prerequisite for unionization; it exists where the unions are militant and very politically active. Many companies, even yours, may not want unions to represent your employees. Union representation challenges your management freedom, adds employment costs and reduces flexibility, which cuts into profits, though the higher wages and benefits, and better working conditions reduces expensive turnover. A union call center is almost always the employer of choice.

Unions also create the specter of strikes, though with proper trust and relations unions can provide a fast, efficient conduit of information to and from the shop floor. If, to save your company, the union agrees to a wage reduction or looser work rules, it is done, unless the union leadership is out of touch with the members on the floor.

Another sign of class consciousness and unionization is a strong social safety net, including generous unemployment insurance benefits and government-provided healthcare, campaigned for by unions and union-backed left-wing political parties. This protects workers who have been laid off and injured and their families. Coupled with high union wages it has the side effect of removing the need to work in lower paid jobs like call centers.

Susan Falcetta of Engel Picasso believes that Canada's wider social safety net, such as health care and liberal workers' compensation, removes much of the incentives for Canadians to work in call centers.

"For example, many people, such as stay-at-home spouses, go to work in call centers in the US part time and full time to earn money for benefits," she says. "That doesn't exist to the same extent in Canada. There is a greater expectation there, especially outside the major cities, that the spouse stays at home."

Yet, for class consciousness to exist there must be attitudes and behaviors by dominant employers in the past and currently to foster them; that they may regard or had regarded employees as no more than lumps of coal or sticks of woods to fire their profit engines. If you look at the history of industrialization this has been the case. Even in supposedly enlightened times, like today, employees are still being forced to work long hours for comparatively little in grueling conditions.

Political scientists and sociologists have long pointed out that cultural attitudes by the workers themselves will determine whether class consciousness will develop. If they feel that they are equal to management, thinking themselves as "contractors" rather than "workers" and believe they can get a job down the road they will not become class conscious because for them classes do not exist. The owners may have more money and power but they believe they can acquire the same money and power if they want it badly enough. If, on the other hand, they feel that they cannot advance, that there are social as well as financial ceilings that they cannot penetrate they will see the work relationship as "us versus them." Although, many times workers feel that unions, with some justification, are another set of bosses that they must pay dues to and obey; one set is enough.

Class consciousness is rarely apparent in the US, except in the big cities like New York. The same apparently goes for Australia. Both countries embrace the belief of individual advancement, of a "classless" society. Class consciousness is a reality in Europe and to some extent in many parts of Canada. I've noticed differences between Alberta, which has a more independent enterprise individual culture, and neighboring British Columbia, where workers are much more militant.

Matt Jackson, manager with Deloitte and Touche Fantus Consulting (Los Angeles, CA), finds that cooperation between individual workers and management is not as common in Canada, even in nonunion firms, compared with the US.

"We interviewed a US-owned call center operation and received feedback that it was having a difficult time in creating a culture whereby employees would share ideas, frustrations and complaints with the existing management team," he says.

Engel agrees. "Canadian call center agents identify with the working class, whereas American call center employees see themselves as white collar and identify with management," he points out.

He also observes that although few call centers in Canada have unions, Canadians prefer union shops.

"While you have higher overall unemployment in Canada, and seemingly lower wages, the presence and strength of unions bring the Canadian wages to or above US levels of $11 to $13 an hour," he says.

However, some US firms, such as outsourcer ICT Group (Langhorne, PA), have found few differences between Canadian and US centers. The company prefers to locate in areas where there is very little secondary industry. ICT Group has six centers in Canada; they are located in the cities of Miramichi, Moncton and Riverview in New Brunswick and in the cities of Halifax, New Glasgow and Sydney in Nova Scotia.

"We have a highly structured and scripted program with advanced technology and thorough training company-wide," explains Paul Pierce, ICT Group's vice president for teleservices in Canada. "We also encourage employees to communicate with management, which has been successful, and we ensure that their concerns are brought forward. As a result we have a very high morale in our call center teams."

▶ Other Site Selection Factors

There are other factors that you should look at in your site selection process. Among them are:

Taxation

Watch out for and examine the impact of different tax rates, i.e., corporate, employment, income, property and value-added between jurisdictions. Between two or three locations that have roughly the same labor availability, skillsets and costs the one that has the best regime could make a bottom-line difference in deciding where to locate.

James Trobaugh, senior vice president of CB Richard Ellis Call Center Solutions Group (Phoenix, AZ), points out that even if a call center does not make money directly for a company (i.e., a help desk or similar "cost centers") they could create substantial tax liabilities. For example, a 500-seat center could create a multimillion dollar liability amounting to 20% increase in the center's labor costs for a firm that generates $2 to $3 billion in net income.

Trobaugh suggests that with careful planning and cooperation from local communities, a company, such as an Internet firm could avoid having to collecting taxes on its customers even if they set up in a state that has a sales tax. If your company makes a profit and is eligible to receive state income tax credits but your call center is a non-profit entity that does not pay income taxes you may be able to gain some of those breaks.

Keep in mind that many places that would make great call center locations because of labor force availability also have high personal income and sales taxes. Many countries have a value-added tax or VAT (called Goods and Services Tax or GST in some nations, such as Australia and Canada) which is applied at each step where value is added to the product or service. Do not let them discourage you from locating there. These taxes are paid by your employees, not by your company. Also, they help finance healthcare and other benefits that in the US would have had to come out of your pocket.

Access

For your agents to start producing at your call center they must get there. The same goes for your senior management and clients to see what they're paying for.

How easily and quickly the labor force that you've identified in the locations that you're reviewing can get to work helps determine how many of them you will tap. The area that lies within commuting distance of your proposed sites is known as a *commutershed*. The size of the commutershed depends on the time your potential workers in those areas want to spend commuting, shaped by transportation mode. More about this in Chapter 8.

Generally the lower the wage the less the tolerance; the workers who depend or prefer mass transit are willing to allocate more time. A 50-minute drive is a headache; a 50-minute bus or train ride less so, unless they're packed in every day like sardines.

Fantus's Shapiro recommends that you limit commuting time by car or by mass transit within 30 minutes of where you expect to draw most of your labor from.

"The acceptable commuting time is typically longer for managers and supervisors," Shapiro points out.

If you need to bring clients and management to your call centers on a fairly regular basis you may wish to look how they're going to get there and weigh that up against the labor market advantages of those locations. And that isn't easy, and will likely get much worse with overpacked airline terminals, runways and overloaded air traffic control systems. In the appropriately-timed day-after-Labor Day, Tuesday September 5, 2000, *The New York Times* reported that aviation experts believe delays, which have risen by 50% over the last five years will get worse. The Federal Aviation Administration predicts that by 2010 that the number of airline passengers will rise by 59%, with 70% at the 28 largest US airports.

Delays plus cancellations and frequent plane changes at overcrowded hubs, coupled with extortionate fares to some locales and bargains to others that change at the last minute, with legalese conditions, and lousy or nonexistent food, have made flying an almost unendurable ordeal. Some consultants strongly recommend against locating in small US and

Carriers that use small aircraft to fly directly between smaller cities, and permit you to visit one or more call centers in the same day or two days, saves time and hassle compared with flying into and out of large delay-riddled hubs. You recoup on the extra costs from hotel room savings and personal wear-and-tear. For example, Bearskin Airlines schedules regular service to cities in northern Ontario, including North Bay, Ottawa, Sault Ste. Marie, Sudbury, Thunder Bay and Timmins. The airline also flies to Winnipeg, MB and connects with Air Canada to Toronto.

Canadian cities if it means changing once or twice to commuter airlines, or enduring long rental car drives.

"There are many areas that we found in Canada that have good labor forces like New Brunswick but which are very costly in terms of money and time to get to," says Engel. "But if your business is within three hours', one way, flying time of a major Canadian city, then access is not a major issue."

Boyd says that some US companies are locating new centers in smaller nearby Canadian cities where labor markets are less saturated than the US cities where they are based. He cites Gage Marketing (Minneapolis, MN), which chose to open a call center in Winnipeg, where the unemployment is double that of the Minneapolis-St. Paul area.

"Accessing your call center is a challenge, especially if you locate a call center in second- and third-tier cities," says Boyd. "But it is a cost of doing business."

In Europe, Japan and in some parts of the US and Canada you can locate your call center so it is accessible by train. Train travel can be just as fast as flying, when you calculate in access times and delays, and it offers you room to work enroute comfortably. Trains also stop at intermediate smaller cities that often do not have air service.

Given today's travel realities you may prefer to teleconference instead of in-person visits. This removes the access obstacle to site selection. New technologies make that even more feasible. CustomerAssistance.com, a subsidiary of leading-edge outsourcer APAC Customer Services (Deerfield, IL) can mount an IP camera over the shoulders of the agents dedicated to your program so you can see what they're doing from anywhere, even from your laptop as you wait *another* two hours for your next flight.

Political stability

When you decide to locate a function like a call center you are making not just a business decision but a political one that will affect the lives of the community that you select. At the same time the local politics, especially outside the US, could affect the cost, timing, functions, viability and in some cases the safety of your investment and your staff. These may give pause of concern to your senior management and could lead them to overrule your site selection decision.

Manufacturing and resource extraction businesses have long located in politically unstable regions, risking quick and radical changes in government, frequent political protests and terrorism and have had to deal with corrupt and often unsavory dictatorial regimes because they have affordable raw materials and markets. Labor-intensive garment firms have been moving their operations from the US to these nations because they have plenty of low-cost people resources and potential markets. Aided by improving voice/data links information businesses and functions like call centers are going in the same direction. American companies are contracting with outsourcers or setting up their own call centers in India, Jamaica and The Philippines to serve US customers.

Companies have also located businesses like call centers quite successfully in unstable regions such as Northern Ireland and Quebec, which are part of more stable countries: Britain and Ireland, under the Good Friday Agreement that set a foundation hopefully for peace in that sad, long-troubled land and Canada, respectfully. Quebec's political leadership, with the fluctuating support of its majority French-speaking population has been trying to pry the province from the rest of the country since the

1960s. This has been a peaceful tug-of-war for the hearts and souls of Quebecers but terrorist violence has flared up on occasion.

On the other hand, it can be argued that many of these unstable areas, such as Northern Ireland are safer than many US cities. People from outside the US often look aghast at the American gun-happy culture.

Many, but not all firms, find that the advantages of locating their call centers in unstable areas outweigh the risks. They often have large numbers of available, educated hardworking individuals; governments have sought investments by granting large direct and indirect subsidies.

John Boyd, who has been skeptical about Quebec in the past, is more optimistic, citing the relative quiet. He notes that new US firms have opened there, such as Nasdaq's Canadian exchange in Montreal and Motorola's multibillion-dollar research center, with the expectation "of uneventful political developments." He also observes that residents of Quebec are less likely than Canadians in other provinces to leave for the US or for other parts of Canada.

"There are now some forward-thinking businesses that believe they can prosper in an independent Quebec," says Boyd. "They think that there will be more economic incentives because the government needs to show Quebec can make it on its own."

Yet, when you look at such a location examine its political stability carefully. You may or may not decide you can live with risking your investment there or tolerate the bureaucracy. While your potential agents and supervisors who live with milieu can cope with the realities; if you are assigning US-based managers for any length of time, including their families, you need to think about how they will feel about going into that kind of situation.

You have a few choices to serve or locate in unstable markets. You can recruit and hopefully find call-center-savvy managers who are there or who can set up and run your operation from there. You can outsource to experienced, technology-savvy local companies — there are, for example many new Indian-founded outsourcers seeking business from US clients — or to multinational outsourcers that already have operations there. Outsourcers know the cultural and political lay of the land.

Or you can locate your center in adjacent more stable nations or areas, where there is an adequate supply of native speakers. There are many

Eastern European language speakers living in the former East Germany, which, with its high unemployment rate and quality labor supply, is a prime call center location. Many North Africans have settled in France, enabling you to serve those countries from there. Excellent telecom links from Spain and Portugal permit you to serve Latin American customers. In Canada, the province of New Brunswick and eastern and northeastern Ontario also have large French-speaking populations. Toronto, Canada's largest city, and to a lesser extent Montreal and Vancouver have large enough European and Asian-language speaking populations to support international call centers there.

Disaster vulnerability

There are few places you can locate a call center where nothing will happen to it. If you place it in the northeast, expect ice storms that crumple power and phone lines; if you site it in the southeast, expect Hurricanes Bonnie and Clyde to rob it of its capability. If you drop your call center anywhere from the midwest to the southeast there is a chance that a tornado may drop pieces of it somewhere else. And if you're on the Pacific Rim, the so-called ring of fire, prepare for earthquakes and mudslides in California and volcanic eruptions and pyroclastic mud flows in Oregon and Washington State. And there's the reasonable chance an asteroid will wipe out everything.

At the same time, many of the most vulnerable places, like the Gulf Coast, make the best call center locations because they have affordable labor. Consultants say damage to call centers from hurricanes have been minimal. People will live in a place, come hell or high water, if they can make a decent living there, especially if it has attributes, like warm weather or the beach. By the same token, some of the safest places, like central Nevada, have too few people to support a call center. And it still won't protect you against an asteroid hit.

If you are locating only one call center, your best bet is to look into disaster vulnerability *after* other key factors, such as labor supply, and then plan for disaster recovery. Otherwise, spread your call centers around in key labor markets, so that if one goes down, such as, your Puyallup, WA facility that lies in the shadow of Mount Rainier — a semi-active volcano whose seemingly peaceful cone dominates the region, calls are automatically switched to the center in Portland, ME.

Says Fantus Consulting's Andy Shapiro, referring to the Gulf Coast: "The risk of not having affordable available trained workers poses a greater threat to call centers than any major damage from storms, provided you have other backup sites."

Technology

Take a close look at available bandwith. There are still many locations, especially in other countries, that lack the voice/data capacity your call center needs. Carriers are adding high capacity networks worldwide, especially as they face competition, but not in every community, especially those in rural areas, and not in every country, particularly developing ones. The available low-cost and educated people you want may be there but they can't access your customers. India, for example, has low cost labor but the country will need more capacity. Alternatives to voice/data lines such as satellites are costly and there are slight time delays as calls are sent over 22,000 miles in space and bounced back.

Some carriers, namely those that are aggressive in seeking call centers as customers may be interested in working with you to supply you the bandwidth you need. You can often find them outside the US, especially in Canada, Europe and in Australia and New Zealand. Other carriers take the usual bureaucratic monopolistic "we're the phone company, we own the last mile it's our money we extracted from you and we can do as we please, so take it or leave it" attitude. If your call center and/or your company is small, you'll have to do just that. But if your firm is prominent and/or is planning to build a large facility in a high unemployment area, you may get local politicians and the business community to go to bat for you.

Governments are reluctant to intervene against private or public companies, especially monopolies but if not doing so risks enough bad publicity or result in shifts of campaign contributions that can give their political opposition the edge, then they will act. If the choice is between their heads and Ma Bell's, well it's fairly obvious who greases the guillotine...

Total Cost

Your call center has to be within and preferably under budget. To meet that requirement there are locations that you may have to pass up because they are horrendously expensive to locate in, even though it has the skilled labor you need, has excellent facilities and provides superior access.

For example, New York City has the world's best sales culture, with people who know how to hustle from cutting deals (and everything else) in the boardrooms to selling batteries while walking through the cars of the uptown subway B train. Lady Liberty in New York Harbor still beckons immigrants worldwide, speaking a United Nations of languages and dialects though they now land at JFK and nearby Newark Airport instead of docking at Ellis Island. Yet, the extremely high cost of everything: from labor to land, has prompted many companies to move their back offices, including call centers, out of New York City.

Only high-valued call centers, such as the ones servicing Internet companies that rely on the city's young, highly educated, cosmopolitan multilingual workforce, seem to prosper there. For example, the outer boroughs, such as Long Island City in Queens and Staten Island have relatively affordable real estate and ready access to workers who don't want to commute into Manhattan or who prefer the easier reverse commutes.

Because call centers require a large amount of relatively low-valued labor and require large amounts of space to house them they are very vulnerable to escalating wages, and to turnover and to real estate prices. The costs and labor availability at a location needs to be monitored constantly. Many locations that once attracted general lower-level customer service/sales call centers, such as, Phoenix, AZ and Dublin Ireland, can now only support higher-valued top-level sales/help desk centers.

▶ Locations Strategies

This section will not tell you the location of the rich veins of affordable people and places. They may be played out by the time you read this. What it will do is suggest some strategies to use when placing your center. While the focus of this section applies to US call center site selection, most of these tips are and will hold true in other countries, especially Canada and Australia.

Look at rural communities and smaller cities with populations under 200,000, but make sure they have suitable real estate and the telecom infrastructure to support your call centers.

Consultants often recommend this approach because such locations often have higher than average unemployment rates, significant underemployment and a loyal workforce with a strong work ethic. Many of these places will be able to make even stronger cases for themselves as call center locations when high-speed telecom and data services become available to them.

If you are planning to locate a large call center, placing it in such communities will make your firm a "big fish in a small pond." You become the dominant or top call center employer, enabling you to have more control over wages and benefits. Everyone else will have to scramble to meet your compensation levels and working conditions. You may lap up enough of the labor market to ward off other call centers.

Old military bases in small towns are ideal for call centers because they have an available civilian labor force, plentiful telecom capacity and one- and two-story buildings with large floorplates. Maine has benefited from such base closures, which have attracted call centers to that state.

"What you should look for in communities that don't have such telecom trunks or military bases is a partnership between the economic development agencies and the telcos, including alternate and competing providers," advises Engel. "They can help you get the telecom and data connections you need depending on the size of your project."

If you plan to set up your center quickly, smaller towns may not necessarily have facilities you can simply move into. Many of these locales have vacant space in office buildings, industrial buildings or shopping centers, all of which can be more costly to convert to call centers than spaces in office parks.

"It takes four to six months to renovate a shopping center and nine to 12 months to develop a build-to-suit," White advises. "If speed to market is critical to you, look at the larger cities because they usually have more suitable real estate."

A potential downside is a stronger more negative reaction from workers, the community and elected officials — especially those who arranged generous incentives to get you there — should you be forced to cut back or close your call center. Losing a 500- or 700-seat call center employing 1,100 or 1,800 agents is a pinprick to the economic life of a metro area with 1.1 million or 1.8 million people, but is a big wound for a small city with 110,000 or 180,000 residents.

Examine the larger cities, including the inside of their expressway rings, but do so with caution.

Downtowns in large and small cities alike are slowly coming back as business locations. While in other countries, such as in Europe, Asia and to a lesser extent in Canada they never went away, many American companies that took flight to the suburbs as soon as the local Interstate opened are taking a second look at what they left behind. Crime crackdowns, cleanups and modernization, amenities like convention centers, malls and arenas and new mass transit systems are making many downtown areas once again attractive and accessible.

Many cities inside their surrounding suburban expressway rings still have higher than average unemployment rates and large numbers of unemployed people. Blacks, Hispanics and in Canada the Metis and native peoples, and in other countries immigrant groups who live in urban areas often suffer from greater joblessness levels than those who reside in the suburbs. Yet with training, such as on job skills for those with spotty work histories, they can provide a great labor source. The Hispanics and immigrants possess vital native language skills for centers that need to serve those markets.

Growing numbers of downtown areas are also becoming magnets for young tech-oriented workers, attracted by colleges, a vibrant nightlife and culture, housed in funky converted and remodeled pre-World War II buildings or their newly-built lookalikes.

New startup firms are establishing themselves in older, renovated districts like Denver's LoDo, New York City's Silicon Alley and northwest downtown Portland, OR., Hoboken and Jersey City, NJ, once derelict with rotting warehouses and rusty railroad tracks are now buzzing with new and converted offices, and/or renovated homes, new light rail lines and so forth.

The downtown areas usually have call-center-suitable convertible older offices, which are popular with younger workers. They also have unused low-rise warehouses or industrial buildings that also work for call centers.

Equis' Cariola agrees that urban centers can work for call centers. "Crime has gone down dramatically in many cities and workers can get there on mass transit," he says. "You have to think out of the box."

Engel advises that you avoid selecting a site solely based on your general perception of cities and suburbs.

"You have to be careful if you are looking to set up a call center in an urban area," he says. "It is particularly important to do a location by location comparison rather than a generalized evaluation of urban versus suburban locations because it may vary for different products, services or job types. Education and orientation differ from city to city."

Look for population inflows

If your call center has a medium to high turnover rate or you are planning to expand the facility once it opens, you need to look for communities that attract more residents — through domestic in-migration and immigration — than those who leave. They are often the archetypical "big city" that draws people nationwide and from abroad like New York, Chicago, Los Angeles, San Francisco Bay, Atlanta and Dallas-Fort Worth in the US, Toronto, Vancouver, Calgary and Montreal in Canada, London and Manchester in the UK, Paris, France and Amsterdam, in the Netherlands.

There are cities and towns that may be business, commercial, cultural and educational hubs for their surrounding areas, which John Boyd calls "regional centers of influence" which also become the regions' employment centers, such as Sioux Falls, SD and Thunder Bay, ON, Canada.

Some communities may also attract new residents for climate and lifestyle reasons, like Arizona, Colorado and Florida in the US and southwestern British Columbia in Canada. They are often, but not always, a "big city" or "regional center of influence." Victoria, BC, the province's capital, serves only the immediate environs in splendid isolation at the southern tip of Vancouver Island, whose quite agreeable weather and laid-back nature-oriented lifestyle continues to attract new residents.

"We put a premium on a city's propensity for growth in order to keep an inflow of labor and to mitigate inflationary wage pressures," explains Boyd.

Open smaller, more distributed and connected centers.

If your optimal center has hundreds of seats, you may want to distribute it, especially if you locate your centers in rural areas or small cities. The days of the thousand-seat megacenter appear to be numbered.

The smaller the center the less daunting it is to find workers, and the more locations choices you have. Breaking up a large center into smaller, more widely-distributed facilities increases the likelihood that your call center operations can continue even if one particular site has an outage or has to shut down.

Military Bases

Communities where there are military bases — active and about-to-be-closed — can make excellent locations, for several reasons. Wherever there is a base there are usually many former service personnel living nearby. Their discipline and toughness make them excellent reliable call center agents, especially for outbound telesales. Many of them have had technical training, giving them skills for help desks.

Spouses of active duty and retired military personnel are also prime call center material. They also share the same strengths as their partners. Military pay is, unfortunately, woefully low. In Canada, military spouses who are French speaking often provide a bilingual workforce in communities where there would otherwise be no or few French-speaking residents.

Military bases that are downsizing or being closed offer superb facilities. The buildings are often large, low-rise with plenty of parking and excellent voice/data links.

Not all military communities are suitable for call centers. For example, those that are boot camps provide few stable households to recruit from.

Follow the Tourists

Remember that great vacation you took, where the people were so friendly, the service was excellent and the prices were low beyond belief? That may be a great place to locate a call center.

Communities that attract tourists, such as with casinos, attractions, entertainment and relaxation also have and require the same type of people who will work well in call centers: those who are friendly, trustworthy and willing to work flexible hours at low but fair wages. Such cities and towns include Atlantic City, Branson, MO, Deadwood, SD, Las Vegas, New Orleans, Niagara Falls, Orlando and new riverboat ports like Tunica, MS. They usually have never-close services like dry cleaning to support this labor force.

Even where the tourist traffic is seasonal there are call center opportunities. You can tap into workforces that would go often on unemployment or out of town to find work, and utilize cheap-to-rent buildings that are closed for the season. With today's smaller, flexible computer and phone hardware and easy-to-setup-and-move workstations you can move right in. A summer vacation area like much of Cape Cod could support a temporary winter call center selling packages for it and for other regions for next summer and for winter get-away-from-it-all trips and cruises to Florida and the Caribbean.

Locating Outside of the US to Serve US Customers

With unemployment rates plummeting and costs rising, growing numbers of call centers that serve US customers are opening up and moving to countries that have higher labor availability, less competition and lower costs, aided by vastly improving and ever-cheaper voice/data networks. These countries include Canada, India, Jamaica, New Zealand and The Philippines. India's call center operating costs are only a third that of the US. Canada's dollar is about a third less valuable than the US dollar; the country has an excellent education system.

However, setting up a call center in another country involves extra time, resources and the ability to cope with different laws, regulations, taxation regimes, cultures and languages. Where dialects can inhibit understanding you will need to hire trainers to help agents speak in tune to American ears.

"The best person you can pick to communicate to an American is another American," points out Engel. "They have that commonality of experience that creates that customer relationship, a bond that is greater than our cultural and geographic differences."

Regional or Satellite Call Center Networks

When companies began opening call centers outside of the US they place facilities in countries where they have customers or a presence, i.e., office or factory. Yet, there are few countries that have or will have large enough markets that want phone-based services and sales in their own languages to economically support their own facilities.

In Europe and to a lesser extent in Asia-Pacific many companies have tried to serve their customers with cost-effective single multilingual pan-European or pan-Asian call centers, in countries and cities that attracted native language speakers from other nations. While this approach worked for awhile, when the countries like Ireland, the Netherlands and Australia had high unemployment, it is becoming less viable as the economies boomed. There are often not enough native or learned language speakers in those hubs.

You may then consider two other methods: regional or satellite networks. A regional network entails opening and linking several well-placed call centers with native and learned language agents. It offers the economies of scale of pan-Asian or European centers with the ability to tap local labor forces and language skills. And the regional approach is more cost effective than opening and running call centers in individual or small clusters of countries.

One example of a regional network is Avis's new call center system. The "try harder" car rental firm has a 170-seat center in Barcelona, Spain that serves customers in southern Europe and a 200-seat center in Manchester, UK, which serves customers in Austria, Germany, Switzerland and the UK. The two facilities replaced eight European centers.

"The churn of people is the major cost in running a call center," says Philip Cohen, a longtime regional call center advocate. "If you haven't got that supply then you lack the prerequisite to open a call center. It is much easier to find Spanish-speakers in Barcelona than in Amsterdam and vice versa. The shortage of language skills among workers is a real threat to the multilingual call center. It pushes the odds in favor of regional, language-based call centers."

The satellite strategy entails opening one large multilingual call center, linked to smaller call centers in each of the countries you market in. This method can work quite effectively in the Asia Pacific, where some countries are only now seeing call centers set up and accepted as employers, and where property costs to support large centers are horrendously high, such as in Hong Kong and Japan. Yet many Asians are very sensitive to language nuance and prefer native speakers. And you may be inviting war if you tried to serve Taiwan from China and vice-versa; China regards Taiwan as a wayward province while the Taiwanese do not trust the mainland regime.

With the satellite system you organize calls and contacts in two ways: to native speakers in the main center or to the satellite center and escalated, if necessary, to the other. The main center can handle overflow calls. The system also provides for disaster recovery through call and contact rerouting: a vital consideration in this region whose countries are often hit with earthquakes, cyclones/ typhoons and volcanic eruptions.

The satellite method is scalable. As call and contact load grows from each country you can then justify expanding each center, to when they become not satellites but regional partners.

Regional networks appear to be the future best method of serving the Asia Pacific market. Martin Conboy, director of ACA Research and CEO of Callcentres.net (North Sydney, Australia), a research firm and news service, reports that while companies want to consolidate or set up one or two call centers, they are limited by cultural and marketplace considerations. While a few companies have successfully set up pan-Asian centers in Australia, many others may have difficulty doing so. He explains that most Japanese and Korean immigrants in Australia are reluctant to work in call centers because they see it as a low-status occupation. Many of them are spouses of relocated businesspeople.

"Companies can only go so far in consolidating their operations," Conboy points out. "They have to address the cultural and local issues by locating call centers in those markets."

Driving this as well is the Asia Pacific region's dense thicket of insular cultures that are often impenetrable by outsiders. Jon Kaplan, president of TeleDevelopment Services (Richfield, OH) points out, for example, that there are three to four level of politeness in Japanese. A person who

DIY Site Selection Research

One of the best ways to find out if a location will work for you is to find out for yourself, directly and indirectly, without letting on that you're interested in opening a call center or any other function there. It is amazing how nice people can be when there's jobs and money riding on it.

Here's some suggestions how:

Research the community. Frequently visit (but don't register at) local Web sites, especially those belonging to media outlets and governments. Subscribe to the local newspapers — circulation departments usually don't ask questions as they just want the money — but have them sent to your home. Pay particular attention to the business pages and the Help Wanted ads.

Find out the lay of the land. There are issues such as zoning that could affect your call center that if you went through 'normal' channels like the planning office, word might get out. The advice that I got, when I was researching opening a bed and breakfast, is to hire a well-known local lawyer. They will tell you what is going on and what you can do, with confidentiality sealing their lips.

See for yourself. Nothing beats being a tourist to see firsthand how a place ticks. Stay at a local hotel, eat in a variety of restaurants and visit and buy in the shops. Go to some of the attractions. Strike up casual conversations with the front desk clerk, or with some of the people at the bar. Bring your spouse and kids along, if the locale is attractive to them; they make great foils. Go back to some of the businesses you first patronized to look for consistency. If you had a bad experience the first time it may be good the next; everyone has off-days. Visit again or have one of your staff travel to the community some weeks later.

What you're looking for is how well you and your family have been sold to and served by the employees, because this is the labor pool you'll be drawing from if you locate your call center there. If the salespeople and waitstaff have been attentive without being pushy then the community might work as a location. If they take their sweet time about getting to you and have an attitude (like the TV commercial where the waitress, having been told by a customer that he didn't want mayo, proceeds to scrape the piece of bread on the side of the table), leave. The place, and the city or town.

learned the language would not know or appreciate the nuances.

He sees regional call centers growing in Japan, Korea and Singapore, which have advanced economies and increasing amounts of phone and Internet use. He sees Korea as a prime call center location to serve that market; he has seen many Koreans visiting the ICCM show in Chicago over the past two years.

Clallam County, WA, which encompasses the city of Port Angeles that sits at the foot of the Olympic Range has been advertising for call centers to locate there in magazines and at trade shows. If you want to know how well the workers there will serve your customers you should go there and see how *you're* served.

"People would rather be served by agents in a call center in their own countries, speaking their own languages and sharing the same culture, than those in a pan-Asian call center, " Kaplan points out. "But you must have a critical mass of customers and that strong culture to support it."

Setting up a call center in some of these countries is viable from labor supply and cost perspectives. Kaplan points out that there are many relatively affordable cities, such as Nagoya and Yokohama within an hour from Tokyo, whose real costs are 1/3 to nearly 1/2 less than in the Japanese capital. Call centers are growing in size; 200-seat facilities are not uncommon. The workforce attracted to call centers are spouses and college students, mainly for part-time. Working in a call center is not considered a career there, he explains.

"You have just as good labor supply in these communities as you do in Tokyo," Kaplan points out. "But as in the US you have to offer good working conditions and wages and benefits to attract and keep them because you're competing against other service industry employers."

Follow the Sun

One locations strategy that could save you labor, facilities and operating expenses is "follow the sun": locating a network of call centers spread out east to west in varying time zones, including in different countries. This way you can have a call center open for only one or two shifts but provide continuous or near-continuous live agent customer service. I had outlined how a follow the sun strategy can work domestically in Chapter 2.

An international follow-the-sun implementation lets you take advantage of different labor costs in other countries. While the British Empire is no more, the sun hasn't yet set on the English-speaking "empire": its most important legacy. You can, for example, have a call center in Wellington, New Zealand handle evening and night calls and contacts from California, permitting you to close down your Fresno facility in that high-cost state: New Zealand is a less costly location. When New Zealand is ready to turn in, you can have them routed to your center in Perth, in Western Australia, then to Mumbai, India, Sheffield, England and back to yours in Scranton, PA.

Follow the sun requires hard work and investment to network your call centers and to train agents to be on the same program to provide consistent customer service. While domestic and international long distance voice/data costs are dropping, additional capacity is coming on stream, and lower cost technologies like IP telephony are becoming reality, such networking is still not inexpensive.

Troll For 'Secondhand' Locations

Call centers come and go, thanks to mergers, acquisitions, loss of clients, business strategy changes and just plain bad business decisions that force the owning company to go out of business (see Chapter 10). As a result at any one time there could be several just-vacated call centers, sometimes in locations that may work for your call center.

These used centers offer several important advantages. Perhaps the most important is that someone else has already done the site selection homework, which means there is a reasonable chance that the location could work for you, with adequate labor, facilities and amenities. The centers are available to be occupied, often with few renovations. Sometimes the previous owner will leave the PBX, wiring and workstations, saving you money. You may be able to hire the former agents and supervisors. All of these factors can radically cut down the time it takes for you to open your new center. There are real estate consultancies such as Arledge/Power and Mohr Partners (Dallas, TX) that track and market used locations.

The downsides are that these locales' workforces may not have the skillsets at the compensation you offer. The facilities and equipment may not be suitable for your operation.

Before you select a secondhand call center be sure to find out not only if it could mesh into your operation but *why* did the previous occupant move out. Talking to previous employees and perhaps the local newspaper's business editor could give you some clues. If the center had been shut down because the company owning it had been acquired or that the firm had retrenched, you need to ascertain why the location drew the short straw.

"While you might find good pickings here and there, you must remember that there is usually a good reason why a merged company chose to close a call center at a particular spot," warns Boyd. "While keeping others open."

Robert Mohr, president, Mohr Partners agrees. "Just because one firm is moving out does not necessarily mean that the same site won't work for you. You may have different needs than the vacating call center. Also, you can take the attitude that you can do a better job than the previous tenant."

Mohr's firm helped iSKY, a Columbia, MD-based outsourcer, make just such a move. The outsourcer enlisted both Mohr Partners and CB Richard Ellis (Los Angeles, CA) to scout out some 30 possible locations for available space. Finally in February 1999 it opened a 96-seat call center in Lafayette, IN in a 12,000-square-foot space that PNC Bank had just vacated.

Jeff Uthoff, iSKY's vice president of communications operations, says that the outsourcer was looking for a pre-existing call center with the goal of saving time and money it otherwise would have needed to recruit and train agents. With the assistance of the two real estate firms, iSKY found what it needed. Besides securing the property, the outsourcer hired more than 50% of PNC's laid-off staff.

"We found we had a highly-experienced, highly-capable tenured workforce that had been there for a few years," recalls Uthoff. "Yet before we decided on reusing the PNC Bank location we did due diligence and asked the bank tough questions to make sure that they were pulling out for the right reasons."

▶ Working With EDAs

When finalizing your site selection plans, you should work with local economic development agencies (EDAs) to get information about underemployment and to ask for help in setting up your call center.

EDAs can put you in touch with local resources, such as community colleges, to provide training for agents and help you through the application and zoning process. If you need extra services, such as arranging for a new bus stop close to your call center, the EDA can introduce you to the local transit authority.

If you are having trouble getting phone service in time from the incumbent local exchange carriers (ILEC) EDAs can connect you with the right people at the ILEC you do business with. In contrast to US practice where the ILECs seem disinterested in call centers, carriers in many other countries, recognizing the revenue call centers bring in, work closely with local EDAs to attract and establish call centers.

EDAs can obtain important information for you that can be difficult to obtain from other sources. Examples include the number of call centers in the local area, the companies that run them and these companies' prevailing wages. EDAs can also fill you in on signing and re-signing bonuses.

"Those numbers are not listed in an area's reported average wage but they can make a big difference on your bottom line," says Arledge.

Do not expect all jurisdictions to help all types of call centers. During a boom economy, regions can pick and choose companies. Some states, such as Arizona and Texas, have set wage floors so that if you pay agents below a certain hourly amount, these states won't offer any incentives for locating your center within them. Some communities no longer want outbound telemarketing call centers because they pay low, turnover is great and they do not stay around. People are also beginning to hate telemarketers.

You need to be as smart in dealing with an EDA as you would with any salesperson. The goal of an EDA is to convince you to locate in its community. Consultants recommend that you obtain as much information as possible about communities you're interested in before you meet with EDAs. When an EDA presents you with data, find out how recent the data is and confirm the source.

According to consultants, EDAs often fund market and competitive assessment research from private firms. Such research usually, but not always, reflects the conclusions and views of the sponsors. "EDAs are a good resource for community information but should never be the only one," advises Engel.

Be wary when an EDA presents testimonials either on paper or arranges you to visit companies that have located there. According to Philip Cohen, in some instances, such firms have been told to say nice things as conditions of receiving generous grants.

"I strongly advise my clients to be aware of the conditions attached to grants and tax breaks when making site selection decisions," states Cohen. "It distorts your entire decisionmaking and that of the entire industry."

Also, be careful of what an EDA promises. Many are private or semi-private organizations that have no real authority. They cannot guarantee planning approval or tax breaks — both come from the government.

You also need to decipher the confusing array of incentive packages that come from EDAs. Governments similarly offer what can be a bewildering variety of job creation grants, loans and tax breaks. Many incentives have strings attached, such as the number and types of jobs your center creates.

"Sometimes, depending on the fine print, you can't take advantage of a tax credit if your firm makes too much money," Arledge cautions. "Therefore, you have to look for grants or training dollars."

Consultants advise that you not tip your hand about your final site decision. If you do, you could risk losing many incentives. "Before you declare your intention to locate your center, you need to have a preliminary written commitment from local officials that details the types of incentives offered, the level at which you qualify and the conditions that you will be required to adhere to," says Shapiro.

▶ Finding Space Quickly

Yes, you can set up a new call center in less than 60 days. Outsourcer ClientLogic (Nashville, TN) got its new Albuquerque, NM center opened in 37 — and over the Christmas holidays yet. The center, which received the go-ahead on December 8, 1998, went live January 18, 1999.

One of its keys to success is *advanced planning*. ClientLogic forecasted seat planning in 30-day, 60-day and 90-day timeframes; needs are reviewed each week. It has in-house, design and human resources project teams. It contracted with site selection firm Jackson and Cooksey (Dallas, TX) to find locations and space.

It had pre-set its center plans, sizes, configurations and facilities requirements and had agent profiles to screen staff with.

Another key is *finding a good EDA*. Albuquerque Economic Development, helped Jackson and Cooksey find space; ClientLogic looked at eight buildings before picking a recently vacated third floor of an office building, which had administrative offices and a call center. The agency introduced the outsourcer to recruitment and training firms, helped it obtain the necessary state and local permits and made contacts for the call center firm with US West, the ILEC.

A third key is *constant communications*, to make decisions in real-time. ClientLogic had cellphone-equipped team members in Albuquerque, Las Vegas, NM, its nearest call center and in Buffalo, NY, where it had offices.

A fourth key is *serendipity*. The office it took over required few modifications; for example, it already had carpeting, which saved enormous time. It reused rooms for office and training space though it did have to install a separate computer/switch room. It also used a tie line from its Las Vegas center until its switch could be hooked in.

"We were on a tight aggressive timeframe spanning two big holidays, " explained ClientLogic senior vice president-facilities Melissa Bailey. "We were pushing US West to connect us on time. The Albuquerque Economic Development office called the right people in the company for us who then enabled us to meet our timeline."

ClientLogic's Albuquerque call center

▶ Incentive Tips

Whisper that you're going to open a call center in a region and you may end up feeling like the rich prince off to find a bride, only to discover someone in your court had leaked the word out. You'll get more offers and promises and see fatter dowries than you've ever dreamed of.

Every city and town, it seems, wants the jobs and tax revenues you will create, even at the price of going broke with grants, loans and tax breaks, and free buildings. And every city and town knows about each others' goodies, just as there are no secrets in the locker and powder rooms.

It is tempting to make your decision based on which community can come up with the best deal. But don't. Like marriage, when you set up a call center you have to live with the decision, and it could be the worst one you'll ever make. You will have to put up with the consequences such as higher than expected costs and turnover, and not enough and/or lower quality agents that annoy your customers.

In the words of one obviously male site selection expert, who will go nameless: "The bigger the dowry the uglier the bride."

Incentives do have a place in deciding between two or three roughly equal locations. They can reduce the costs of setting up in that community, improving your bottom line. Senior management likes such deal-making. It shows that you're a good businessperson.

CB Richard Ellis Call Center Solutions Group offers these tips on incentives:

- Have you worked with the community to create a beneficial incentive package that will help you and them?

- Has someone explained to the community which incentives do not apply to your company? It is imperative to give specific reasons and support to the local community contacts. Remember that a community official may have to sell your incentive package to other local agencies and/or governments in the same way in which you have to sell your projects to your company's management. One of the best ways to help the community understand how your company will be affected is to provide a detailed analysis of their taxing structure in comparison to other communities;

- If a community offers incentives that cannot be utilized, work with the community to create alternative solutions;

- Involve your tax/finance department and check to ensure that administrative requirements for tax credit programs are reasonable. Do not assume that your tax department will have the time and/or resources to follow through with your negotiated incentive programs.

Location Factors

According to site selection consultants, you should consider many factors when deciding where to locate your center, and you should center these factors around three main categories: labor, legislation and community

Labor:

Availability

Wage structures

Local fringe benefits

Education

Language skills

Labor force participation

Legislation:

Telemarketing laws

Taxation policies and rates

Unemployment insurance and workers' compensation rates and rules

Right-to-work laws

Incentives, such as training grants and tax credits

Community:

Time zones

Climate

Telecom and electrical infrastructure

Transportation (roads, mass transit and inter-city air and rail access)

Cost of living, including housing

Public safety

Property and site availability

Local business attitudes (e.g., whether the community is pro-business)

Real Estate

If you have done your labor market analysis correctly and you have either picked a community (or short listed three or four) with roughly the same worker availability, cost and skillsets, you now need to find or construct a building to house your call center. To repeat from Chapter 7, do not let the presence of desired property sway you over labor cost and supply. Real estate accounts for about 10% of a call center's operating costs compared with 60%+ for employee wages and benefits.

One good example where the labor force presence makes the difference despite property hassles is with Cigna Health Care's new call center, near Scranton, PA. Construction workers blasted through bedrock to create a three-story

Looking for a home for a call center? One of the best ways to find what you need is to use the same technique you use looking for a house. Check out the areas where you want to be. You may find some great leads simply by watching for signs. And you'll get an excellent feel of what the area is like. This is taken in St. George an old but reviving downtown section and transportation hub in the New York City borough of Staten Island. The building is in walking distance of the Staten Island Ferry to Manhattan and to a new minor league ballfield.

160,000 square foot (sf) facility situated in the Glenmaura Corporate Center that will house 1,200 to 1,500 workstations. Ed Diazlo, Cigna's assistant vice president of corporate real estate told *Call Center* in an interview published May 2000, that the effort is worth it, citing the area's excellent labor force. The firm had researched other land sites and determined that location was the best despite the terrain. "We had done a demographic study and it rated the Scranton area very highly," said Diazlo. "The work ethic ranked above average, the region's education system is excellent and the business support from the local chamber is outstanding."

▶ Call Centers' Unique Property Requirements

Where you set up the call center in a city or metro area will determine how many of the intended workforce you will tap, their demographic composition, and amenities requirements. Also, when the labor force factors are similar between competing locations, available reasonably priced buildings and property can make a difference in siting a call center, especially if you have a short timeframe. Lastly, the building type, the individual structure and its features will make a difference in how the center functions, and how your agents, customers and senior management perceives your company.

When picking the right property you must first recognize that in the realm of commercial usage call centers are *unique*. They're an office function, or more accurately back office since most support departments such as customer service, marketing and sales. Yet, they have higher density than other uses. Call centers fit more people in a given amount of room than other functions, as much as seven persons or agent/seats (going back to measurement in Chapter 5) per 1,000 sf expressed as a ratio: 7:1 compared with 4:1 say for administrative or marketing.

The greater density has vital implications for every function of that property. You will need more of everything, including parking (usually to the same ratio as your density) greater air circulation, washrooms and the attendant plumbing, break space, and wiring to accommodate your agents and workstations.

Also, unlike many other uses, call centers work best if they are on the same floor. This lets you orchestrate your layout and supervision more easily, as opposed to having people run among different floors or play elevator roulette.

On the other hand if your call center performs several functions, such as training, outbound sales and inbound sales or if you work for a service bureau with shared and client-dedicated agents, a multi-story building can work for you. This setup lets you take advantage of economies of scale provided by the building and site, and may give you a greater choice of property in your desired labor market, when you need it.

"We recommend that call centers go into single floor buildings," recommends Bob Stinson, president of the Stinson Design Group (Houston, TX). "But if you have limited time to get your call center operational and the available single floor space does not have expansion room then a multi-floor building can work for you."

Because your customers are valuable, your call center can't afford to go down. You will need high capacity and quality voice/data links (T-1 at minimum; ISDN if your volume is not high) and power, preferably with multiple feeds. Yet don't be surprised if these fat pipes and additional power connections are not available. If "Hurricane Brendan" threatens most offices just shut down and go home and they work a standard business day and require 'normal' business phone lines. And, unlike call centers, the normal office doesn't get swamped with hundreds of calls in a matter of minutes for orders for a new FDA-approved miracle fat dissolver.

"Few developers or lease managers will go out of their way to lay T-1 or additional power on site as standard practice, " Roy Young, president of design/project management firm Young, Bickley Geiger (Boston, MA), points outs.

If multiple power feeds are not available you can make do with an online (always on) battery-fed uninterruptible power system (UPS) and generator system; which set-up is also necessary to smooth out power loads and prevent damage to your equipment.

Bear in mind that not every building or development can accommodate generators and/or UPSes. UPS systems are very heavy; the battery cabinets alone are an I-beam-bending 400 lbs. per sf when a typical aboveground space permits 45 lbs. per sf of floor loading and the cabinets come in at a total of 3,000 lbs.

Generators, which are more costly than UPSes, also churn out noise and fumes (although some models are amazingly small and quiet), need fuel sources that must be transported, such as gas, or stored, such as diesel and propane, and must be in code-compliant locations. You will need approval from the building architect and mechanical engineers. However, some properties now have tenant-shared on-site generators.

If your call center will or will eventually be open 7x24 (all the time) you will need better security and be located in safer areas than offices open 9 to 5. Your property access should be through computerized pass keys. The building and property, especially parking must have excellent lighting, with no dark corners, high bushes or outside transformer alcoves for perps to hide in. Adjacent and nearby streets should also be well lit. There must be monitoring at all times by cameras covering entrances and exits.

Also, after daytime hours the building should have a security guard that can escort employees to their cars or to the street. One development, Netpark Tampa Bay, a shopping mall converted into offices, including a call center in Tampa, FL, can drive your agents to their cars in golf carts. If employees must use parking garages they must be kept clean, well lit and camera-fitted.

Up until relatively recently, many landlords have been reluctant to lease to call centers. They have seen them as a lower-paying, here-today-gone-tomorrow tenancy, than other office types and as being more trouble than they are worth. The higher densities create parking problems and more demand on building air systems. Also, the failure by some call centers to provide adequate smoking areas have led to the ugly, filthy and grossly unhealthy practice of agents smoking their butts off outside of entrances, leading to complaints from other tenants. The fumes often infiltrates into other offices.

Snobbery can also play a role in why landlords sometimes say "no" to call centers, Many want better-dressed professionals in their building rather than the more casually garbed call center agents. Fortunately, as call centers become more professional for longer-term, higher-paying customer service and sales, rather than fly-by-night outbound telemarketing, all of these factors are changing . Offices are now gradually being built to the same densities as call centers, with air quality and parking improvements, and higher quality voice/data links including multiple feeds and reportedly, with backup generators. With more workers of all classes dressing casually it is becoming more difficult to tell, at first glance, the salaried professionals from the hourly agents.

There are also more designers and developers such as The Alter Group (Lincolnwood, IL) that build-to-suit and create speculative structures specifically designed and suitable for call centers. The Alter Group's *CallCore* series, available in single and multi-story configurations have been engineered with open space, lighting, air quality and parking, that call centers need, with 7:1 to 10:1 densities and parking ratios.

This points to the Economics 101 truism that if the demand is there, the price is right, the market will supply it. But sometimes not right away, when some buyers need it.

▶ Property Types

There is a wide range of structures that are potentially suitable for call centers that you should look into, each with their strengths and weaknesses. They fall into two broad categories, which I call *conventional* and *conversion*. Conventional offices are buildings that are purposely built to house business functions from managerial to clerical, data processing, sales and secretarial. Conversions are former industrial, retail, transportation/distribution and warehouse spaces that have been converted to office space.

You can divide both conventional and conversion into pre- and post-World War II or *"prewar"* and *"postwar."* There are some very important differences between the two types. The two eras are separated by the ascendancy of the automobile as the primary transportation means and by the design trend to spartan "Modern," away from fancy, rich and fascinating exterior details such as gargoyles and scrollwork.

Postwar properties

A *postwar* office or conversion usually, but not always, has large open floorplates with few fat columns or other obstructions. With this design you can change your layout to your heart's content.

Postwar buildings are often sited outside of the downtown area, with on-site parking and little mass transit access. They generally have no more than four stories, each with large level floorplates. The exceptions are downtown headquarters buildings in large cities; these 'skyscrapers' are 10 stories and up, usually with small floorplates and little parking. Conventional postwar offices often have glass and steel or panels made with stucco or other similar materials on the exterior but with little adornment; conversions are made with brick and concrete and have little or no designed-in natural lighting.

Postwar conventional and conversion spaces in non-downtown locations are the most popular property types for call centers because they possess efficient large floorplates and plenty of parking, while the lease and construction costs are reasonable. Suburban and smaller cities also tend to have less planning bureaucracy than their big city counterparts.

These building types and their demand by business functions like call centers and corporate offices reflect the reality that most people live and work outside of the downtown area, especially in the service sector, both part-time and full-time employment. Workers at all levels usually don't want to drive far or take inconvenient mass transit alternatives that tend to be little or nonexistent in the sprawled out suburban areas and small cities.

Many workers don't want to go downtown because of lack of parking and security concerns. The suburban buildup, partially driven by racial flight of businesses and residents, but also by the birth of expressways and ensuing ripping up of streetcar and interurban rail systems, turned many smaller US cities to become human and physical wastelands. That situation is now being addressed through the help of economic development agencies (EDAs) and this era's run-away, booming economy.

Companies and workers have also moved out to the suburbs from downtowns in other countries but not to quite the same extent as in the US. Consequently downtown and near-downtown properties remain popular; more people also use mass transit outside of the US. Many cities, especially in Europe try and restrict urban sprawl while encouraging downtown vitality by making car-free areas and investing in mass transit.

Postwar conventional

Postwar conventional is what everybody thinks when you say the word "office." Nicknamed "bankers boxes" they feature fluorescent-lit "cube farms" stretching as far as the eye can see, surrounded by rifle-slot-sized windows, set into boring, if cost-effective featureless solid colored flat exteriors, often located in so-called "office parks." So-called because rarely do you see people enjoying them as "parks," surrounded by fumes and noise from passing vehicles. Instead, the individuals who occupy the structures are too busy driving in and out as if they were metal-clad wheeled beetles, or Beetles.

Postwar conventional buildings are popular because they work for most business types, including call centers. They have the large floorplates and the parking and they look corporate. You know what to expect when you sign a lease for or build such a structure. You don't have to spend much money and time renovating them into an acceptable call center. Your employees know what to expect when they move in.

What you may want to watch for is whether the buildings have the required density and parking, and whether this will cause problems for you either directly, or indirectly by other tenants complaining. There may also be hassles from adjoining communities. Many postwar nondowntown offices are located near residential neighborhoods. Large bursts of traffic, and vehicles coming and going in the wee hours of the morning, or the specter of that happening, once word gets out that your call center is going in, may prompt complaints and possible political action to try and stop your center from going live. To shut them up (or more politely, to 'ameliorate their concerns') may require you and/or the landlord to spend money to alleviate the problem, like adding a traffic light or turning lane.

Also, you may not find the voice/data and power quantity, quality and multiple feeds that your call center requires in such buildings. Until relatively recently, offices usually did not consume much power or voice/data. Bob Stinson of Stinson Design suggests that you might be better off seeking an existing building or doing a build-to-suit in an office/distribution park, where office and light manufacturing and distribution are located.

"The electrical system is robust, there's room to grow and there's more parking," Stinson points out. "And there's going to be less complaints about your traffic."

Renovate or Build to Suit or Spec?

If you select to go with a conventional office you have two main choices, build to suit or renovate. With build-to-suit, you are the sole occupant and the owner, although in some cases, the developer is the owner and you are the

The Oak Creek Center in Lombard, IL, built by The Alter Group, is an excellent example of a call-center-suitable speculative building. Its one story has 35,000 sf with a 6:1 parking ratio.

sole occupant. The main advantage with building to suit is that you get the kind of building you want, finished the way you desire, whereas with renovations you have to work around the existing structure and lot.

The principal disadvantage with build-to-suit is that, well, it has to be built, Lead times to complete these buildings often range between five and seven months and they can sometimes run longer depending on the building and zoning approval process, the climate and the terrain of the site. However, if you lease and renovate you can be ready to take calls in weeks.

A third and increasingly popular option is leasing in a speculative building. You can open your center within a new and attractive modern space in as little as 30 days. The downside is that the structures are made for conventional offices for maximum marketability, which means they may have smaller floorplates, multiple stories and be located in metro areas that are suitable for head or regional offices, such as Phoenix, AZ, whose labor markets are too saturated for call centers. Yet, as the call center industry grows, developers are more willing to adapt properties and locate them in the right labor markets to attract call centers.

Mike McElwee, manager of call center services for real estate consultancy Mohr Partners (Dallas, TX), says that properties built to specifications are great for call centers and developers. "Spec buildings are becoming more suitable for call centers," he explains. "They tend to be in shell condition with plenty of open space, and they lend themselves to be open to various space plans."

If you decide to build to suit, or take possession of a building for renovation — lease, don't buy — unless you want a call center or office as a symbol for your company, have full control of your property and prefer the benefits of landlordism, like leasing to other tenants. With leasing you tie up far less capital and you have greater flexibility to expand or contract your call center. In an industry as fast changing as this one, having maneuvering room usually pays off.

Postwar conversions

The one big downside to conventional offices, either existing and especially build-to-suit or spec is that they may not be where your desired labor force is. Many small cities that are great call center locations because they have plenty of friendly, loyal, hard-working people willing to work for less than what you pay in larger cities, lack such buildings.

In contrast, you can find in nearly every city, no matter their size and location a postwar conversion candidate, usually commercial but sometimes factory/distribution. Wherever you want to open a call center, chances are that there will be several potentially suitable properties.

That is the main reason why you should consider them. They have the same if not more floorspace and parking: 8:1 to 10:1 ratios than a postwar conventional office. It can give you, therefore, many of the same benefits of constructing your own building, without the time lag and potential zoning hassles.

It is amazing the types of buildings you find call centers located in. I now have to take a second look when I see what I think is or thought was a lumber store, a discount outlet, a WalMart or a bowling alley. The only clue is that there are no flashy signs, but plenty of cars in the parking lot. WalMart (Bentonville, AR) even has a separate real estate division that markets its older smaller properties.

Postwar conversions also have some unique advantages. The main one is that potential agents know how to get there: which is important when you are recruiting and retaining employees. "Everybody knows" where the old K-Mart or Ford assembly plant is. The same can't be said for some lookalike building in a mass-produced office park, hidden behind noise-limiting grassy mounds. Another is excellent voice/data and power. Conversion candidates are either on main roads that they are routed on or under or had these fat pipes laid in for their original owners and tenants. Line crews won't get lost looking for them.

Conversion candidate buildings also have high ceilings, which help to reduce noise, unlike conventional offices. This gives you the option to make some nifty additions, like adding a mezzanine housing offices and training facilities.

Their main downside is that they often require extensive structural and infrastructure renovations; there is little if any cost savings with them compared with other building types. You will probably need to add heating, ventilating and air conditioning (HVAC) units, toilets and attendant plumbing, including sewer lines to the street, and power, as these structures weren't designed to accommodate large numbers of people sitting inside all day. You will probably need to punch out skylights and windows to bring in natural lighting.

Also, especially with a retail conversion, like those in strip malls, they tend to look what they were, a former discount department store or mall, no matter how nice you make them. This may be a liability if your company places a premium on "corporate" appearance.

There are pros and cons to each of these conversion candidates. Commercial conversions are close or convenient to amenities like restaurants, pharmacies, gyms and child care services, unlike many conventional offices and factory/distribution conversions that tend to be in out of the way places. Your employees won't have to spend half their lunch hour going to and from the friendly neighborhood "Kolesterol Kate's". If a commercial conversion candidate is a strip center or converted mall your agents and supervisors can simply walk next door.

Also, if some of your employees come by mass transit, commercial conversions, especially shopping centers are often on major bus routes or near suburban rail stations. Many conventional offices and factory/distribution candidates lack this.

"Remember, with shopping centers all the hard work — parking, traffic and site selection — has already been done," says site selection consultant John Boyd of The Boyd Company (Princeton, NJ).

One great example of a commercial conversion is a 1,100-seat CompUSA call center that opened in May 1998, it is made out of a former WalMart in Plano, TX. Stinson Design and Carter and Burgess (Fort Worth, TX) renovated the building, including adding a second story for meetings and training. To limit noise there is a stepped suspended ceiling with sound-absorbing fiberglass tiles. There are two new generators and multiple utility feeds that back parallel UPS systems.

"CompUSA figured that it would be less expensive if it renovated rather than implement a build-to-suit, but it came out even," explains Bob Stinson. "But the project cut the time involved and avoided any zoning hassle that could have happened with a new building. Another benefit CompUSA saw was a 40% increase in agent retention because their employees loved the new building."

Some real estate developers lease large renovated spaces to call centers within malls, including properties that were stores, movie theaters and food courts. Then the developers rent out smaller spaces within the same malls to restaurants and childcare providers.

"The call center gets space where there is a lot of parking, amenities and visibility," says Ron Cariola, VP with Equis (Chicago, IL), a real estate consulting firm. "The mall management gets daytime traffic from employees."

You can also find commercial conversions in other countries, including in the downtowns. In Canada the T. Eaton department store chain recently closed, leaving many empty prime-located downtown and suburban buildings. Woolco has also closed the doors on its stores there. Call centers are now moving into these properties; RMH Teleservices (Bryn Mawr, PA) opened a call center in a former Woolco in downtown Sault Ste. Marie, ON.

Commercial conversions can be risky in a major metropolitan area. You have to consider what properties your call center will replace when it moves into a former mall or store.

"The numbers may say there's availability of suitable conversions but when you take a hard look at it there's not," Cariola points out. "Many times a retail center or mall failed because it may not have been located in the best neighborhood. A strip center where there's a pawn shop, a church and a vacant department store is not really where you want to put a call center."

Factory/distribution conversions offer one unique advantage over commercial conversions: they are bland and faceless so they can be made to look more corporate than the other type. They are big, usually featureless boxes, though many also have clear and tinted windows for direct light and opaque glass brick, providing indirect light. You can also co-locate fulfillment operations in these structures with little hassle from the neighbors.

Moreover, these sites tend to have robust power and phone connections. You also won't have a problem installing and running a backup generator. Chances are there will be a generator pad already there or one easily constructed for such units.

You may find considerable assistance from local EDAs and the community if you pick such a conversion candidate. Some of these buildings have become eyesores, home to vandals and the like. Some states encourage "brownfield" (reuse) redevelopment as part of efforts to limit "greenfield" sprawl. In many cases the property will not be used for its intended purposes again, especially if it is older and smaller.

Unless the property is completely demolished and the grounds unearthed and cleaned up there is scant chance there will be other uses, such as residential on them, since they have to be in the "right spot" for many other uses.

Such conversions are also available and popular outside of the US. When I was talking to an EDA official representing Blackburn, England where my family is from and where I lived on two separate occasions, he mentioned they had a former Philips plant that would make a great place for a call center. I chuckled. I said I knew about that factory. I have an aunt who had worked there and in the British terminology "was made redundant." The silent gulps on the other end of connection were deafening.

The big problem with such conversions is that you may incur more renovation costs, especially if there is environmental cleanup. Many buildings have pits, such as for processed steel looping and vehicle maintenance that must be filled in. The grounds have to be cleared up.

And they may be in the wrong spot for your call center labor force.

"You would consider a factory or warehouse conversion if there is nothing else available in your location," advises

This is what a factory conversion candidate looks like, and could look like, with extensive renovation work. There are many such properties in the larger cities.

King White, a call center site selection consultant with real estate company Trammell Crow (Dallas, TX). "You would need more on-site amenities such as a cafeteria or gym in a warehouse conversion because these buildings are in more isolated industrial areas."

A prewar office or conversion will typically be in or near a downtown, and tend to be multi-story, to minimize the amount of costly land they take up, and have plenty of natural lighting. The structures are strong and attractive, with brick, stone or terra cotta facings, often with attractive outside detail, like gargoyles and trim. Prewar offices and conversions are also popular in Canada and Europe.

The voice/data systems and power to them tend to be very reliable and in plentiful supply; the telcos and electric companies started out from downtowns. The cables are usually laid in weather-and-traffic-proof and out-of-sight underground conduits rather than on ugly, vulnerable poles. Also, many landlords, seeing the Internet boom, have renovated older structures with fat pipes and quality wiring.

Prewar offices and conversions, such as Villanova Capital's Miquon, PA call center, located in an old paper mill just outside of Philadelphia are "cool." They have plenty of lighting, highly functional interiors and interesting design features, such as exposed supports. The call center has on-site parking plus a bikeway and its own electric suburban train station.

There are often excellent amenities, such as clubs, restaurants and shops nearby. There is no driving 15 to 20 minutes on a traffic-snarled cookie-cutter street only to find an overcrowded blaah franchise 'barfeteria' with snotty kids playing food fight accompanied by clueless preoccupied parents and five-years-out-of-date teenagers attempting to look "cool."

For these reasons — appearance, functional and amenities — such buildings are very popular with young people. If that is the labor force you want to tap, such as for an Internet multimedia help desk, you should consider a prewar conversion.

At the same time prewar buildings have little or no parking, except if it had been provided later on site or nearby, as most people in that era commuted to work on foot or mass transit. If many of your agents will come to work that way you avoid paying for on-site parking; if you have them driving in you need to arrange for it.

Many, but not all, prewar buildings have small floorplates. Also, depending on the building, they often have fat support columns, taking up room. Real estate consultant Susan Arledge, principal, Arledge/Power Real Estate Group (Dallas, TX), estimates they can soak up 25% to 30% of your space requirements.

Safety is an issue with prewar buildings because of where they are located, though this is becoming less of an issue as crime rates decline and as the neighborhoods where they are situated make their come back. Denver, CO's, LoDo, Portland, OR's northwest and New York City's

Silicon Alley are just three of the many booming worthwhile locales to consider. There are many others. Also, many cities have invested in excellent, frequent and well-used mass transit systems.

Companies who occupy such spaces will concede that they may have had to make design compromises and be much more careful in where they place their workstations and wiring than in postwar buildings. Yet their officials, such as John Mulherin, COO of Villanova Capital that moved into a renovated prewar former paper mill in Miquon, PA, just outside of Philadelphia, point out the location and building's advantages far outweigh the installation challenges. Villanova's center will eventually have more than 200 workstations there.

"Villanova Capital is about conserving your capital to make the right investments for your future," explains Mulherin. "The buildings fit our image and the kinds of employees we want to attract, who also think the same way. What better way to project that image than being in a restored building? The call center has access to that labor pool."

▶ Explaining Office Property Classifications

There are three classifications of office property: Class A, Class B and Class C. CB Richard Ellis's Global Information Standard Reference Manual defines them as follows.

These are taken from the Building Operators and Managers Association (BOMA):

Class A - The most prestigious buildings competing for premier office users with above average rental rates for the area along with high-quality standard finishes, state of the art systems, exceptional accessibility and a definite market presence.

Class B - Buildings competing for a wide range of users with rents in the average range for the area. Building finishes are fair to good for the area and the systems are adequate, but the building does not compete with Class A at the same price.

Class C - Buildings competing for tenants requiring functional space at rents below the average for the area.

Robert Marsh, senior vice president, CB Richard Ellis's call center solutions group (Phoenix, AZ), points out that buildings such as former supermarkets that had been classified as Class C can be renovated and upgraded to Class B or in some cases Class A, depending on the level of work.

"You can renovate and upgrade building classifications by making substantial improvements to the structure's interior and exterior," Marsh points out.

Consultants report that call centers rarely occupy Class A property because they lack sufficient parking and are too costly. Yet there may be some quality Class A space available at lower rates, depending on the location.

"Some Class A space can be good for call centers," King White, a call center site selection consultant with real estate company Trammell Crow (Dallas, TX) points out. "Depending on the city, they can be in active, busy locations with access to labor. You may find them in enterprise zones, which means you can get them at lower rates. But we've never seen call centers move into downtown Class A buildings."

The cost and supply advantages of Class C over Class B space is often outweighed by having less efficient HVAC systems, inadequate voice/data and power systems and parking. That said, if you're interested in particular Class B and Class C spaces, and you observe that they don't have sufficient room for parking, you may find the landlord willing to expand the lot if he or she has enough property nearby to do so.

"As companies expand, many of them are moving out of the Class Bs and Cs into newer buildings," explains White. "To fill this space, the landlords will try to accommodate new tenants. We've seen them expand their parking lots to ratios as high as 10:1."

▶ What to Look For When Examining Property

Before you sign on the bottom line and take the keys and/or signal to the bulldozers, make sure you have carefully examined the building, the property and the terms. The decision to locate a business is one of the most important managerial decisions you'll ever make; you'll be stuck with it. And, as with many business decisions, if your choice succeeds, no one will remember it, if it fails they'll make sure *you* remember it.

The best way to think about locating a call center is to think of what information you need about a prospective space when buying a home or renting or leasing an apartment. Realtors will advise you to have an idea beforehand of how much square footage, the number of rooms and floors and types of amenities (e.g. laundry room, outside deck) you want before going home hunting. The real estate Web sites, such as Realtor.com let you input that data and they will come back with houses or apartments that meet those specifications.

The bottom line with a home is people. How many people are there or will there be in your family? What are their activities? Does your family entertain others or are they solitary homebodies? Do they like to exercise? Do you have pets: a dog that needs a big back yard or a cat who could care less? Do you want room for a home office?

Also, what are your transportation needs? How many cars are there in your household? Is your preference a garage or is outside or on-street fine? Or will you be taking mass transit or walking or riding bicycles instead?

Here are a few of the key factors to go over when looking at real estate for a call center:

Access

Your call center depends on people, and for them to work for you they must get there. Where you open your call center, in a given labor market, determines how many of them will be able or will want to come to work at your building. The general rule is the lower the income and the hours the shorter the distance and time people are willing to travel to get there, and the less hassle they are willing to incur, according to the acceptable standards in that area. While consultants recommend limiting the commute time by car or mass transit to about 30 minutes, that may be longer in many areas and shorter in others.

Few people will drive 45 minutes to an hour for a $9 an hour job hawking titanium steak knives, unless that's the only job in the region. But, if they live in a larger city, like Baltimore, Boston, Chicago, Philadelphia, Montreal, New York, San Francisco, Seattle, Toronto or Washington, DC, which have excellent mass transit, they will ride the train or bus for that

Getting to work is not just by car. Growing numbers of cities in the US, Canada and worldwide are rediscovering mass transit and rebuilding, reintroducing and expanding their bus, rail and ferry systems. Many people now prefer riding, like on Portland, OR's popular MAX light rail seen here, to driving at just above walking speed on traffic-snarled roads.

period of time to such call centers.

That's because there is greater time endurance on mass transit than in driving, because somebody else is responsible for getting people there. From Staten Island to Manhattan I and many other commuters from the borough spend 90 to 100 minutes each way on a bus, ferry and bus or subway to reach our offices. If I had to drive for that amount of time I'd fall asleep at my desk, if not at the wheel.

This also means you have to determine *where* the bulk of your workers will be coming from and by what means. If they are mainly suburban spouses or your center is in a small city they will come by car and will want to stay in the suburbs or that city. Your call center will need to be in a location (almost always a suburb) with good road access and the property must have excellent parking. If they are college students, trendy young people or live in downtowns or older suburbs they may come by mass transit, or by bicycle, with some by car. Therefore your call center must be on a transit route, near a station or downtown.

If your call center serves the high-tech industry it should be in a pre-war conversion. Most young trendoids won't go downtown or come to your center just to work in a postwar 'bankers box'.

The only occasion where suburbanites will go to a call center or any other employer at or near a downtown is if the mass transit system is the only way to travel because of horrendous traffic jams and parking costs. The transit system must be attractive, convenient and enjoyable compared to driving.

Your supervisors and managers will endure longer more hassle-ridden commutes than your agents will. They can also stay in touch with what is happening at the call center on their cellphones (where permitted by law — many communities are now banning "mouthing and motoring") and laptops.

Andrew Shapiro, site selection consultant with Deloitte and Touche Fantus Consulting (New York, NY), recommends that you can turn this longer drive or ride to your advantage by locating one large call center and several satellite centers as much as two hours apart. The hub and spoke centers serving different labor markets.

"This way you can manage two centers with one team, instead of having two separate teams, provided they can commute acceptable distances to both sites," says Shapiro.

Competition

Call centers in the same area are like having two or more cats sharing the same house. Each is jealous of their territory.

If you are not bothered by other call centers being in the same labor market that you plan to enter, fine. You may even benefit from them. If your company has a great reputation with customers, clients and employees, pays well, you'll be able to pull other call centers' experienced and trained workers into your labor pool.

If the presence of other call centers troubles you investigate to see who is out there, whether they have the same function as yours and compete for the same labor pool and if they are in the same immediate area as where you plan to locate. A job handling inbound order taking for a catalog company requires quite different skillsets than one selling day-glo vinyl siding. However there is growing sales and service skills convergence occurring, as companies want every agent to provide both functions.

Therefore, you may or may not run the risk of a staffing war. Instead, you may want to locate your call center elsewhere in the same region, tapping into some but not all of the same workers as the other centers. Consultants advise that if you are the first center on a piece of property that you lock the doors on others by negotiating exclusivity arrangements or noncompete clauses in your lease.

Security

Whether in a downtown, suburb or small town your call center must be safe to get to and around or else you won't get people to work and stay. When poking around sites look for the obvious: empty beer and liquor bottles, graffiti and litter both inanimate and two-legged, and buildings with gates and grates, daytime and nighttime. If employees will be coming by mass transit or using a parking garage, check them out. Look at nearby buildings. Abandoned, decrepit structures, chop shops, seldom-open evangelical church storefronts, liquor stores and pawn shops are, ahem, 'dead' giveways of trouble, as are falling-apart houses, apartments and housing projects.

Don't think these conditions just exist "in the big city." Many formerly pristine postwar suburbs are just as dangerous as their downtown counterparts. Small cities, including their outskirts can be just as rundown, decrepit and unsafe.

Use your street instincts. If you don't feel safe, chances are your workers won't either. On the other hand, be careful not to let class and racial preferences distort your thinking. What may be anathema to you as a middle to upper-class professional, like riding the bus or subway or being around people of a different socioeconomic class, skin color or first language may not bother the people coming to work for your call center. They may *be* of that class, color and/or ethnicity.

Before you decide get some objective information. Ask around, by going into shops and restaurants and talking with the owners. Avoid the chains because they are usually run by kids with no managerial or life experience or authority. They'll also be too scared to talk because they'll be worried about what will happen to them if "the big cheese" finds out.

Check with the police. They'll tell you the deal. They don't want any more accidental "customers." A good local newspaper editor will be equally as honest. Then, armed with this information, have a chat with your economic development agency or real estate/site selection consultants and discuss what you found. If you don't get any good answers, or alternative sites in the same labor market, look elsewhere.

Yet even if you find a building in a "good area" don't assume the building or development is safe. Check the doors, accessways and parking lots, day and night and on weekends. See who's hanging around.

If the building has security and you require it for your call center watch the security guards. Before leasing space check out the company that has the security contract. Do similar due diligence if you decide to have guards at your reception desk. Some firms and 'rent-a-cops' are good, with alert, well-dressed-and-groomed officers insisting that workers sign in and show passes, and who escort employees to their cars, others are good only for a good night's sleep. I've worked as a security guard in offices, apartments, factories, warehouses, construction sites and parks. I did security work for the 1978 Commonwealth Games in Edmonton, Alberta, with my radio connected to the Mounties and I've seen both kinds. You get what you pay for.

Is the Building Healthy?

When looking at leasing space in an existing building, or having it built for you, make sure it is designed healthy. Many structures are about as safe as working in a closed garage with your car's engine running.

Business Week reported June 5, 2000, in a cover story "Is Your Office Killing You?" that today's efficient, insulated zipped-tight buildings may be drawing and keeping in poisons like carbon monoxide from vehicles and smokers, volatile organic compounds in furnishings, fumes from exterminators, bathroom molds and ozone from printers and fax machines. These chemicals create an aerial toxic stew that can cause ailments from headaches, dizziness and nausea to nervous and respiratory damage. Other consequences, such as short-term memory loss and irritation, could affect how agents deal with customers.

The magazine said that 20% to 30% of the office workforce could be affected from these afflictions. Doctors report that sick-building-related symptoms have climbed by 40% in the past decade. Lawsuits are also increasing. Bad air is also damaging equipment. The article cited reports from Telcordia Technologies scientists that say indoor, polluted air creates film that coats circuit boards and phone switches, causing costly failures. Fixing faulty wires alone costs telcos more than $100 million over the past 10 years.

One of the culprits is not enough outside air. American Society of Heating, Refrigerating and Air Conditioning Engineers (ASHRAE) standards recommends that you provide 20 cubic feet of outside air per person. The *Business Week* article on sick buildings reports that some buildings suck in only 5 cubic feet; just enough to keep humans living. According to the story the Environmental Protection Agency ranks bad air as one of the top five environmental risks. While there are no federal or state air quality standards for offices, expect to see them soon; the ASHRAE standard is voluntary.

Another bad air culprit are fresh air vents located, for some perverse reason, over loading docks and parking garages. There is an appropriate and obvious penalty for the idiots who drew *those* in. Still another trouble source is buildings that allow smokers to puff away at entrances; the toxic smog gets sucked in through the doors into the offices.

If you plan to lease space in a building where you share the air, be aware that other tenants could cause problems for you. Examples of harmful practices include locating copy machines next to vents, not cleaning bathrooms for mold and permitting or not cracking down on people smoking in their offices. Smoking is also a major fire hazard that could kill or injure your employees and visitors. One lit butt into a trashcan and your call center goes up in smoke. When you move in make sure *you* don't undertake harmful practices that could injure others.

There are clear benefits from healthy buildings; cleaning the air could save businesses $58 billion and improve employee productivity by $200 billion annually. The *Business Week* article cites Lawrence Berkeley National Laboratory researchers William Fisk and Arthur Rosenfeld who said the benefits are eight to 17 times greater than the costs.

To ensure your prospective building is clean, check for the obvious, like the air changes, vents and smoking practices. Track down the previous tenant and see if there were any problems (with this and with any other matter, like security). Raise the concern with the landlord/developer and ask them to give you records of past air quality complaints. *Business Week* recommends that you bring in your own indoor air specialist to measure air quality. If there are differences that cannot be resolved, go elsewhere. There's always another building.

Is the Building in Good Shape?

Just like buying a house or condominium you need to find out if the building and its upkeep are sound. You should bring in your architectural and trades experts to inspect the structure, HVAC, electrical and plumbing to see if they are in sound shape and if they comply with the building codes and with laws such as the Americans with Disabilities Act. Be prepared to add more HVAC capacity.

Don't overlook the small things, like the condition of the common areas, the entrances, foyers, elevators and stairwells. Sloppy painting and repairs, garbage and butts not being picked up and elevators frequently out of service are signs of trouble. Talk to the other tenants and see what they say.

Voice/Data/Power Reliability

"Things" like earthquakes, fires, hurricanes, ice storms and volcanic eruptions happen that could cripple your call center. Both power and voice/data lines can be ripped apart by idiots on backhoes.

Even on bright sunny days your systems can go bye-bye. High electrical demand that creates computer-killing voltage sags while aging phone switches and lines can fail.

The best backup system is having your calls and contacts automatically switched to another call center. If the weather is bad enough to knock out telephone and power lines then it will also sever roads and rail lines that will prevent your agents from coming to work.

But switching to another call center is not always possible or desirable. Your call center may perform *truly* mission-critical work such as handling 911 calls. It may be the only one you have and you need the revenue and

When you hear the words "backup generator" you probably think of big, hulking diesel engines that look like they were stripped from railroad locomotives. While many are that large there are also smaller compact and noise-baffling enclosed units like this Kohler set that has a twin cylinder 15 hp engine that runs on LP or natural gas.

want to service customers who may not understand or care *why* they can't get through; it's not *their* problem. Or your call center taps into an important area-specific skillset, e.g., French-speakers. Or you may not have the capacity at your other call centers.

You can arrange for disaster recovery "hot sites": pre-arranged temporary emergency call centers but they may be miles from your stricken center, causing transportation hassles for your staff. You can outsource your calls and contacts to live agent or IVR/Web service bureaus, but this requires arranging, scripting and training beforehand. If maintaining a consistent high service level is vital to you, outsourcing will not work. There is no way a service bureau agent can be trained to handle, on short notice, highly complex, knowledge-laced calls and contacts.

There are also mobile on-site recovery — temporary cellular or satellite transmitter/receiver trucks and services — you can contract with to provide emergency voice/data connections into your call center. Yet they take time to appear and go live.

While all of these techniques should be looked at and employed, you should also examine to see if the prospective property has or can provide backup power and voice/data. This is accomplished by two means: multiple feeds, so if one dies the other lives, and on-site. Of the two systems: power and voice/data, the former is less reliable than the latter. While they could go out together, there is a good chance that they will not. You hear more instances of power than phone being down. Electric power transmission between communities depends on high voltage overhead lines supported on exposed poles and towers; low-voltage voice/data communications rely on buried or easily accessible (and less risky to fix) copper or fiber cable, microwave or satellite transmission. Therefore, you may have a dial tone at your call center but you will need a candle or flashlight to find a phone.

Electric power is also essential to keep your phone lines open. While the local telco's CO, which usually has power backups, provide the juice for PSTN lines, ISDN and T-1 circuits must be powered at your end, the same with PBX.

"The question that you have to ask yourself is how long and how often can you stand for your power to be down," says Ted Fredericks, Mohr Partners' project management director. "If you have an outbound call center and either your program or your clients find interruptions acceptable, then you can probably tolerate outages. If you have an inbound center, robust power is more critical."

If your call center needs robust power then you may have to consider property that has multiple electrical feeds and voice/data trunks that loop through more than one central office. To reduce risks further these connections should be underground, free from weather disturbances.

If multiple power ties are not available then you should see if the building can accommodate UPS and backup generators, preferably together. UPS systems usually have a 30-minute lifespan, which is more than adequate for most outages that usually last only a few minutes. If the power loss is longer than that they allow your files to be transferred to another call center, outsourcer or disaster recovery site before you shut down your call center.

A backup generator, which is more expensive than UPS systems, can last for as long as you have or can get your gloved hands on fuel. Many of them are very small, quiet, yet powerful, often packaged in noise-baffling enclosures. UPS suppliers recommend that you hook in an on-line (where power is routed through the batteries at all times) UPS bank to the generator to smooth out voltage kinks when the engines kick in.

Another reason why you should consider installing UPS and generators is because US power supplies are reportedly becoming erratic; multiple feeds won't help you if there's not enough electricity in the wires. Voltage sags caused by insufficient power can play havoc with your computer and phone systems. According to an August 2, 2000 *USA Today* article, a growing power-hungry economy is being increasingly restrained by a limited and aging generating and transmission capacity.

Yet community opposition to power stations has halted new capacity from coming on stream. Who wants a chimney in their back yard, even if it is attached to a quiet, efficient and clean combined-cycle gas turbine? Even windmills, which are clean, seemingly benign power source, have been attacked by some groups because they despoil the scenery.

Already some major e-commerce firms have gone to DIY power. *InternetWeek* reported June 26, 2000 that Exodus Communications, which hosts popular sites such as eBay and Yahoo at its 20 data centers has installed generators to handle short-and-long term outages. "The trend is for more frequent outages, and they will continue for some time," the magazine quoted Mark Wilhelm, vice president of the Electric Power Research Institute, a utility research firm.

Expansion and contraction rights

When you look at the contract documents, make sure you have enough wiggle room for expansion and contraction. Most leases are 5 to 7 years in length.

Ensure before agreeing that there is space and land available on site should you need to grow, *if* your labor market projections show you will have the people to make/take contacts at the additional workstations. It is almost always easier, definitely is less costly, and there is less hassle incurred to expand on-site than going through the ordeal of finding another property and opening another call center, though it may give disaster recovery protection and access to new workers.

Consultants recommend that you insist on a *right of first refusal* on adjacent space, where if the landlord makes it available then the landlord is obliged to ask you first. They also advise that you examine having and agreeing to a *must take* in the lease where you pay rent on a certain amount of additional space within a year or so after you sign the initial lease.

"If you are not sure when negotiating and signing what your space needs will be then you might want the right to first refusal," advises Susan Arledge. "If you know that you are going to need the space then a 'must take' might be a better deal."

Because call centers do close (Chapter Ten), you need to prepare for the

---

How Much Downtime Costs Your Center

This worksheet determines the estimated dollar savings that a UPS can provide your company. simply fill in the information to calculate your cost of downtime for one hour.

1. Number of critical loads
2. Number of employees using critical loads
3. Employees average hourly earnings
4. Estimated cost of lost business per hour of downtime ($1,000, $5,000 $10,000...)
5. Cost of service calls per hour (average cost is $100 per hour)
6. Cost of replacing hardware (if applicable)
7. Cost of reinstalling software (if applicable)
8. Cost of recreating data (if applicable)
9. Lost employee time (lines 2 x 3)
10. Lost business (line 4)
11. Service (line 5)
12. Replaced hardware and software (lines 6 + 7)
13. Recreating data (line 8)
14. Estimated total cost per hour of downtime

Backup power isn't inexpensive but neither is having your call center down. This worksheet from Exide Electronics (Raleigh, NC) helps you decide whether a UPS system is justified.

inevitable in your lease. This can take the form of landlord-approved subleasing rights, lease cancellation and termination options. You also need to find out if the building and property is desirable to other future tenants, by doing research into the local market, should you need to move out.

While these methods usually have penalty clauses, Arledge says paying them is "certainly cheaper than paying rent for space you don't need."

▶ Compromises and Options

Unfortunately, you may be under severe time restraints to get a new call center set up. You have to hire and train staff (see Chapter 9). In addition to finding employees and worrying about turnover and costs, you are probably facing time constraints to be up and running quickly. And then you have to buy and install the equipment needed to run the center (see Chapter 6).

This may not leave you with much opportunity to design, approve and prepare the ideal workplace. You might need that corporate-looking office but your site analysis shows that the best places to locate your center, which you must have up and running in two months, lacks enough desirable conventional space. Or that you had found locales with plenty of great, ready-to-move-in space but the labor supply, skillsets and costs do not meet your needs.

In both cases compromises have to be made on property and design. If the two or three candidate locations rank close together on labor, choose the one with the best building option. However, you should *never* choose better building availability over quality labor supply.

Think of this like being told you're being transferred to a new office or you change jobs out of commuting distance from your existing location, and you only have X amount of time to pick, remodel and set up in your new home. What would *you* prefer, a slightly older rundown house, say a 1950s vintage ranch a 40-minute drive or 60-minute bus and/or train ride away from your office but in a safe neighborhood with good schools? Or a fantastic mini-mansion that is 10 to 15 minutes away but walled off with gates and pointed fences, with window grates on the buildings lining the access roads?

"You can always find property," says Bob Mohr. "But is it where your desired labor force is and when you need it?"

If you are facing the time/space crunch and want to watch your wallet here are some of the options you should examine:

Conversions, even for high-visibility corporate call centers. Architects and developers are not alchemists but they do so much with old stores and factories that they can make you think you're inside a Class A, even though it had been a Caldor;

Multifloor space. Such occupancies may not be ideal for managing a call center, because you have to split up your operations, but they do give you greater choice in conventional offices. You may also find benefits in having your administrative and training functions and agents working for different and sometimes competing clients on separate floors;

Property near mass transit terminals. You may find good buildings and building sites near major bus and train stations and ferry terminals. Mass transit brings in people. The new and renovated older systems are safe, fast and accessible. Because uses like call centers also generate transit ridership, cutting down on high-polluting car use, transit agencies and local governments may be quite willing to work with you. This alternative is limited, however, to those locations and sites that have good and popular mass transit access by your workforce. There may be zoning and traffic issues to cope with;

Staged occupancy. With this method you can add staff incrementally rather than opening an entire center at once. If you have a 500-seat center, for example, you can add 100-seat sections over a period of time instead of having to commit to hiring a full staff by the time you open the center or resort to overtime or premiums;

The tradeoff with staged occupancy is that you get more time to build and staff your center. But also, it is unattractive if your facility is not completely built out and you have clients and management going through it;

A variation on staged occupancy for build-to-suit projects is *phasing*. Applicable in build-to-suits and renovations through lease options such as must-take and right-of-first refusal, it lets you test the labor market with a smaller sized center. You can then expand later;

Hoteling. This is the arranging for temporary facilities for certain activities like training for agents and taking and making calls. Some countries' economic development agencies and telcos, such as in Belgium, France, Ireland and Northern Ireland offer this option to allow you to test that market and for disaster recovery;

Co-location. This is where you combine your call center and other functions, such as administration, accounting, data processing and distribution. Co-locating different business and office functions with your call center can save you money through economies of scale, and they give you greater leverage with landlords and your community.

Xerox at its Webster, NY call center successfully uses co-location; the building is shared with engineers who can directly listen in and learn from calls. Other firms such as phone switch maker Mitel also discovered this co-location advantage when it moved its US help desks back into its Kanata, ON Canada headquarters a few years ago.

If your call center is in the same building as your marketing and product development offices, you create potential synergies among these departments. You also show a physical career path for your agents that helps attract staff and improve retention.

A contributing factor to this trend is companies installing and integrating powerful new customer relationship management (CRM) software and adopting business processes to efficiently use them to permit anyone within a firm to access and update information about a customer or user. This enables easy interdepartmental communication. Before CRM software came along, companies had to rely on separate, unconnected, incompatible and often proprietary data systems.

But co-location requires a considerable amount of time-gobbling buy-in among different departments. It requires that the center and the other departments draw their labor from the same commutershed, which isn't always possible. A location that attracts administrative and managerial personnel may not be able to pull in sufficient, affordable call center agents. A building that works for a call center may not work for other types of operations.

Roger Kingsland, principal with architects Kingsland Scott Bauer Associates (Pittsburgh, PA), sees pros and cons of co-locating, especially for high-tech and information-heavy financial services firms. He points out that co-location makes efficient use of expensive high-volume high-powered networks and computer resources among many users.

"What you must watch out for is your labor markets," advises Kingsland. "A location that may work out fine for accounting or data processing personnel may not draw enough qualified call center agents at your price point and vice-versa. You have to ensure you get the right people to make them work."

Mohr argues that co-locating is unnecessary for most companies. He says that when a firm's call center exceeds 50 seats, it becomes difficult to find space in the same facility for different functions, and he doesn't believe that outsourcers have to be physically close to their clients to work with them successfully.

"You can manage and keep in touch with your senior management or your clients by not being in the same building or vicinity," says Mohr.

CHAPTER NINE

Staffing, Training and Retention

You now have your dream call center. The lights work, the switch is connected, the dust is off the workstations, the contractors' empty cola cans are out of the hallways, the paint is dried and the AC is cranked up, while the asphalt in the parking lot has a never-to-be-seen again deep black, if odiferous, hue. You've got a rent-a-sign out front flashing "Good Jobs! Good Pay! Excellent Benefits! Child Care! Jacuzzi! Just Come On In! Yes, open it and they will come. The "Field of Dreams" in the call center league.

Well it doesn't quite work that way. You must have your staffing and training worked out and ideally the people lined up *before* you open a new center. Finding and retaining the right people to provide service and sales is the most critical and challenging aspect of setting up a successful call center. All the labor-saving technologies in the world won't help you without qualified, friendly, intelligent, hard working and reliable agents, managed by competent and dedicated supervisors.

If you want to keep your call center viable for as long as possible at the new location, which caused you to pull so many hairs out while researching, selecting and outfitting that the baldness cures and toupee telemarketers are calling and e-mailing you — your attention should be focused on selecting and keeping the right agents. Which is what this chapter will explore along with training strategies.

You're not the only one looking for people to work in a call center. The challenge is making your company stand out from the rest. The best way to do that is to make your firm worth working for.

▶ Staffing

This is the best and the worst of times to be running a call center. Never before has there been so much demand for people-delivered phone and online-based service and sales, with the growth of e-commerce and the need for information and service instantly, wherever the customer is. And never before has the image of call centers been so great.

Once upon a time, when someone thought of call center agents, what came to mind are the rattle-jawed telemarketers calling at dinner time and the TV ads for miracle-grow hair enhancers with the voice (not comb)-over "operators standing by." When I heard that I used to think 'you mean they don't have chairs?' These soundbites are now being replaced by TV ads, such as, for insurance that show friendly, smiling, helpful agents talking to customers. One of the classiest ads is for the OnStar system showing Batman pressing the OnStar button in his Batmobile and the voice of a friendly agent comes on the line, advising where to fill up on jet fuel or an alternative route to trap Joker...

This growing elan can only help to find people to work in your call center. Call centers already possess certain key advantages over other service center employment, such as gas stations/minimarts, restaurants, retail and warehousing/distribution that helps to lead many recruits to your door. Your pay is usually higher, there is less physical labor, security is greater, the environment is office-like and professional and employees get to work on computers, including Internet/e-mail. Depending on the company, you may also offer flexible full time and part-time hours.

This attractiveness will also grow as call center functions become more professional, where the agents become service and sales consultants, empowered to solve problems and make deals. The basic drudgery calls are being increasingly handled by lower-cost customer self-service IVR and Web site self-help sections and automated e-mail systems.

"Even in a tight labor market, call centers will always draw people from other service jobs," observes King White, vice president, of real estate firm Trammell Crow (Dallas, TX)'s site selection consulting group.

This means you can tap into a greater labor pool than other industries, beyond what the official unemployment rates tell you. This includes college students, new labor force entrants, at-home spouses and retirees and people who have been out of work for a long time. Those potential agents with mobility and, depending on the job requirements, sense impairments can and do make great agents. Someone who cannot see can make and take calls; there is now text-to-speech software to help them. A person who cannot hear can communicate with text chat. There are often government grants to assist hiring and placing such workers. And it makes your firm look good.

LiveBridge, a Portland, OR based outsourcer, has worked with Oregon agencies and non-profit organizations to hire the long-term unemployed. A driving force behind this company's efforts has been the experience of its co-founder, Patrick Hanlin. When he was younger, his father, a sportscaster, lost the use of his legs following an accident; in his day announcers had to climb on ladders into boxes overlooking the stands to give the play-by-play.

"After the accident people would talk to him about their day-to-day experiences in the outside world but this hurt him because he had very little of his own," recalls Hanlin. "Today our disabled employees have the same kinds of experiences as their co-workers. They can talk about the sales they've made and the customers they've dealt with. They have the life that disabled people a generation ago did not."

On the other hand, call center work, though becoming less humdrum is still high-pressure and not everyone's idea of a career. Dealing directly with the public often causes stress while the compensating pay and benefits are still low, especially when compared with employment in manufacturing, programming, transportation and construction trades. There is not the direct professional and personal satisfaction from working in a call center that exists in nursing and teaching. Also, the hours are often irregular and inadequate to make a living as a call center agent, and it plays havoc with personal lives. Consequently turnover, which costs anywhere from 50% to 100% of the agents' wage in the form of hiring and training expenses, tends to run upwards of 25%+ per annum, depending on the local labor market.

Yet, just because the economy is booming and labor is scarce that doesn't mean you have to accept and keep every warm body that walks in the door. Your agents are your company's voice: what they say and do on the phone or through the Internet and on e-mail reflects on you, both on the positive and negative sides. You need agents who can accomplish the tasks well, especially communicating with customers, who will show up and leave on time and who can work with others.

Designing Your Ideal Agent

Before you begin recruiting your workers you should have a set of parameters or a *profile* of what makes a good agent for each position type. You then use the profiles to attract, screen and select the employees that will work best in your call center. Ideally you should have the profiles created *before* you begin your site selection process so that you can find out if the labor force in the targeted locations match them, and in the quantity and quality needed for the life of your call center.

There are some common characteristics that call center agents must have and should be in your profiles. These include communication and customer service skills, judgment, and stress tolerance. Your profiles should also incorporate personality attributes and backgrounds so that you will have employees that have the right aptitudes and attitudes for your center.

These characteristics and skills can vary from center to center. If your agents sell products and service, inbound and outbound then you should state that applicants must have the ability to offer and close sales. If they need to perform detailed calculations, your profile must stipulate math ability. If your center sells insurance, real estate and securities, your agents will need licensing and certification. If they will handle mainly customer service, the applicants should have listening, understanding, problem identification and resolution skills.

If you're running a help desk, your agents should be acquainted with computers *and* must empathize with those who have the simplest of problems. Technical wizardry is not enough. Many computer-smart people have little patience for those who are not on their exalted knowledge level. My wife, a mainframer turned Web programmer is one of those happy exceptions. On top of her busy workload she often handles customer service inquiries that come through the Webmaster's e-mail address on her firm's Web site.

Also, if you serve domestic or international non-English speaking customers from your call center your profiles should include other language skills or create a separate profile for non-English speaking agents. In developing the profiles you need to look at whether your customers prefer native speakers and in which languages. If so, you need to decide if the market is large enough to warrant serving them with native-speaking agents, or if you can get by with learned language-speaking agents or whether you should outsource some or all of your language needs to a translation service, such as Language Line.

These profiles can vary by call center type and function. If your center makes outbound cold-calls the attributes you need for your agents — aggressive, persistent, goal-oriented — are different than the passive, patient, and problem solving attributes necessary for customer service and help desk. Yet, if your customer service/help desk involves cross-selling and up-selling — which they should as part of the customer relationship management (CRM) trend — the profiles should include some selling attributes and skills.

Your profiles are also molded by your corporate culture. Dave Burdette, business development consultant with Development Dimensions International (DDI) (Bridgeville, PA), uses the example of two call centers that provides customer service in competition with each other. One has a by-the-book process with a well-defined process and procedure, including escalation to succeeding levels while the other has a less rigid system by which agents are empowered to make their own decisions to solve problems accurately without escalation.

"The first call center would look for employees who can understand and follow instructions while the second would look for employees who are creative and problem solvers," explains Burdette. "Yet they would have the same type of job serving the same type of customer."

Kathyrn Jackson, associate with Response Design Corporation (RDC), (Ocean City, NJ) and Rosanne D'Ausilio, president, Human Technologies (Carmel, NY), also recommend you develop employee attitude profiles. These are based on your center's best practices and those of other call centers. Such benchmarks help you decide what characteristics you list in your help wanted advertisements and job descriptions and refines applicant qualification and screening.

Make sure that when you use profiling that your standards are high but realistic, so that you don't unnecessarily limit your labor pool, and exclude good applicants. You don't want to leave seats vacant which lowers your center's performance levels when you don't have to.

One common, simple and sometimes misused staffing profile element and screening device is having a college degree. While it is nice to have the intelligence and prestige of college grads on your phones and keyboards you may also find the applicants that have this education level are not your best performers. They may view a job with your center as a temporary position and leave as soon as they accept an offer from an employer in their studied field.

"For example, one best practice company we worked with found no correlation between success and significant prior customer service, but some correlation between success and a stable work history," reports RDC's Jackson. "They also found some correlation between success and college experience, but an inverse relationship between success and having a college degree. Therefore, it believes that the profile of an agent most likely to be successful is one with some college, between six months and one year of customer service experience and a stable work history. "

Also, see that you're not excluding individuals that may not fit one set of agent positions but who are quite suitable in others. There are different tasks in call centers requiring their own skillsets, aptitudes and personality types.

"A detail-oriented person may not work best in general customer service," Burdette points out. "However they may be ideal in an upper level desk where they're solving more complex problems."

Remember, profiles are not living human beings but your applicants are. Use profiles as a model of what your agents should be like and measure your applicants against them. However, when you interview these prospective agents, look at them as people, with bright and dull spots, to see if you can see them working for and with you.

"You can interview someone that has all the skills and qualifications, who fits the model, but if they show no life, no spark, no enthusiasm for the position, then what good are they to your center and to your customers?" D'Ausilio points out.

Screening for the Right Agents

Before you get to the in-person interview you must first attract and sift through a slew of applicants. Therefore, you should have effective qualifying, screening and assessment methods and systems in place to sift them out for aptitude, skills, and interest. The methodologies and tools you employ can introduce the position, describe the work and sort out applicants' skills and aptitudes before they ever sit down with you or your supervisors. At each step they let the applicants deselect. This saves them and you from saying no to each other's face.

Most screening methods today are highly automated; they use a combination of inbound and outbound IVR, the Web and computers. They can screen for voice and for online contact handling. These tools work closely with your agent profile: you use the profile's components to devise questions and score answers.

The qualifying tools usually work the same way: an interested employee calls up or through an on-line-contact reaches a call center and is asked a series of questions that they respond to. The applicant is given a job description and is asked to see if they have the basic qualifications and interest. If the answers meet your criteria the applicant is asked what dates and times they would like to come in. These tools are open 24/7, meaning people can apply at any time.

Rosanne D'Ausilio is a big fan of qualifying tools. She says they can significantly cut down on time and costly human intervention. Because they are uniformly programmed, the responses are consistent, allowing for fair efficient evaluation.

"The great thing about these tools is that if I'm a call center manager I can have an ad placed in the Sunday papers and Monday morning I could have a list of pre-screened applicants and appointments," says D'Ausilio. "That's opposed to the old system where I get resumes arriving, or people stopping by at random to fill out applications, sorting them out, calling the ones I liked, then playing voice mail tag and that's before these individuals come in for an interview. That's in between doing my job managing a call center."

The qualifying tool sets the applicant for the next stage, which should be a phone assessment. This is conducted either by outbound or inbound at an appointed time. Allocate 15-20 minutes for each recruit.

Phone assessing is the single most vital tool in call center recruiting. You can eliminate a lot of applicants — separating the wheat from the chaff — with this method. Unless your agents are doing nothing but e-mail, which is extremely rare in call centers, your applicants will need to know how to respond by phone.

"If a person cannot conduct a phone interview successfully, they are unsuited for the job," RDC's Jackson points out.

In your assessment you should look for characteristics such as proper enunciation, grammar, timing of responses, organization of responses, *especially* if those agents are going to handle online communication. D'Ausilio advises that you engage the applicant in a casual conversation and get them comfortable, then ask important questions such as "how do you handle stress" and hear how they respond.

"When someone calls a call center in most cases it isn't to say 'thanks for doing a wonderful job'," she points out. "You need to know if the applicants can take the complaints and the problems that customers present."

Once they've shown their phone skills, you then call them in for screening, although there are some highly detailed phone assessment systems that can combine that function. You conduct screening either through written tests and/or with new, sophisticated computer-based call center simulators. Recruits sit down in cubicles, are given sample role-playing situations, and are gauged on how well and quickly they responded. The process takes 30-45 minutes.

The screening usually tests potential agents in three areas: computer skills, math and voice. The computer skills identify people who are able to navigate using the keyboard and mouse. The system will give a simple math test for addition, subtraction, multiplication and division.

With the voice test the applicant will receive a sample call from customers with a question and respond to the question. In addition to assessing problem-solving skills, this will help assess the agent's ability to use proper grammar, enunciation, and quality service skills such as empathy.

You can also screen people for e-mail/Web handling. You set up a terminal, transmit the types of e-mail questions you get to the applicants and have them reply; the response doesn't leave your building. With this method you gauge not only how they responded but how quickly and accurately, like a traditional typing test.

When seeking qualifying and screening tools, Jackson advises that you see if they are customizable and if so, be prepared to spend additional money. The packaged scenarios, questions, answers and scoring may not fit your business. If possible have your management team test them. This goes back to the corporate culture issue; the assumptions that went into the system's designs may not be shared by your company.

"If the vendor can't customize the scenario or range of answers, at least ask if they can customize the scoring to reflect the most relevant answers to your call center," suggests Jackson.

Interviews and References

Those that pass the screening and assessment are usually given a conditional offer. It is then that you interview the applicants. It is at this stage that you must discover what kind of people they are.

"What the manager should do when they see the applicant is find out about their attitude," advises D'Ausilio. "See what that applicant's hobbies are and what are their likes/dislikes. How alive they are."

RDC's Jackson recommends having interviewers ask questions that lead to an understanding of how well the potential agents line up with the profile. Interviewers ask questions around real situations and look for actions the applicant took and the results of such actions.

"An example of this sort of question may be 'Have you ever handled an irate customer? And, if so, describe the situation and how you handled it,'" she says.

Jackson also advises that you give leading applicants a chance to sit down with experienced agents to get the feel of being on the job. If your firm does not allow this because you're working with confidential customer material see if you could permit your potential agents to watch interviews of experienced agents and client and resource specialists and then talk to them about what their job will entail.

She urges that you give them a picture of their long-term future with the company. The first interview should include a discussion about what the potential agent wants to do now and in the future. It should also include the commitment the center expects from the agent.

"All best practice managers we studied demanded a commitment of the potential agent from Day One that he or she would stay on the job for (usually) 18 months before he or she would be eligible to move into other areas of the company," reports Jackson. "One manager was so philosophical about it that she took to introducing applicants to the managers of other areas of the company. She would say: 'This is Joe, he wants to be in your department in three years.'"

In devising your screening program it is critical that you communicate what your center does and your agent profiles to your senior corporate HR department and the college/government employment offices and staffing agencies you choose to work with. This way they can deliver the applicants you need.

We all know and gulp when we get to that line on a job application that says: "Please list your references." Immediately we think of those people who will say nice things about us, and hope they do. If we're really smart we'll contact them ahead of time and prep them.

And that's the point. For that reason Rosanne D'Ausilio argues references are meaningless. She also points outs that work-related ones can be difficult to find as it is rare for people, especially managers and their supervisors to be in any one job in any field for a long period of time.

"Be realistic," she says. "Is your applicant going to give a bad reference?"

RDC's Jackson points out, for legal reasons, corporate HR departments tend to give nothing more than confirming that the applicant had worked there, and at the position, and the length of time that they stated on their application. However, if applicants give former co-workers and friends as references you can often gain additional insights on how that applicant worked if you ask the right questions.

"You have to pay close attention and ask behavioral questions to ensure that the reference is giving valid examples of the applicant's work behavior," says Jackson.

Call centers rely on feedback to monitor and improve performance. That also goes for staffing and recruiting. Once you've selected and trained your agents and they've proven out in your call center, say 60 to 90 days after hiring, you may

Job fairs are an excellent means to recruit agents; Willow CSN's booth is seeking independent agent contractors for its service. They are also an invaluable tool to gauge the labor supply in a candidate location.

want to survey them on what they thought of the process.

"The value for you is seeing how the job fits the description you had given, the skills you tested to and the profile you've developed," explains Jackson.

Recruiting Channels

There are four main channels for recruiting agents, *word of mouth, advertisements, job fairs* and *contract staffing.* *Word of mouth* is just that: employees telling family, friends and acquaintances how great or terrible your place is to work. *Advertisements* include newspaper display and classifieds, job board and Web site postings, on your site or on others. *Job fairs* are events, either sponsored by you or by a college or a local economic development agency (EDA) to draw in potential workers to ask questions, fill out applications and be screened and tested. *Contract staffing* is outsourcing your agent staffing to a staffing agency that handles all recruiting and training for your call centers; these individuals are their employees under your management.

If you are setting up a call center in a new location, your EDA is probably the best source of assistance; they want your call center to provide jobs to local residents and the good ones will do what they can to help you. They know what channels people use in that community to find employment. They have links to all of the local colleges and staffing agencies and social services organizations. They will also arrange for call center training.

You can also use these recruiting methods to test the local labor market, prior to making a final decision on a location. You can do this semi-covertly by placing a blind ad in a local paper, drop a hint to local officials, who will spread it like wildfire to the respective media outlets that you are looking to expand there, but no decisions have been made. Or you can be open by holding a job fair. Even advertising it will flap the word of mouth network.

For example, Stream International (Canton, MA) tested the waters by sending out a release on June 8, 2000 stating that it was sponsoring, what it billed as an "Informational Open House," in Belleville, ON, Canada to be held the following week. The release also featured quotes from the city's mayor, Ross McDougall.

"We are confident that the City of Belleville and the entire Quinte region can provide the labour force that Stream International requires," Mayor McDougall continued. "It is essential that all persons with either a customer service or technology background who are interested in an exciting career with a world-class high tech company express their interest at the Open House or directly to Stream using the Internet or by mail. We strongly encourage residents within the Quinte region to step forward, not only to demonstrate their interest in employment with Stream International, but also to demonstrate that this region is capable of providing the labour component so essential to the success of this company in the City of Belleville."

The "open house" worked. Stream sent out another press release July 27 announcing that it had picked Belleville. Over 3,000 people submitted job applications at the open house; the resumes the outsourcer saw revealed a "solid pool of people" with customer service skills and with technical certifications. Stream also received a strong commitment from the local colleges to work closely with them in the future to provide career opportunities to their graduates.

"We were extremely pleased with the level of interest shown by the Belleville community and by the strong technology expertise of those that submitted applications at our job fair in June," said Larry Schumer, Stream's Worldwide Senior Vice President of Human Resources. "We expect to be able to hire a large portion of our senior site management ranks from the local community for various finance, information technology and human resources positions. In addition to a large talented pool of customer service candidates, we are excited to have such a great number of MCP and MCSE technically certified and Internet skilled people apply for higher level technical support positions at Stream."

Word of mouth is the most effective of all recruiting methods. They make the others happen; they will prompt potential agents and supervisors to go to the job fairs, read the wants ads and scan the Web sites or go to a staffing agency.

It is also word of mouth that is will make or break your call center when it comes to agent retention once it goes live, and govern its potential to expand. That's because word of mouth has long proven as one of the most effective recruiting means. According to DDI's Burdette about 39% of all employment is with this technique. Firms (including CMP Media) have recruiting and retention bonuses.

"One of the prime target call center employment markets are young people," he explains. "They are very social and they frequently network. Those that have good experiences with an employer will quickly tell their friends."

This ties back into developing and implementing agent profiles. If you hire based on them, these agents will recommend your firm to friends and family who will likely fit them.

"Recruiters can prove recommendations (e.g. family, friends, next-door neighbors) from agents make the best potential agents," RDC's Jackson points out. "These referrals seem to understand a company's culture and expectations from the beginning."

If word of mouth is going to work then you must have a call center and a firm worth working for. If you followed the advice in the previous eight chapters and followed up with the consultants you will have done much of that already, by providing an excellent facility and work environment in a convenient location. But also, your company must manage people correctly, by empowering them and treating them decently and fairly, and compensating them likewise. It should also have a positive image with its customers, delivering quality products and service.

Nobody likes working for a terrible firm, *especially* agents. They're the ones that deal firsthand with the angry customers who call up and send e-mail to complain or who must try and sell to them. The verbal and written abuse is hydrochloric acid on the soul.

Service bureaus can piggyback onto companies with excellent images. Some clients allow bureau partners to use their names to recruit people. After all, the agents they hire will be working for that client, just as if they were hired directly. However, make it clear to applicants that they're working for and being paid by you.

"Money is not that high of a factor in recruiting people," D'Ausilio points out. "It is way down the list in what people are looking for in an employer. Flexibility, amenities and motivation all rank higher. One day you won't be able to give any more money. What's going to happen?"

While in a tight economy you should try all recruiting means, some work better than others for different types of call centers. If you have a basic unsophisticated low paying inbound order taking or outbound telemarketing center, newspaper ads, campus and government employment center job boards and staffing agency listings may work very well. Listing such positions on the Web or featuring the Web site will not be very effective.

Still, if your center is targeting the Web-savvy 18-30 age group, provides high level customer service/help desk and is for or is serving the high-tech industries, you need to offer online recruiting, either through job boards and/or on your corporate Web site. To take full advantage of your Web site's potential you should consider deploying a Web-based qualification system.

"The number of people who are accessing the Web is growing," Burdette points out. "As well as reaching people you can find out much more about your applicants and in real-time than other recruiting methods."

Contract staffing is becoming a very popular alternative to staffing and training a call center. They will send in X amount of worker(s) who perform their tasks directly for you. The vendor recruits, qualifies, screens and pays for the agents (but only for the number you need) under your management and supervision. If they don't perform or the tasks they've been assigned to accomplish are finished, they're out. You call up the agency and say: "We don't need so-and-so tomorrow."

Contract staffing agencies also offer "temp-to-hire" programs where if one or more of their employees is working out real well in your center they can be placed on your staff, usually after four to six months. That gives the temps extra incentive to perform well and to get to know your company and customer needs. You can also insource with some staffing agencies, letting them run your call center day-to-day.

Formerly known as "temping agencies" companies such as Adecco (Melville, NY), FurstPerson (Chicago, IL), Kelly Services (Troy, MI) and Manpower (Milwaukee, WI) have call center staffing expertise. The biggest benefit of contract staffing is that the agencies bring in large numbers of qualified people to your center quickly. This is especially helpful if you are setting up a call center in a new community and/or your center requires high and fluctuating volumes of part-time and short-term employees.

They're also very handy if you're setting up a center in another country. By knowing the cultural and legal lay of the land these agencies quickly get your employees in place, and with less hassle than if you tried to recruit them yourself. By contracting with them to directly pay for your labor they may free you from being covered by onerous and often union-favoring labor laws that govern your vertical industry, i.e., banking/finance, which are especially prevalent in Continental Europe.

Staffing agencies rely on their large and frequently updated personnel databases. To fill them they effectively use all the recruiting means: word of mouth, ads, the Web, job fairs and college and government job boards. Their core competency is people: the good ones know how to attract and keep workers. They also use an array of qualifying, screening and testing methods, and incentives to select and retain the right candidates.

As with outsourcing to service bureaus, there are some downsides to contract staffing. You are leaving recruiting/selection in the staffing agencies' hands. They may not screen as well for exactly the employees you're looking for as you could in-house. And they're still the agency's employees, not yours. Turnover is usually higher than in-house; people often go to staffing agencies when they're making career or life changes.

For a staffing agency to work for you, your center must be in a community where there is what site selection consultant John Boyd (Princeton, NJ) calls a "temp culture." In a temp culture there is a workforce that is accustomed to going to a staffing agency to find permanent or, more often, temporary employment, commonly in fields unrelated to their main area of expertise. Cities that have a large service industry: such as offices, healthcare/institutional restaurant/hospitality and cultural/entertainment have a "temp culture."

Also, when working with a staffing agency, ensure that they have an excellent understanding of your culture as well as your skills needs. Monitor their performance. Kathryn Jackson recounts that one company that hired a staffing agency for their call center had one of their HR personnel doing just that, including attendance at the same job fairs when they recruited for the call center.

"There are some very good staffing companies, devoted to quality and excellence," Jackson points out. "But the success of the relationship is dependent on the strength of the partnership between recruiter and the client, as in any outsourcing partnership."

What Makes A Good Agent

There are many characteristics that go into a good call center agent. Kathryn Jackson, associate with Response Design Corporation reports the following characteristics for one insurance client. Its management and local management (the managers involved with the performance of the agents on a daily basis) developed a list of the competencies of a successful agent.

- Oral communication.

- Customer service orientation.

- Tolerance for stress.

- Sensitivity. Agents must be advocates for the customer.

- Teamwork/cooperation. Agents must be able to cooperate with their team members and understand internal customers. According to a site visit host, "It is not enough for an agent just to be nice to the customer. The agent must function in a team environment to solve problems, both internally and externally."

- Analysis. Agents must be able to analyze the patient information and identify the type of problem the customer is facing to provide a quick solution. Agents must also be able to analyze customer billing statements and understand the best way for customers to use their prescription benefits.

- High work standards/work ethic.

- Motivational fit.

- Ability to learn. The insurance business is complicated and agents must understand its nuances.

- Resilience. If agents are discouraged by an interaction with a customer, they must recover quickly and go on.

► Training

If you've done your staffing correctly then you should have a fine crop of recruits to be trained on your front lines. They need to be taught the mechanics of the job: how to work the phones and computer hardware/software, what are the contact handling procedures and rules and how performance is measured. You must also teach them on individual products and services, and in their specialties, if that is what you are hiring them for, such as help desk, and insurance and securities sales.

Last, but not least you must train them on the "soft skills": such as listening, understanding and responding appropriately and on the "hard skills": customer service and sales. In this CRM era you need to train *all* agents on *all* of them, where feasible, the principal exception being agents who are outbound selling fire-and-forget products like wax steak knives and outdoor winter ski vacations in the Bahamas. The caller who wants to know about how your video-enabled cellphones work is a prime candidate for a sale; the called party that you sold the phone to and you're offering an add-on, like cable TV, may have a complaint about picture quality and reception while driving through the Holland Tunnel.

Veterans with sales and service experience as well as raw recruits with skill aptitudes need training, and time to get up to speed. Every business has their own procedures; also, people pick up bad habits from their old employer that are exposed in their new job.

"Training a new agent in the "art" of customer service should always be part of the new hire training," says RDC's Jackson. "An agent who does not possess strong customer service skills is apt to alienate callers and you face the potential of losing business. Call centers tend to focus on product/service training (i.e., specialty) initially and consider the "soft skills" as a secondary training. Customer service skills should be incorporated throughout the new hire training, regardless of the specialty."

There are a variety of training methods and tools. You can train by people, such as your trainers or those provided by consultants and companies and by technology, through a growing array of computer, online and video tools. One set should not substitute for another. In-person gives immediate, direct human feedback to individual trainees and sets up role playing to reinforce lessons while technology-based aides enable information retention because agents can review at their leisure what has been taught.

The length of new-hire training typically ranges from 40 hours to 12 weeks. You should also test periodically to ensure that the information is getting through; don't wait until the end. After the agents have been trained they should be brought up to speed under close supervision. When they meet the same standards in the rest of your call center then they can be given the same level of attention as the other agents.

Don't make the mistake of focusing too much on product training at the expense of hard and soft skills training. It is the people who sell the product, not the other way around. You can have that practically impossible acme of an offering: air service that is on time, safe, with direct routes, ample and cushioned seats and edible food at reasonable fares, or sheer, comfortable and affordable pantyhose that never runs, or Windows-compatible software that never crashes and quickly boots up. But if you don't have agents who can sell and service them and build relationships with your customers you will get little initial or no repeat business. There are few proprietary products or services; if yours is popular your competitors will soon mimic them; those Asian prison factories and copy shacks can turn on a dime.

Centralized Marketing Company (Cordova, TN) is a unique training firm in that it practices what it preaches; the firm operates a service bureau. CMC believes in gradually immersing its trainees. Its training floor is not in some basement or far off room but in a glassed off section of its call center. Agents pass through the firm's exacting standards apprentice with a 3:1 agent/supervisor ratio in its Academy Bay, seen here, on a non-partitioned section of the call floor. Once passed agents move to the main section.

"The priorities, between product training and soft skills, which I call 'context training,' should be reversed," argues D'Ausilio. Today, the competition is just a click or a call away. The only way your front lines can keep your customers is if they have these skills."

Training doesn't end there. Consultants recommend refresher sessions to keep skill levels up and to provide new techniques, in this fast changing industry. Refresher training particulars and frequency depends on the company.

"Timing of refresher training should vary from center to center, based on each ones unique need," says Jackson. "What is triggering the need for training? Have the monitoring scores gone down across the board? Are we launching a new product? Has there been a process or policy change? Will the system be changing?"

Staffing and Training for Online Customer Service and Sales

Staffing and training for text based communication presents a unique set of challenges. It takes one set of skills to understand and respond to a customer complaint or pitch them a product with your voice. It takes quite another to do so in writing. And just because a person is great on the phone doesn't mean they will do well in e-mail and chat. The challenge is screening and training agents to handle the growing volume of online communications, e.g., e-mail and text chat.

When researching the issue with the American Productivity & Quality Center, Response Design Corporation had expected to find that a majority of agents would be able to alternate between answering the phone and answering e-mail. RDC even thought that it might prevent boredom and possibly agent burnout. Yet, it learned that few organizations were able to maintain a large group of agents cross-trained in both phone and e-mail handling.

"Most managers select a group of agents and train the agents to handle e-mail exclusively, although they may return at times to handling phone calls during peak call volume periods," says Jackson.

Underlying this experience are the pros and cons of text-based communications. Its great advantages are that you can carefully review what you receive, and what you send out before hitting the "send" button and you have easily-accessible and incontrovertible records of what is said. You are also not facing the pressure of someone on the line wanting answers *now*.

The key disadvantage of e-mail and text chat, from agent staffing and training perspectives, is that you have to be painstakingly accurate in your grammar, syntax, spelling and meaning. There is little tolerance for dropped words and factual errors, and no opportunity to quickly correct mistakes as there is with voice.

In writing English, as opposed to speaking it, you are stripped of accent, emphasis, tone and vowel length that gives context and meaning to language. Trainer Rosanne D'Ausilio says you can fall prey to homonyms such as "the farmer does produce" which can have two quite different meanings but if you heard or spoke this line you will know which one. If the o is short produce means agricultural goods; if the o is long it means that the farmer makes something.

Unfortunately, today's all-too-lousy American primary and secondary schools and colleges are spitting out too many graduates and students who lack essential grammar, spelling and composition skills. Computer-screen spell and grammar checks make even the best students lazy.

This isn't limited to call centers. Publications like *Call Center* which require a very high level of language competency, have seen some horribly written resumes from applicants.

In an August 11, 1999 *The New York Times* op-ed, former federal Labor Secretary Robert Reich said that one out of six Americans are functionally illiterate. Training consultants have seen a drop in agents' basic grammar and spelling skills.

In his argument for more funding, Reich pointed out that federal education and training investment declined amidst rising school and college enrollment to 0.58% of the gross domestic product in 1999, compared with 0.61% in 1992.

Training consultant Stephen Coscia (Havertown, PA) has seen agents with word usage problems, such as differentiating between "to," "two," and "too." Another common area of confusion is between the words "their" and "there." No spellcheck could pick up on *those* errors.

Another problem with text is that because it takes longer to communicate in those media than with voice users often tend to abbreviate, CAPI-

TALIZE and key in symbols to express thoughts, such as :). Many people who casually e-mail and engage in text chat use them. This practice is akin to the shorthand and codes used by telegraphers — the original e-commerce practitioners — and later, by ham radio operators and by CB radio enthusiasts in the 1970s for the same reason. A "QSL" card, which ham operators and CBers used to send to each other, stands for "confirmation of communications." Railroads were big telegraph users; they depended on the technology to operate trains safely. Signal towers were not known by the cities they were in but by two-to-five-letter designations, e.g., "Shell" for New Rochelle, NY.

The problem is that poor language usage and punctuation, coupled with informal abbreviations and symbols, can not only radically alter the meaning of a sentence, but also what the agent is attempting to convey. This leads to misunderstandings, lost business and possible legal action if the misunderstanding caused damage. A poorly-worded e-mail message from a help desk agent could lead a customer to make an error on a computer, causing a crash and either losing valuable data or disabling the machine. It also shows a lack of professionalism by your agents. They should keep the "chat" language for their friends.

Coscia points out that the decline in language skills places a burden on human resource managers, as they must screen more carefully or offer supplemental grammar training, both of which add to costs. "This is one of the conditions that is causing such rapid growth in HR management," Coscia says.

Ideally, you should have screened and hired individuals for your online team who have proven written communications skills. There are technology-based screening tools, such as Assessment Solutions Inc, (ASI) *REPevaluator* that tests for these and for how well candidates respond to e-mails and chats. Yet you may not have enough people with these increasingly rare gifts.

Trainers such as Human Technologies now offer grammar and spelling modules. "If your agents don't know how to use words the right way then they are misrepresenting your company to your customers," says D'Ausilio.

There are differences in text based communications that you need to be aware of. Text chat requires phone-like immediacy and quick thinking, unlike e-mail response, which is more deliberate.

"Managers are telling us they are having better luck selecting chat representatives from their pools of phone agents rather than their pools of e-mail agents," says Jackson. "It seems the attributes agents must have to excel in chat mimics the attributes of phone agents more so than the attributes of e-mail agents."

▶ Supervisors: Your Call Center's NCOs

The task of determining when your agents need retraining or other improvements to keep up their performance and to keep costly agents from falling down between the cracks falls onto your supervisors and team leaders. They are the non-commissioned officers of the call center. It is their mission to translate your decisions and see that they are carried out, and at the same time to report to you what is happening: with the customers and the agents, to enable you to make accurate decisions, closing the loop. Without good supervision, your staffing, training and call center site selection investment has been wasted.

The first step to having good supervisors is recruiting for them correctly. Unfortunately, many companies fail to do so. They will pick someone on the basis of seniority or because they are an excellent agent, without looking for leadership abilities. They expect someone to supervise or train by osmosis. Yet not everybody is cut out to be a leader or wants to be one.

What separates supervisors from non-supervisors is *management*. This is a 'you have it or you don't' skill. Supervisors must tell those that they are supervising what to do in a way that a person being instructed believes the order is in their best interest, and that in carrying it out correctly helps them and their colleagues. They must watch for, listen to and help resolve agent problems that might hinder the completion of your goals. They must hear without being personal and advise without bullying.

Human Technologies founder Rosanne D'Ausilio had this quote on her online August, 2000 newsletter:

"Leadership is the ability to get a person to do what you want, when you want it done, in a way you want it done, because the person wants to do it. — Dwight D. Eisenhower

To find a supervisor look for someone who has demonstrated managerial experience, even if not in a call center, such as in hospitality and retail which are also demanding customer service/sales fields. The key is the ability to motivate and get the most from your people. Volunteer experience also helps, such as organizing a Girl Scout troop, coaching a Little League team, acting as president or vice president of a very active civic or fraternal organization or putting on fundraisers like a car wash, dance or scavenger hunt for a nonprofit organization.

Some of the best supervisor or coach candidates are those who serve or have served their country in the military, Coast Guard and in police and emergency services. They may be in Reserves or in the National Guard or in Canada, a Canadian Forces militia unit, or who are in volunteer fire or EMT/paramedic units. If these fine people are in your workforce, support them when they get called up. They make an important contribution to our freedom, security and safety. They know what to expect, and what is expected of them, in *truly* mission-critical situations.

Also, make sure they get proper leadership and management training. Todd Beck, who is market director-Web-based training for AchieveGlobal (Tampa, FL) and was once a call center supervisor, lays the responsibility at both management and the supervisors, many of whom do not want to take the time to go to classes or take technology-based training. His firm offers supervisory training through its Frontline Leadership and Leadership for Results programs.

"From my own experience and from focus group sessions, I found that while a company may tell a supervisor about a new workforce management tool, I did not see a lot of training on how to become good managers or trainers," says Beck. "I also found that many managers and supervisors were reluctant to take training. The reasons, I suspect are time and the fact that many of them don't want to admit to the agents they too need training."

RDC recommends that successful supervisors utilize "full spectrum coaching" to train their agents. Supervisors' methods should include setting clear expectations; providing consistent, timely and accurate performance feedback. They should also develop expert agent skill through educating, modeling, practicing, applying and inventing successful behaviors.

There are other excellent training courses to teach supervisors how to manage their charges, including spotting for signs of poor performance and how to motivate others. CMC's Supervising for Performance Leadership program helps supervisors build respect and create a fair and consistent work environment. It trains them on how to establish credibility and earn employees' respect along with teaching them a positive communication style to motivate employees to achieve their potential.

The best programs ensure that they are exposed to the same front line conditions as agents. Just as in the military, a "paper sergeant" who hasn't been exposed to incoming blasts is useless on the front lines and gains little respect from the troops.

"How will supervisors and managers be able to help their agents, if they have not been able to be successful at it themselves?" explains trainer Kathy Sisk, of Kathy Sisk Enterprises (Clovis, CA). "Managers and supervisors need real world experience in order to effectively coach and train others."

▶ Live Versus Technology-Based Training

Providing training sessions cost time and money. Agents and supervisors must be pulled off phones and computers, leaving you to scramble to cover lost productivity. Sometimes there are meeting room and transportation expenses, as well as the costs of hiring the trainers and providing the materials.

An increasingly popular alternative is technology-based training, such as on CDs, over the Web and on video. The main advantages are convenience and retention. Each agent can tap into their sessions at their leisure, when they have a few minutes and, in the case of Web-based training, at their desktops. They can easily review them to refresh their memory and go over key points.

Yet, there are several distinct advantages to live training. The first is feedback. Your agent and supervisor can ask questions, be asked questions and take part in role playing exercises and will be told practically right away the answers and what they are doing right or wrong and how to improve. Your employees cannot escape the eye of a good trainer; you can't switch or click them off. If your agents are not paying attention, the trainer, like a teacher, will notice.

The second benefit is motivational. Good live trainers leave you, like a fine preacher or speaker, with an inspirational buzz to act, to do better. There is an emotional impact from being in the presence of a live person speaking that does not exist in a broadcast, Web cast or video.

To minimize the time drain on call centers some trainers offer part-day as opposed to whole-day training. D'Ausilio's training takes 16 hours but she breaks them in 4-hour sets, say over one month.

It is also easier and less fatiguing for someone to retain information if they come back for it, say two or three times, even if the material is new each time because attending the sessions and seeing the trainers reinforces the lessons.

Many trainers have or will introduce technology-based training. They provide the best of both worlds: the human touch and the convenience and reinforcement of instant review.

"It is more cost effective to duplicate your training through video, audio, and the Internet, so long as it can be interactive," says Kathy Sisk. "However, every company should have an on-site trainer. Nothing can replace the human factor when it comes to dealing with people. We have become so high tech that I believe we are failing to recognize that most people still prefer the human touch and are more receptive to it."

Nancy Friedman, The Telephone Doctor (St. Louis, MO), also offers instructional videos for classroom training. Her newest set, the Discussion Catalyst series, provides eight wrong way vignettes on a common theme where either the caller or the agent is at fault. After viewing each scene your class then discusses the mistakes. One of the tapes addresses, for example, common e-mail errors. She also offers Web-based access to animated customer training movies.

"The trends of training are not nearly as important as the fact that you do the training," Friedman points out. "You could show an old 16mm film and if it proves a point and gets the job done what does it matter how it's presented?"

▶ Unions (boo!)

There is one word that is guaranteed to frighten many businesses, especially those with call centers: unions. To many firms they raise the frightening specter of higher wages and benefits costs, grievances and strikes, and, underlying them, the biggest evil of them all, another powerful force telling them how to run their business.

Many site selection consultants are often told by clients to avoid locations where there are "union cultures," i.e., where the communities support strong unions, like the Northeast and much of Canada and Europe. Even if a company or operation isn't unionized — most call centers are not — there is social and economic pressure to raise wages and benefits to near-union levels. In "union towns" there is often also a poisonous "us versus them" attitude between workers and management that could seep into agent attitudes to your managers.

On the other hand there are good reasons why there are strong unions and union cultures. Many industries that have been unionized, such as manufacturing, resource extraction and transportation, exploited their employees by making them work long hours, under tough backbreaking conditions, for little pay and no benefits, laying them off at a whim and giving them no respect.

Management often regarded their workers as less-than-human —"wage slavery"— to rationalize their ill treatment of them. Unions emerged, after many bloody battles, as protectors of workers' rights. Their wage gains laid the foundations for today's middle class. A union wage, such as the increase in the average hourly base pay to $29.25/hour from $26/hour for Verizon's customer service agents that had been won in 2000 after a bitter strike, is much more livable for a family facing the Northeast's horrendous house prices and rents than the $10/hour to $15/hour wages typically paid by non-union companies.

Yet, just because call center agents and supervisors work in nice clean offices many think that conditions can't be tough; perhaps not enough for them to consider joining a union. It is difficult to sit electronically tied to a cubicle taking a never-ending barrage of often abusive calls and e-mails and making calls to similarly impolite people, knowing that every nanosecond of your behavior is being measured, recorded and judged remotely by management in supervisory towers or behind walls. Call center agents do come down with painful injuries caused by repetitive motion, such as keyboarding, including carpal tunnel syndrome and tenditinitis. OSHA and individual states are looking at or promoting regulations to curb these ailments.

On top of that are the hours and shifts, which vary radically, and change at a spur of the moment and in doing so can wreck an agent's personal and family life. Sometimes the wage and the hours worked are not enough to pay the mortgage or rent. There is also the usual 'Dilbertian' capriciousness of top management: ignoring workers' needs and opinions and deploying new hardware and software and rule changes with little training and notice.

According to the August 21, 2000 *The New York Times*, Verizon's workers won several important issues in their strike: to organize non-union wireless division workers more easily, limits on the right of the company to transfer out jobs like call center agents and the lowering of mandatory overtime. They also receive up to five 30-minute periods each week in which they can do non-call work. But does it have to take a strike to make these changes?

Your company may or may not have Verizon's local carrier monopoly or can or cannot afford those types of wages. And yes, you can relocate your call center anywhere there is enough cheap, loyal labor, like India: if you can find qualified local managers or have some adventurous types on your team who'd like to move.

But you might be better off if you made your call center a decent place to work, designed and well located, with excellent amenities, paying decent but affordable wages and benefits, and employing fair, productive work practices including listening to employees and acting, where merited, on their suggestions. That's how many other companies have avoided unions, if that's what you want to do. Employees have the right to be represented by unions. The propensity of workers to join one is, therefore, up to you.

▶ Agent Retention

To retain agents, attract others and to satisfy your customers, thereby achieving a return on your substantial resources and time investment, your call center must be a "good place to work." How do you accomplish this? You must be an employer who is firm but fair, who is empathetic but not sympathetic, who knows how to constructively motivate employees and who takes a genuine interest in them. Who helps workers to see how they can 'be all they can be' for their company. Your company must also make and sell products and services employees and their customers can be proud of.

This isn't a revelation from "above." It is only common sense. Unfortunately, common sense isn't that common, which is why the phrase exists. If it were *truly* common it would not need attention drawn to it. Alas, to maintain and improve competency and effectiveness is a never

In today's hectic economy, if you run your call center like this, you'll soon find your benches empty. There's many other call centers and other service sector employers that value good employees.

ending struggle against the entropic forces of carelessness, laziness and stupidity encapsulated in the iron rules of the Peter Principle: where people rise to their level of incompetence.

There are three proven methods to retain agents that together can help make your call center a good place to work. The first and the most important is *listening and responding to your employees.*

Call centers are tough places to work. Your agents are working with people, who can be kind and polite or rude and obnoxious at any one time. Like the concept of the "law-abiding citizen": it only applies to that person at that one moment in time. Like your kindly neighbor who looks after your house when you are on vacation then decides to see whether the side panels in the SUV that cut them off in the mall parking lot are *truly* bulletproof. The same individual who is polite one time they call and then who can pass for a 'goodfella' making a 'collections' round the next.

Your employees can't walk away from this; they have to deal with it. They are tethered to their seats; they can't, without permission, get out, wander around or destroy some aliens that pass for their last callers on a video game they loaded into their PC. They can't give dumb stupid customers diving instructions or an anatomically-not-recommended place to insert the product they're having problems with because they didn't read the "friendly" manual.

RDC advises that you look for signs of burnout such as health problems, sickouts, short temper, bad co-worker interaction and lack of responsiveness to corporate communications. For agents, in particular, this is shown in lower monitoring scores and increases in escalated customer calls and poor attendance. In supervisors the symptoms are less monitoring being done, unavailability for questions and decrease in coaching sessions.

To handle burnout RDC recommends you should consider:

- Measuring job satisfaction — conducting employee surveys, providing opportunities to serve on committees, working with management to improve the environment of the call center;

- Job rotation, i.e., having agents/coaches work on projects from time to time;

- Ensuring appropriate training is delivered, offering access to gyms, aerobic classes, etc.

- Providing defined career paths relieving the "dead-end job" syndrome;

- Providing voluntary time off — allowing agents to go home (without pay) when call or contact volume does not require their services;

"Managers noticing these signs should have one-on-one sessions with coaches, and coaches noticing these signs should have one-on-one sessions with agents," says Jackson. "Causes of burnout could include reaction to understaffing or personal problems."

You also need to be flexible with your working hours in case employees have family responsibilities. Don't limit this to those that have families: single and childless workers also have personal needs and they can get resentful to time off given to others.

You should also solicit employees' input. Who knows more what is going on than the front lines? That way they feel that they are making a contribution to what they regard as *their* company. The second method is *rewarding and recognizing performance.* Everybody likes to be praised for a job well done, especially if everyone else in the office is told of the accolade. It is the best motivation tool there is.

Again, there are many methods to accomplish this, such as gift award programs based on employee performance measurements. Equally, if not more effective, are where recognition is personal, such as awards ceremonies and special walls where compliment letters are posted. DDI's Dave Burdette suggests having the most desired parking spots designated for "employee of the month."

RDC's Jackson recommends that fair and consistent reward and recognition programs should be built for all employees and that they should be part of the development process. Managers should create a "wish list" by surveying the call center employees. You can personalize a reward list that can be customized for each employee based on his or her selections from the master list.

"Reward and recognition programs should be built on a balanced foundation of quality, productivity, and time utilization, " says Jackson. "Once a program has been built it should be rolled out with solid, clear communication to the agents."

One increasingly popular method, for management and employees is teleworking (see Chapter 3). Agents who have proven that they can work without direct supervision make the best candidates. Many people love what they do for a living but hate the commute: which is growing in time and stress and takes away from their personal lives. You'll likely find that you can keep agents longer and get more out of them as well as attract new employees if you offer this option.

The third technique is *career and personal development.* Most employees who are any good do not like to sit still; they want to learn. Learning doesn't stop until your brain stops. For example, online response, for those agents that show a language aptitude and keen interest in using computers. Another is visual response, if you plan or currently offer video-enabled services. Still others, if your company is in these fields, is licensing for insurance, real estate and securities.

You also need to provide career paths from your call center; not everyone wants to be an agent for the rest of their life. You can do this by creating different performance skills levels, leading to supervisory and management positions within your call centers. Or you can provide a route into other departments, such as administration, HR, engineering, marketing, product development and, of course, sales.

Who knows your customers and their needs better than your agents? If you make, install or sell computer hardware and software, the best trained people to fix problems and help create new applications are found on your help desk, who have been solving them.

"Providing a career path is especially vital to attract and retain the new generation," D'Ausilio points out. "They don't want just a job. They want to be going places. A job has to be interesting and worth while for them."

▶ Accents and Dialects

The most important yet potentially the riskiest skillset a prospective agent must have is the ability to hear and speak clearly in the language(s) they are hired to communicate in. If a potential employee can't talk and listen well they can't, by definition take or make voice calls, which is what most, but not all, agent positions require.

Yet, some individuals may overreact if you turn them down and could threaten legal action on the grounds of discrimination. There are enough attention-hungry lawyers and political wannabes with their agendas to jump at and capitalize on such cases.

Clarity and enunciation is essential in any language. Your agents don't have to speak the King's or Queen's English (or the more common variant in the UK known as 'BBC English' after the droll monotone of the venerable broadcasting corporation's announcers) or Castilian Spanish or Parisian French. But they do have to be understood.

Most callers are tolerant of accents and dialects, and have become more so as societies become globalized; but they must be able to understand the agents. Southern drawls are more acceptable to Yankee ears than they used to be and vice versa. The same holds true for foreign-accented English.

One of most amusing stories I heard about accent and dialect was about an inbound campaign in England being handled by Convergys (Cincinnati, OH). In 1996 Convergys, then known as Matrixx arranged to overflow calls from its Newcastle, UK call center to its Ogden, UT, Omaha, NE and Pueblo, CO centers . In preparation of that, the bureau trained its US agents on British dialects by having them listen to British soap operas. One of them, Coronation Street, is set in a mill town just north of Manchester, which is roughly the area where my family is from and where I lived on occasion.

I could just imagine one of my relatives in the UK, sitting in front of the television, likely with a fag (cigarette) in one hand, watching the infomercial, dialing the number and talking "to someone in America." 'Bloody hell, did you hear that? I was on t'phone and some Yank answers it. They've sent th' bloody call to America!"

But the overflow program went spotlessly. Matrixx also tested UK agents handling calls from the US, where the British employees were taught how to recognize US Hispanic accents. Americans and Britons understood each other quite well. No rendering asunder of the great transatlantic relationship, pesky little incidents like the War of Independence, the War of 1812, the Monroe Doctrine and that to do about a big chunk of rock, trees and snow known as Canada, notwithstanding.

Said Robert Ashcroft, general manager of Matrixx Europe: "We've found the UK and US consumers were very accepting at hearing the different accents. [But] agents must not only have a good command of the language but know the cultural nuances of the country they're calling, such as form of address."

Yet, if the dialects are too strong and the words spoken too fast that they can't understand the agent then they cannot get the service or buy what they need from your company. Often customers will call back at another time, hoping to get someone else, which adds to your costs. Ultimately they may get so annoyed they will go elsewhere.

Therefore, when you set up your call center you must carefully screen out applicants that you feel your callers and called parties cannot understand. Make sure, however, of your grounds for not hiring them based on speech. While speaking and listening are essential job competencies, like knowing how to hit a nail if you're applying for work as a carpenter, the lack of which are grounds for not hiring, in this lawsuit-happy society you can never be too careful.

Be sure, though, that you don't fall for the nonsense that there is virtue in, as they say in northern England, "talking broad," i.e., with accents. That is talking down to people: a big customer service no-no. Many people perceive strong accents in their own language as lower class; most individuals aspire to upper class. And under no circumstances should your agents copy the twangs of callers or called parties. Such fakery will get them and you unprintable but quite unmistakable words, loud and clear.

There is an old joke from northern England, recently updated that illustrates job competencies. A man walks by a mill and sees a sign 'Handyperson Wanted. Apply Within'. He does just that. He sits in the hiring office, fills out the application, and hands it in to the secretary. She then hands it to the manager. A few minutes later the manager asks the man to come into his office.

"Mr. Bloggs, I see you've applied for the handyperson position," the manager says through his wire-rimmed spectacles. "Tell me, have you done any mechanical work? We have a lot of machinery in this mill that has to be taken care of."

"Sorry, can't help you there," replies the man. "I can't even fix the lavatory when it runs too long."

"Hmm. Are you experienced with wiring: electrical and telephone?"

"Electricity?" the man shuddered, all concerned. "All them electric and magnetic fields that can cause cancer? Candlelight for me, squire. And them phones, well, I had one once. Nobody but bloody telemarketers calling. I ripped it out of the wall. I showed them!"

"I see," said the manager, knitting his brows. "Well, what about something more simple, like painting, tidying things up, a little janitorial. I'm sure you can handle that."

"Sorry, sir," the man shrugged. "I'm a real mess with things. I get one touch of paint on my hands and it goes all over me. And I got a bad back. I can't pick things off the floor."

The manager stood up and tossed down the application. "Well, Mr. Bloggs, explain what's so bloody handy about you?!"

"Me?" grinned the applicant. "I just live around the corner!"

When sorting your applications, you should also see if the applicants can read and reply accurately in text. Many people especially those from India or Pakistan, or of that heritage, that speak fast are very well educated and can respond well in e-mail and text chat. India is becoming popular as a location to handle US-based customer contacts, but those centers have handled text-based first, before training their agents to handle voice. On the other hand there are applicants who write as poorly as they speak.

You should also look for strong signs that the applicants have other key skills such as friendly and helpful personalities and who want to learn to become good agents — those you can train to speak clearly. For example, US firms are now reportedly helping to train Indian call center agents to speak to Americans.

The last step is to see if there are any other non-call center positions that they might be interested in or suitable for. You may offer them a job such as in programming or distribution that is better suited for their skills.

With all of these steps you should structure the screening to let the applicant self-select out by realizing that being an agent may not be the job for them. The steps may also protect you in case some disgruntled applicant goes after you. More importantly, they will help you find value to your customers and to your company from those applicants.

▶ The Pros (and Cons) of Prison Labor

When looking to staff your call center there is another, if controversial, source of labor: prisons. Many US states permit companies to hire convict labor for work inside prisons including for inbound reservations and outbound telemarketing. There are airlines and service bureaus that have used prison labor.

There are several advantages to having prisons handle your calls either directly for you, or through a service bureau. They are available for a lower cost per hour than law-abiding citizens on the 'outside', which lets you keep your calling operations in the US. With the American mania to incarcerate for even the smallest offenses there are no shortages of, ahem, 'captive' workers.

Hiring cons and having them trained as call center agents also gives them job skills and experience that they can readily use when they've done their time and ready to go outside. Many prisoners are released literally on the street, and many of them commit crimes and head back in. Some of the money prisoners earn goes to restitution: paying back the people they victimized, whose acts led them to jail in the first place.

On the other hand you run the risk of entrusting individuals who had violated society's trust before with personal information about innocent people, such as their names and telephone numbers and addresses. The cons could then memorize this data and use it to rob, rape, assault, abuse, kidnap and kill once they're released or have their pals on the outside commit these acts for them. While prisons are reportedly careful with personal data, no system, like no jail, is totally secure and protected.

Do you want to permit the possibility of that happening? Can you and/or your company weather the resulting hellish media and legal firestorm? Can you withstand the heat from customers knowing that you use convict workers, which raises these understandable fears?

Using convict labor raises another issue: is it right to deny law-abiding citizens, in the US and elsewhere, employment opportunities just because you wanted to save a few pennies? Is it not more morally right, when faced with this choice, to employ decent hardworking Canadians, Filipinos, Indians or Jamaicans and help them support their families, than Americans who assaulted, robbed, stole from and murdered others?

If your competition doesn't use cons you risk them using your practices against you. Your customers may respond to these fears and moral concerns and go elsewhere, or they may not care as long as they get good service.

If you are concerned about convict labor but do want to give them a chance to rehab their lives, wait until they have paid back their debt to society. If they apply at your call center screen them very carefully. If they have the skills you're looking for let them gradually build your trust, such as doing non-phone functions, like fulfillment. If they have fine writing skills put them on e-mail and text chat — all of these interactions are instantly recorded and retrieved.

Off and on the phones — monitor these former prisoners carefully and correct them when they make errors. Many of them did not have or lost job-retaining skills such as showing up to work on time so let them know what is permissible and what is not. Let them know that you're giving them another chance but they have to earn it by proving that you and society can trust them.

Because much of the work is entry-level, call centers are a great place for people to begin or begin anew their careers and that is the opportunity you offer them. A former prisoner who by their own free will applies for a job with you may have more success assisting and selling to your customers, and in rebuilding their life, than one who is still on the inside and who looks at phone work only as a way to make their existence easier behind bars.

CHAPTER TEN

The End (Literally)

Everything comes to an end, from the universe and our solar system to our lives and yes, even to call centers, and to books about them.

There are many good reasons to close down or cut back a call center. They are very costly to set up and operate. You may then wish to drop smaller centers and consolidate into newer, larger facilities, or move out of locations whose labor pools are drying up or becoming too costly, i.e., high wages and high turnover.

If your business is expanding you may have outgrown your old call centers and their labor markets. You may have also had added new capabilities, such as technical help desk or are branching out into new markets, such as Asian or Hispanic-speaking customers, requiring that your centers be in communities whose workers have those skillsets. The volume of available, qualified workers may not be sufficient to keep the old facilities going.

You may also find, for example, that the sales and qualified leads from your outbound telemarketing operation are declining, in which case you should look at quitting the technique or outsourcing it to a service bureau. While you could have agents take inbound calls, you may already have an inbound center that is not growing rapidly, or you may find that the workforce which lives in commuting distance of the outbound center does not have the right customer service skills or attitudes.

After reviewing your inbound operations you may find that you can't afford *not* to have IVR and Web self-service with live agent "call me" buttons deliver many key functions, such as dealer locator, first level problem resolution and order entry. The cost benefits: pennies per transaction compared with the dollars per interaction conducted by your agents are too good to pass up. You believe that the customer friendliness of speech recognition and their acceptance of the Web vis-a-vis live agent contact will make these changes acceptable to your customers.

You could have also realized that while your customers prefer live agents, the low value of each call and contact and the sharp demand peaks and valleys make providing enough agents uneconomical, prompting you to consider outsourcing. Or you've bought into the CRM philosophy and decided to shift a fair-sized chunk of lower-valued customers away from always being served with live agents to automated self-service.

Mergers often cause companies to close down offices and back offices, including call centers. Every expense in the ledger is keenly examined to see if it is justified. Some of the bought firm's product and service lines and functions like customer service and sales may duplicate yours — whose potential cost savings are what helped drive the merger/buyout. There may be excess capacity with the combined call centers: theirs and yours. While your senior management hopes to grow the business, the revenue projections and the number of new customers and their value you plan to acquire may not be enough over the short-term to justify keeping the centers open.

The same factor applies if you are with a service bureau. You may have lost a contract or had one end and while you hope for additional business you can't carry dead assets. Or your management could be taking the business in a completely different direction or into new markets, rendering the skillsets of the agents at one or more of the centers obsolete.

Keep in mind that a merger or acquisition does not mean you have to close down a call center. A Gartner Group study released in 2000 on developing call center strategies, Financial Services Call Center Banking Benchmarking, points out only 33% of companies surveyed who were involved with such an event had consolidated any of their centers as of June, 1999. More than 40% of the total number of surveyees had been in a merger or acquisition, between January 1998 and June 1999. This rose to more than 60% for those with deposits over $10 billion.

When the event resulted in a closure, usually one location was shuttered, though the number varied widely. The report cited two reasons why more closings had not occurred: the logistics of shutting them down and moving functions to remaining facilities often outweighed the cost savings and recent advances in networking strategies and technologies have erased some of the cost and support challenges of maintaining multiple sites.

"Still the elimination of even one site is not trivial and can result in significant cost savings and efficiencies," says Brad Adrian, Gartner Research Analyst. "It's just not consolidation of the scale that we thought we might see." At the same time you may witness declining sales and numbers of customers in given product or service lines, despite the best efforts of the Marketing and Product Development departments. This forces you to cut back the infrastructure, like call centers that support them, unless you can reuse these assets somewhere else in your business. Or you may be going out of business and have to dispose of the facilities, equipment and lay off the people.

▶ Community Reactions

Whatever the rationale, ending a call center, like preparing for death, is painful but necessary. Expect anguish and possibly lawsuits from the doomed call centers' employees. They will try to come up with ways to save their centers, such as agreeing to more flexible hours and wage/benefit cuts, and help you drum up business, which may justify reversing your decision but more often than not these tactics just delay the inevitable.

You should also prepare for a lot of bad press, especially if your call center received a lot of tax breaks and other goodies to get you to that locale in the first place. Business closures and layoffs always make news; reporters almost always interview the doomed workers and their families and explain the impacts of the shutdown on their lives and on the local economy. Elected officials would feel that you had betrayed their trust and made them look like fools putting their necks out to get your business to set up in their community. Their political opponents will have a field day with this one. Don't be surprised to hear rumblings of a local but usually ineffectual boycott against your company for such heinous acts. And calls for a "savior" to rescue the business.

These feelings are amplified geometrically in small cities and towns. People who live there "adopt" your business. You are not just a company you are part of the community. Shutting down and relocating is like abandoning a child while closing down altogether is akin to murder. While closing a 500-seat center in a large metropolitan area with 5 million people is a pinprick on the economy, shutting down one of the same size in a community of 50,000 is like a knife slash into its artery, especially if your center has become the leading employer.

The only possible upside is that there is a good chance that there may be a "white knight" to keep the call center open and save the jobs, if the labor market and location is viable for other companies. Real estate consulting firms such as Arledge/Power and Mohr Partners, both of Dallas, TX, are experts at finding, tracking and turning around closed call centers for clients who need to open one yesterday.

▶ **Strategies for Closing a Call Center**

There are information sources that can help you deal with the human resources, property and asset disposal issues involved in closing down businesses in more depth that what this book attempts to cover. What it will deal with are some general techniques that pertain to call centers:

Design and locate your call center effectively

If you had done your site selection and call center design homework outlined in preceding chapters correctly, and had selected and trained agents and supervisors effectively you may not need to close the centers that you had applied these methods to. But sometimes even the best-designed and located call centers have to be shuttered.

All is not lost: a fine facility and people that had made sense for your business could make sense for others. This makes the sale and disposal of your call center easier; you could have new businesses move in almost right away. This lessens the economic and public relations impact of the closure, and makes exiting from your property commitments easier.

Also, take special care when you pick a small city location. Make sure it has the labor to support a longstanding call center. Don't go in there making big promises of lots of jobs but thinking you can easily pull out two or three years later, especially if you work for a brand name company that people recognize, and particularly if you have your hand out for incentives. Some local officials and residents may be more powerful than you think. In the US and Canada backcountry politicians are very influential, especially at the state/provincial levels as the electoral systems have long been weighted in their favor.

Carefully review your location options

If you are deciding which call centers to retain, say after a merger/acquisition, or in the event of downsizing, you should look at their locations as if you were going to open a new call center. Find out which sites make the most sense for long-term labor availability, skillsets, costs, property suitability and implementation.

It may be that you need a new call center because the underlying demographics and costs have changed so much since you last examined these locations to make the existing facilities no longer viable. Also, as with any acquisition there is inevitably "old team" versus "new team" corporate cultural conflicts that may not be easily resolved, especially if you had planned to fill excess capacity at your center to house workstations and agents from the acquired firm. The technologies of the acquired firm's call center may also not mesh easily with yours. A new call center, with new technology, represents a fresh start for your company.

Negotiate exit clauses in your lease

Writing in exit clauses enables you to get out of a lease, which typically run five to seven years: an eon in the fast-changing call center 'business'. Susan Arledge, of Arledge/Power says examples of such clauses are landlord-approved subleasing rights and lease cancellation or termination options.

"There are penalty clauses involved, but which are certainly cheaper than paying rent for space you no longer need," she points out.

Leo Orsi, vice president, The Paladin Group (Tampa, FL), added that if an exit or termination clause is a part of your lease, you should carefully negotiate your obligations to restore the property you occupied to its original condition, especially if subleasing is not an option.

"While you may have the right to terminate your lease early, you certainly don't want to be responsible to return the premises to shell [original] condition," explains Orsi.

Seek imaginative ways to utilize your employees

When you close a call center you lose the recruiting and training investment that you made in your agents plus the valuable knowledge of your customers and products/services that they gained. While you may offer positions at another center, depending on how close it is, few people will relocate for the comparatively low pay that call centers remunerate.

To keep your people investment, consider looking into having the top performers from the old call center telework. This way you retain their value, expertise and loyalty and save on hiring and training new recruits and productivity losses as they come up to speed at the new call center.

Resources Guide

Here is a list of companies and consultants who graciously helped me with this book, and/or who I had cited in this tome and in past *Call Center* articles. Their knowledge, expertise and services may benefit your firm. Please call them and/or visit their Web site. I have also included the contact information for trade associations. Please note that the telephone numbers change often, much more so than their Web sites. If you reach non-working numbers check the web sites and recent issues of *Call Center*.

ACA Research (also Callcentres.net)
+61-2-9955 1966
www.acaresearch.com.au or
www.callcenters.net

AchieveGlobal
813-977-8875
www.achieveglobal.com

Alter Group
800-637-4842/847-676-4300
www.altergroup.com

American Teleservices Association
877-779-3974
www.ataconnect.org

Arledge/Power Real Estate Group
214-696-4800
www.arledgepower.com

BC Group International
888-428-2232/214-821-7962
www.bcgroupinternational.com

The Boyd Company
609-452-0077

Burkettdesign
303-595-4500
www.burkettdesign.com

CB Richard Ellis Call Center Solutions Grp
602-735-5566
www.cbrichardellis.com

Centralized Marketing Company
800-925-1974
www.cmcmax.com

Centralized Marketing Company
(Performance Training Group)
800-699-9788
www.performancetrain.com

Philip Cohen
+46-910-199-88

Deloitte & Touche Fantus Consulting
212-436-3649 and 213-688-5592
www.dttus.com/realest/specialties/fantus

Digby4Group (Jane Laino)
212-883-1191
www.digby4.com

Direct Marketing Association
212-768-7277
www.the-dma.org

eLoyalty
877-2-ELOYAL
www.eloyaltyco.com

Engel, Picasso
505-341-0001
www.engelpicasso.com

Equis
215-568-4330
www.equiscorp.com

Federation of European Direct
Marketing (FEDMA)
+32-2-779-42-69
www.fedma.org

Hellmuth, Obata & Kassabaum (HOK)
314-421-2000
www.hok.com

Human Technologies (Rosanne
D'Ausilio)
845-228-6165
www.human-technologies.com

Intecom (professional services)
800.INTECOM
www.intecom.com

Kathy Sisk Enterprises
800-477-1278/559-323-1472
www.kathysiskenterprises.com

Kingsland Scott Bauer Associates
(KSBA)
888-231-KSBA/412-252-1500
www.ksba.com

Kowal Associates
617-521-9000
www.kowalassoc.com

Incoming Calls Management Institute
800-672-6177/410-267-0700
www.incoming.com

Mohr Partners
972-239-0394
www.mohrpart.com

Oetting and Company
212-580-5470
www.oetting.com

Paladin Group
813-968-1943
www.paladin-group.com

Phone Pro
800-888-4893
www.phonepro.com

Purdue University Center for
Customer Driven Quality
765-494-8357
www.e-interactions.com

Response Design Corporation (RDC)
800-366-4732
www.responsedesign.com

Janice Reynolds
212-628-8271

Service Intelligence
206-621-7367
www.serviceintelligence.com

Laura Sikorski (Sikorski, Tuerpe and Assoc)
631-261-3066
www.laurasikorski.com

Stinson Design
713-223-3610

TeleDevelopment Services
330-659-4441
www.teledevelopment.com

Telephone Doctor
800-882-9911/314-291-1012
www.telephonedoctor.com

TManage
512-794-6000
www.tmanage.com

Trammell Crow Site Selection
Consulting Group
214-979-6193
www.trammellcrow.com

WalMart Realty Group
501-273-4535
www.wal-martrealty.com

Willow CSN
888-899-5995
www.willowcsn.com

Young, Bickley, Geiger
888-489-8008
www.ybgsolutions.com